ITIL®
Foundation Exam
Study Guide

Helen Morris

Liz Gallacher

WILEY

John Wiley & Sons, Ltd.

Acquisitions Editor: Chris Webb
Assistant Editor: Ellie Scott
Development Editor: Connor O'Brien
Technical Editors: Jane Holmes and Richard Webber
Production Editor: Christine O'Connor
Copy Editor: Kim Wimpsett
Editorial Manager: Pete Gaughan
Production Manager: Tim Tate
Vice President and Executive Group Publisher:
   Richard Swadley
Vice President and Publisher: Neil Edde

UK Tech Publishing
VP Consumer and Technology Publishing Director:
   Michelle Leete
Associate Director–Book Content Management: Martin Tribe
Associate Publisher: Chris Webb
Marketing
Associate Marketing Director: Louise Breinholt
Senior Marketing Executive: Kate Parrett
Media Project Manager 1: Laura Moss-Hollister
Media Associate Producer: Shawn Patrick
Media Quality Assurance: Josh Frank
Book Designers: Judy Fung and Bill Gibson
Proofreader: Josh Chase, Word One New York
Indexer: Robert Swanson

This edition first published 2012

© 2012 John Wiley & Sons, Ltd

Registered office

John Wiley & Sons Ltd, The Atrium, Southern Gate, Chichester, West Sussex, PO19 8SQ, United Kingdom

For details of our global editorial offices, for customer services and for information about how to apply for permission to reuse the copyright material in this book please see our website at www.wiley.com.

ISBN 978-1-119-94275-7
ISBN 978-1-119-94363-1 (ebk.)
ISBN 978-1-119-94364-8 (ebk.)
ISBN 978-1-119-94365-5 (ebk.)

A catalogue record for this book is available from the British Library.

Set in [9.5/12 Sabon] by MPS Limited, Chennai, India

Dear Reader,

Thank you for choosing *ITIL Foundation Exam Study Guide*. This book is part of a family of premium-quality Sybex books, all of which are written by outstanding authors who combine practical experience with a gift for teaching.

Sybex was founded in 1976. More than 30 years later, we're still committed to producing consistently exceptional books. With each of our titles, we're working hard to set a new standard for the industry. From the paper we print on, to the authors we work with, our goal is to bring you the best books available.

I hope you see all that reflected in these pages. I'd be very interested to hear your comments and get your feedback on how we're doing. Feel free to let me know what you think about this or any other Sybex book by sending me an email at nedde@wiley.com. If you think you've found a technical error in this book, please visit http://sybex.custhelp.com. Customer feedback is critical to our efforts at Sybex.

Best regards,

Neil Edde
Vice President and Publisher
Sybex, an Imprint of Wiley

We dedicate this book to our long-suffering partners, Gary Cleaver and John Callaghan, who kept us supplied with food, drink, and encouragement while we slaved over our laptops every evening and weekend writing this book.

Acknowledgments

We thank our colleagues across many organizations over the years who have assisted us in our attempts to put best practices into practice. In particular, Liz Gallacher would like to thank Dave Cousin, who encouraged her to follow her instincts and gave her the opportunity to do just that in two major projects.

We thank the teachers who shared their passion for service management during our ITIL V2 Manager courses all those years ago: Ben Weston, Andrew Jacobs, and Mark Haddad, who taught Helen, and Dave Wheeldon and Lloyd Robinson, who taught Liz. Our commitment to focusing our careers in IT service management can be traced back to those few intense weeks.

We thank all the students we have taught for sharing their experiences with us and the clients who have had faith in us and our ability to put theory into practice. Our understanding of service management grows and develops with every organization we work with.

We thank all the ITIL trainers, wherever they are, spreading the service management message every week of the year.

We thank Jane Holmes and Richard Webber for checking the content of this book and for the helpful suggestions they made.

About the Authors

Liz Gallacher is a service management consultant and trainer with 25 years of practical experience. She placed in the top 5 percent of candidates in the ITIL Manager certificate and was invited to join the ISEB V2 Managers Certificate Examiners panel. She holds the ITIL Expert certification and is a certified ISO/IEC 20000 consultant.

Liz provides consultancy and training on all aspects of IT service management, focusing on the ITIL framework and the ISO/IEC2000 standard. She has designed and implemented improvement initiatives covering many areas of service management for a variety of organizations, large and small. Her experience over the past 25 years has been a mixture of consultancy, training, and implementation, including setting up service desks for many large organizations, working with clients to design their service management processes, and evaluating and implementing service management toolsets that met their requirements. She also advises organizations seeking certification against the ISO/IEC 20000 standard, performing gap analyses, advising and mentoring improvement plans, and so on.

Liz has worked for global organizations, central and local government departments, the U.K. National Health Service, and many others. She has set up service management organizations from scratch. In each case, she designed and documented the processes, procured the service management tool set, recommended the organizational structure, drafted job descriptions, and recruited several hundred staff over a number of projects. She then trained the staff and devised appropriate marketing campaigns to publicize the new service desks to the customer base.

She has implemented service improvement initiatives for several clients, combining improvements in processes and tools with customer awareness coaching for IT staff. For a national railway infrastructure organization, she implemented a 24×7×365 service desk to replace 18 other sources of support, delivering a service that was assessed by the Gartner and Maven organizations to be "world class" and "highly efficient."

She has provided consultancy on many aspects of service management, including service-level management, change management, request fulfillment, and incident and problem management. She has compiled detailed service catalogs.

For many clients, Liz has gathered tool set requirements, evaluated products, and recommended the purchase of products that matched the requirement. She has also specified the tool configuration to support the processes, delivered the required reporting, and overseen the implementation. She has also delivered user training.

Liz has developed and delivered bespoke training for clients covering particular aspects of service management. She has also coauthored classroom and distance-learning courses covering the ITIL framework. She delivers ITIL foundation and intermediate training and consultancy worldwide, with courses this year in India, China, Australia, New Zealand, the Philippines, Germany, and South Africa, as well as the United Kingdom. With Helen Morris, she has devised an innovative blended approach to mentoring and supporting clients remotely.

Helen Morris   provides quality training and consultancy to organizations, assisting with delivery of IT service management. She specializes in providing cultural change support and training to organizations to enable the full exploitation of the benefits from implementing service management best practices.

Helen has 20+ years of experience in service management including operational management of service desks, technical support teams, and service-level management. She holds the ITIL Expert qualification and has delivered service management training for many years. She now delivers ITIL foundation and intermediate training in the United Kingdom, Europe, and the United States. She has coauthored and recorded distance learning courses covering the ITIL framework. Helen is also a certified ISO/IEC 20000 consultant.

Helen is an experienced trainer, consultant, and service delivery manager focused on providing customer satisfaction and business benefits. Many of her assignments involve an initial assessment against best practices, recommendations for improvement, and target setting. She leads programs to achieve significant improvements in customer satisfaction, quality of service, reduced costs, and better control.

Helen has presented at a number of international service management conferences, and she blogs regularly on service management topics. With Liz Gallacher, she has devised a unique approach to mentoring, providing assistance and resources to clients while encouraging them to develop the skills they need without the need for expensive on-site consultancy.

As an experienced consultant, Helen has led a number of successful service management improvement programs, working with organizations to develop their service management strategy and being a key player in the implementation of the strategy within the organizations. She has delivered strategic improvements in customer satisfaction, service delivery, and regulatory standards.

Helen managed the support environment for a Microsoft partner and supported the launch of Windows 95, implementing an improvement initiative to achieve the required customer satisfaction targets. Throughout this period, Helen was also leading a team to achieve and maintain successful ISO 9001 compliance within the division. This included extensive process reengineering in the support division to ensure efficient and effective process to support the customer satisfaction targets.

An assignment with a blue-chip telecommunications company allowed Helen to implement strategies for introducing best practices into the service delivery management team as the lead for the rollout of ITIL. This formed part of the company initiative to achieve BS15000 (a precursor to ISO 20000), in which Helen was a key player, specializing in incident and problem management.

Many of Helen's assignments have involved assessing and restructuring the support environment to provide improvements in cost efficiency and customer satisfaction. This has often required working across a broad spectrum of the business to achieve an agreed-on approach within the organization. Helen was the lead consultant in delivering the service improvement program for an outsource provider; she provided support services and networks for a large number of blue-chip and financial institutions, delivered by a service support function of more than 120 personnel. Helen achieved and maintained an improvement in service levels from 80 percent to 95 percent (target) within three months across all service areas.

Contents at a Glance

Contents

Introduction

IT service management is an increasingly important area of study for all IT professionals. IT managers are realizing that, whatever the technology in use, the requirements to manage that technology efficiently and effectively and to deliver services that are aligned to the business requirement have never been more important.

The internationally recognized ITIL framework is the best-known approach to IT service management; in the first three months of 2011, 54,500 people took the ITIL foundation exam worldwide, with no sign of demand reducing. For most IT staff members, the certification is now regarded as an essential addition to their resumes, with many job ads specifying the foundation qualification as a mandatory requirement. The popularity of ITIL has spread around the world, with an enthusiastic take-up in India, the Middle East, and China in particular.

For those IT staff members who are funding their own training, the costs and time required to attend a classroom course has been unattainable. Distance learning does not suit everyone. For those who do attend classes, it is a common comment that there is too much material to cover in the time allowed. By providing the ITIL course in a book format, these difficulties have been overcome; the book is an economical alternative to a course and can be studied at the student's own pace. The many practice questions help reinforce understanding. It can be used by itself or as an addition to attending a course.

ITIL Foundation Exam Study Guide provides foundation-level training for IT staff and customers of IT to gain an understanding of the ITIL terminology. Readers will gain knowledge of the ITIL service lifecycles and the ITIL processes, roles, and functions. They will also gain an understanding of how the service lifecycle provides effective and efficient IT services that are aligned to, and underpin, business processes. The book covers the full syllabus, preparing students to take the foundation exam at a convenient local test center.

There are no prerequisites, although it is expected that readers will have worked in an IT department or are studying IT at university level.

The book covers each area of the ITIL syllabus, examining each of the five areas of the service lifecycle, explaining concepts, highlighting terms that need to be understood for the exam, and providing real-life examples. These five stages include the following:

Introduction to IT Service Management and Service Strategy The design, development, and implementation of service management as a strategic asset to align with business processes

Service Design The design and development of service and service management processes

Service Transition The building, testing, authorizing, documenting, and implementation of new and changed services into operation

Service Operation   The day-to-day support and management of live services

Continual Service Improvement   Creating and maintaining value for customers through monitoring and improving services, processes, and technology throughout the lifecycle

How to Contact the Authors

The authors are experienced trainers and consultants and use practical examples and explanations to help the students grasp each content. We provide support to all our students; emails seeking further explanation or clarification will be answered within 24 hours in most cases. You can contact us at enquiry@helix-services.com.

ITIL Foundation Exam Objectives

The following tables map each of your study requirements to the chapters of this book. We organized the contents of each chapter to be read in an order that will make your study easy.

Unit 1: Service Management as a Practice

TOPIC	CHAPTER
1-1. Describe the concept of best practices in the public domain	1
1-2. Describe and explain why ITIL is successful	1
1-3. Define and explain the concept of a service	1
1-4. Define and explain the concept of internal and external customers	1
1-5. Define and explain the concept of internal and external services	1
1-6. Define and explain the concept of service management	1
1-7. Define and explain the concept of IT service management	1
1-8. Define and explain the concept of stakeholders in service management	1
1-9. Define processes and functions	1
1-10. Explain the process model and the characteristics of processes	1

Unit 2: The ITIL Service Lifecycle

Unit 3: Generic Concepts and Definitions

Unit 4: Key Principles and Models

Service Strategy

TOPIC	CHAPTER
4-2. Describe value creation through services	2

Service Design

TOPIC	CHAPTER
4-3. Understand the importance of people, processes, products and partners for service management	4
4-4. Understand the five major aspects of service design	4
▪ Service solutions for new or changed services	4
▪ Management information systems and tools	4
▪ Technology architectures and management architectures	4
▪ The processes required	4
▪ Measurement methods and metrics	4

Continual Service Improvement

TOPIC	CHAPTER
4-9. Explain the continual service improvement approach	13
4-10. Understand the role of measurement for continual service improvement and explain the following key elements:	13
▪ Relationship between critical success factors (CSF) and key performance indicators (KPI)	13
▪ Baselines	13
▪ Types of metrics (technology metrics, process metrics, service metrics)	13

Unit 5: Processes

Service Strategy

Service Design

Service Transition

Service Operation

Continual Service Improvement

Unit 6: Functions

TOPIC	CHAPTER
6-1. Explain the role, objectives and organizational structures for	
▪ The service desk function	10
6-2. State the role and objectives of:	
▪ The technical management function	10
▪ The application management function	10
▪ The IT operations management function	10

Unit 7: Roles

TOPIC	CHAPTER
7-1. Account for the role and the responsibilities of the	
▪ Process owner	7
▪ Process manager	7
▪ Process practitioner	7
▪ Service owner	7
7-2. Recognize the responsible, accountable, consulted, informed (RACI) responsibility model and explain its role in determining organizational structure	7

Unit 8: Technology and Architecture

TOPIC	CHAPTER
8-2. Understand how service automation assists with expediting service management processes	1

Unit 9: Competence and Training

Unit 10: Mock Exam

Exam units are subject to change at any time without prior notice and at ITIL's sole discretion. Please visit ITIL's website (www.itil-officialsite.com) for the most current listing of units.

Assessment Test

This test checks your level of understanding of service management before you undertake your study. It will form a baseline of your current knowledge. Each question has only one correct answer, and there are no "trick questions." Read the questions carefully.

1. What is ITIL?
   A. Rules for achieving recognized IT standards
   B. Good advice about how to manage IT services
   C. Advice on managing projects
   D. Advice on the technical requirements for infrastructure

2. What is an IT service provider?
   A. An internal IT department
   B. An external outsourced IT department
   C. Either an internal IT department or an external IT department
   D. A business unit

3. Who "owns" ITIL?
   A. The U.S. government
   B. Microsoft
   C. The U.K. government
   D. The Open Group

4. Which of these is *not* a stage in the ITIL service lifecycle?
   A. Service design
   B. Service implementation
   C. Continual service improvement
   D. Service operation

5. The knowledge management process maintains and updates a tool used for knowledge management. What is this system called?
   A. The service management tool
   B. The knowledge base for service management
   C. The service knowledge management system
   D. The service management database

6. A service must provide which of the following to deliver business value?

    A. Sufficient capacity, the agreed level of security, and alignment to the organization's project management methodology

    B. Sufficient capacity and the agreed level of security

    C. The agreed level of security and alignment to the organization's project management methodology

    D. The agreed level of security

7. In the ITIL guidance on incident management, what is one of the key purposes of the incident management process?

    A. The purpose of incident management is to restore normal service operation as quickly as possible.

    B. The purpose of incident management is to prevent incidents from occurring by identifying the root cause.

    C. The purpose of incident management is to prevent changes from causing incidents when a change is implemented.

    D. The purpose of incident management is to ensure that the service desk fulfills all requests from users.

8. A service catalog contains which of the following?

    A. Details of all services being developed

    B. Details of all services being considered

    C. Details of all services currently available to the users

    D. Details of all services

9. The predicted costs and benefits of a proposed new service are documented in which of the following documents?

    A. The project plan

    B. The service strategy

    C. The business case

    D. The improvement register

10. The agreement between an IT service provider and their customers regarding the services provided is called what?

    A. Service charter

    B. Service contract

    C. Service level agreement

    D. Service targets

11. What is meant by the term *request fulfillment* in the ITIL framework?

    A. Request fulfillment is a means of managing the changes that users request in the IT environment.

    B. Request fulfillment is used to deliver non-IT-related business components to the users.

    C. Request fulfillment is a process for managing the requests from users to the IT department.

    D. Request fulfillment is the report produced on the number of password resets carried out by the IT department.

12. Which of the following should be considered when drawing up a capacity plan?

    1. The business plan to streamline its operations

    2. The possibility of moving a business operation such as a call center overseas

    3. New advances in technology

    4. Plans to restructure the IT department

        A. 1 and 2

        B. 1, 2, and 3

        C. All of the above

        D. 1, 3, and 4

13. An availability plan should consider the requirements for what period?

    A. For the next 24 hours

    B. For the next week

    C. For the next month

    D. For the next 12 to 18 months

14. Which of the following is true about change management?

    A. All changes, however small, must be approved by the change advisory board before implementation.

    B. Emergency changes are too urgent to need approval before implementation.

    C. Low-risk changes may be preapproved.

    D. The change advisory board is for technical assessment and approval of changes *only*.

15. Which of the following is *not* a category of supplier described in ITIL?

    A. Strategic

    B. Operational

    C. Preferred

    D. Commodity

Strategic: Partnering relationships, sharing confidential information to facilitate long-term plans

Tactical: Those involving significant commercial activity (for example, server hardware maintenance organization)

Operational: Suppliers of operational products or services

Commodity: Providers of standard or low-value products and services (for example, paper or toner suppliers)

More information can be found on supplier management in Chapter 6.

16. Who should have access to the security policy?

   A. Business users

   B. IT staff

   C. Senior management

   D. Everyone

17. Which of the following statements is false?

   A. Planning for a number of different disaster scenarios that could affect IT services is essential.

   B. Ensuring the business is able to continue operation is the responsibility of IT.

   C. It is impossible to plan for disasters, because there are too many different possibilities. The IT department should be ready to quickly devise a recovery plan following a disaster.

   D. Continuity planning requires an understanding of the key business processes.

18. What is the purpose of the continual service improvement (CSI) stage of the service lifecycle?

   A. The CSI stage is concerned with the management of improvement across the whole service lifecycle.

   B. The CSI stage considers only the improvements needed for the business outputs.

   C. The CSI stage focuses on improving the operational processes in the service lifecycle.

   D. The CSI stage manages the improvements between project management and live operational services.

19. What is the Deming cycle?

   A. The Deming cycle is a set of questions for managing processes.

   B. The Deming cycle is a set of standards for quality management.

   C. The Deming cycle is an approach for managing quality improvement.

   D. The Deming cycle is concerned with the delivery of security controls.

20. What is the continual service improvement (CSI) approach?

A. The CSI approach is used to manage processes in the operational environment.

B. The CSI approach is focused on the delivery of quality management systems into IT.

C. The CSI approach is used to manage improvement activity in line with business requirements.

D. The CSI approach is focused on the introduction of projects into the operational environment.

21. Which of these statements about asset management and configuration management is *not* true?

A. Asset management is concerned only with purchased items such as hardware and software.

B. Asset management considers the value of items, and configuration management considers the interdependencies between items.

C. Configuration management may include locations and documents.

D. Configuration management information is held in a database called the configuration repository.

22. How is the seven-step improvement process in the continual service improvement lifecycle stage used?

A. The seven-step improvement process is used to manage improvement initiatives in line with business requirements.

B. The seven-step improvement process is used to gather, analyze, and present data to assist in decision making.

C. The seven-step improvement process is used to format the improvement reports delivered to the business.

D. The seven-step improvement process is used to manage the improvement program across the organization.

23. The ITIL framework refers to a number of operational functions. What is meant by the term *function*?

A. A function is a collection of technical infrastructure elements designed to manage an IT service.

B. A function manages the requirement of controlling costs in an IT department.

C. A function is used to deliver the security requirements across the service lifecycle.

D. A function is a unit of the organization specialized to deliver particular processes or activities.

24. Event management is a key operational process in the service operation lifecycle stage. What is the purpose of event management?

   A. Event management detects events that are significant for the management of the service and ensures the appropriate actions are taken.

   B. Event management monitors the infrastructure of the IT services and guarantees that no outages occur in peak times of business usage.

   C. Event management manages failures in the infrastructure and ensures that services are restored to normal working as quickly as possible.

   D. Event management monitors the underlying causes of failures and ensures that changes are made to prevent further failures from taking place.

25. How is the process of access management used in the service operation stage of the service lifecycle?

   A. Access management is used to manage the security technology in the infrastructure.

   B. Access management is used to ensure the correct people are able to use the correct systems in the correct way.

   C. Access management is used to ensure the active directory entries are audited for accuracy.

   D. Access management is used to maintain security controls over the business environment.

26. Problem management is an important process in the service operation lifecycle stage. How does the process define a problem?

   A. A problem is an incident that has become extremely serious and is causing significant business impact.

   B. A problem is an issue that has no solution and needs to be raised to the senior management for a decision.

   C. A problem is the unknown, underlying cause of one or more incidents.

   D. A problem is a set of incidents that have been linked together in a customer report.

27. The service operation lifecycle stage has a number of key objectives. Which of these statements best reflects the key objectives of service operation?

   A. Service operation should ensure the day-to-day service is delivered according to the agreed requirements of the business.

   B. Service operation ensures the financial obligations of the IT department are met and reported to the business.

   C. Service operation should ensure the details of the IT infrastructure are captured in the service asset database.

   D. Service operation should agree on the strategy for delivering IT services to the business.

28. The release and deployment process covers a concept called early-life support. What is meant by early-life support?

   A. Early-life support refers to the end of the project lifecycle and the management of the post-implementation project review.

   B. Early-life support refers to the handoff between service transition and service operation, ensuring support for the new or changed service in the initial stages of operation.

   C. Early-life support refers to the introduction of new processes into the operational environment, using service transition processes to ensure a complete integration of the new processes.

   D. Early-life support refers to the step in the release and deployment process where the project team deliver the documentation of the infrastructure to the service management team.

29. An important focus for the service lifecycle is the capture and management of knowledge relating to IT service provision. How does the process of knowledge management work in the service lifecycle?

   A. Knowledge management is solely concerned with the transfer of knowledge when implementing new or changed services.

   B. Knowledge management is used across the lifecycle stages of continual service improvement and service operation to ensure that improvements are managed effectively.

   C. Knowledge management is used solely in the service operation stage of the lifecycle to ensure that operation issues are managed efficiently.

   D. Knowledge management is used across the whole service lifecycle to ensure that appropriate knowledge is delivered to enable informed decision making.

30. The service transition stage of the service lifecycle has a number of different processes. Which of these is the process most concerned with the management of the whole approach to service transition?

   A. Transition management and support

   B. Transition planning and support

   C. Service transition release and deployment

   D. Change management

Answers to Assessment Test

1. B. ITIL is a framework of best practice advice based on processes for the management of IT services that provide value to the business.

2. C. An IT service provider is the provider of IT services for the organization; it can be either internal or external. More information regarding this can be found in Chapter 1.

3. C. ITIL is owned by the U.K. government, which drew up the guidance in the late 1980s, based on best practices used by successful IT organizations. It has been periodically refreshed, with the most recent edition being released in 2011. More information regarding this can be found in Chapter 1.

4. B. The five stages of the ITIL service lifecycle are service strategy, service design, service transition, service operation, and continual service improvement. More information regarding this can be found in Chapter 1.

5. C. The tool is called the service knowledge management system (SKMS) and is a repository for information, data, and knowledge relating to service management. This has important connections for managing information and knowledge throughout the whole service lifecycle. More information can be found on the SKMS in Chapter 9.

6. B. Every new or changed service must be capable of delivering the service without running out of capacity. It must also be secure enough to protect the organization's data. There is no requirement to use any particular project management methodology. More information regarding this can be found in Chapter 1.

7. A. The purpose of the incident management process is to restore normal service operation as quickly as possible, while minimizing the adverse impact to the business of outages in service. Normal service operation is the agreed level of service documented for the delivery of the service. More information can be found on the incident management process in Chapter 11.

8. C. The catalog includes services that are available to users. The services being considered or developed are in the service pipeline. Details of *all* services, including those being developed, the operational services, and the retired services, are in the service portfolio. More information regarding this can be found in Chapter 6.

9. C. The business case contains the justification for a significant item of expenditure. It includes information about costs, benefits, options, issues, risks, and possible problems. More information regarding this can be found in Chapter 2.

10. C. The service level agreement contains information about the service to be provided, the targets that need to be met, and the responsibilities of both customer and IT provider. More information regarding this can be found in Chapter 5.

11. C. Request fulfillment is a key operational process in the service operation stage of the service lifecycle. This process is used to ensure that requests made by users for information, advice, or standard components are handled efficiently. More information on request fulfillment can be found in Chapter 12.

12. B. Plans by the business to reduce its head count or number of locations would affect the capacity required. New technology may offer increased capacity at the same or lower cost. The structure of the IT department should have no effect on capacity requirements of the business. More information regarding this can be found in Chapter 6.

13. D. The availability plan looks ahead to ensure that the design that is delivered meets the availability requirements when the service is delivered and for the next 12 to 18 months. More information regarding this can be found in Chapter 6.

14. C. Low risk, or "standard," changes may be preapproved by the change manager and require only to be logged before being implemented; only higher-risk changes need approval before implementation. Emergency changes need to be approved by a small number of key people who make up the emergency change advisory board. The change advisory board should include business representatives and others (such as training department representatives) to ensure that all aspects of the change have been considered. More information regarding this can be found in Chapter 8.

15. C. ITIL describes four types of supplier.

16. D. The security policy should be communicated to all users and staff. More information can be found on information security management in Chapter 6.

17. B. Ensuring that the required IT services are available to help the business to continue operation is the responsibility of IT; it is the responsibility of the business to have a business continuity plan. IT services are only part of that plan. More information can be found on IT service continuity management in Chapter 6.

18. A. The CSI stage applies across the whole of the service lifecycle and is key in the management of all improvements across all service stages. More information on CSI can be found in Chapter 13.

19. C. The Deming cycle is used to manage the ongoing quality improvement of services and processes, as part of the stage of continual service improvement. More information on the Deming cycle can be found in Chapter 13.

20 C. The CSI approach is a set of steps that can be used to manage improvement initiatives in line with the requirements of the business. More information on the CSI approach can be found in Chapter 13.

21. D. Configuration management information is held in a configuration management system (CMS), which may contain a number of federated configuration management databases (CMDBs). More information regarding this can be found in Chapter 9.

22. B. The seven-step improvement process is the process used as part of the CSI lifecycle stage to ensure that the correct data is gathered, analyzed, and presented to the correct audience in order to enable informed decision making. More information on the seven-step improvement process can be found in Chapter 13.

23. D. The ITIL framework identifies four different functions, which are units of the organization specialized to deliver certain processes, activities, or capabilities. An example of this is the service desk, which is used as the single point of contact for the users to IT. More information on functions can be found in Chapter 10.

24. A. Event management is the process that uses the automated monitoring capability of the infrastructure to identify significant issues that require management. It is used to ensure that proper notification of issues is received and the appropriate action taken. More information on the event management process can be found in Chapter 12.

25. B. The process of access management ensures that access to systems and services is managed and controlled according to the security policy in place. This includes providing access to users and monitoring their actions. More information on access management can be found in Chapter 12.

26. C. A problem is defined as the unknown, underlying cause of one or more incidents. Problem management is the process that investigates the root cause of incidents so that the incidents may be prevented from recurring. More information on the problem management process can be found in Chapter 11.

27. A. Service operation ensures the day-to-day running of the services is managed according to the agreed requirements of the business. This is where the business sees the value of the services being delivered, and it is service operation that should maintain the status quo. More information on the service operation lifecycle stage can be found in Chapter 10.

28. B. Early-life support is the handoff that takes place between service transition and service operation, during the deployment phase of release and deployment. It ensures the support of the deployment and development teams is still available as the new or changed service is introduced to the live environment. More information on release and deployment can be found in Chapter 9.

29. D. Knowledge management is a process that has influence across the whole of the service lifecycle. It is used to capture and present ideas, perspectives, data, and information to all stages of the lifecycle, ensuring that the appropriate decisions can be made. More information on knowledge management can be found in Chapter 9.

30. B. Transition planning and support is a process that enables all activity taking place in the service transition lifecycle to be managed. This includes understanding the allocation of resources and resolving conflicting demands for resources. More information on transition planning and support can be found in Chapter 9.

Chapter

1

Service Management as a Practice

THE FOLLOWING ITIL FOUNDATION EXAM TOPICS ARE COVERED IN THIS CHAPTER:

- ✓ Describe the concept of best practices in the public domain

- ✓ Describe and explain why ITIL is successful

- ✓ Define and explain the concept of a service

- ✓ Define and explain the concept of internal and external customers

- ✓ Define and explain the concept of internal and external services

- ✓ Define and explain the concept of service management

- ✓ Define and explain the concept of IT service management

- ✓ Define and explain the concept of stakeholders in service management

- ✓ Define processes and functions

- ✓ Explain the process model and the characteristics of processes

- ✓ Describe the structure of the ITIL service lifecycle

- ✓ Generic concepts and definitions:
    - Service provider
    - Supplier
    - Types of services
    - Outcomes
    - Customers and users

- ✓ Understand how service automation assists with expediting service management processes

This chapter introduces the concept of service management and explores a number of key areas that enable the management of services in an operational environment. It also introduces the ITIL framework, which is a source of best practices in service management.

The ITIL framework consists of five publications, which detail the content of the service lifecycle. Each publication covers a lifecycle stage, and each lifecycle stage shows how processes are used to improve service management in an organization. In this chapter, you will explore the basic concepts of the ITIL framework and learn about the terminology used throughout the lifecycle.

This chapter contains a number of key terms that will be important for your understanding of the framework and that also frequently occur in examination questions.

Best-Practice Approaches and ITIL

ITIL is recognized worldwide as a best-practice approach for delivering IT services and IT service management. It focuses on the processes, functions, and capabilities required to support IT services in business.

Organizations need to remain competitive in the marketplace and can compare themselves to peers to identify where they can gain a competitive advantage. Commonly, they look to industry best practices to ensure they are using the best available methods and techniques to deliver a service. A number of best-practice approaches to IT are available, and organizations can use them as a benchmark to ensure that they are delivering IT services efficiently. It is important to recognize that these approaches must enable IT service providers to meet the needs of the customer, while remaining cost-effective and within the customer's budget.

As shown in Figure 1.1, there are many sources of service management best practices.

FIGURE 1.1   Sources of service management best practices

Knowledge fit for business
Objectives, context and purpose

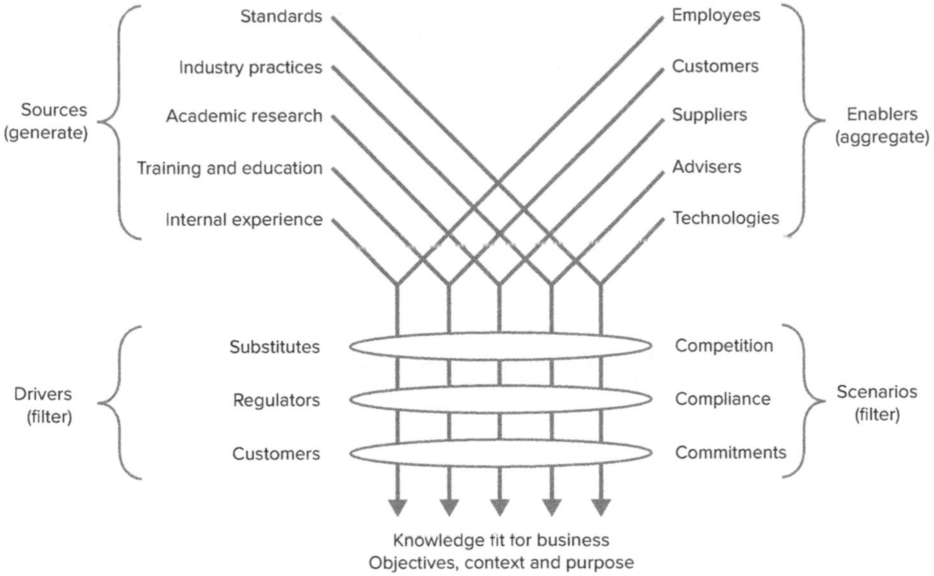

Based on Cabinet Office ITIL material. Reproduced under license from the Cabinet Office.

The sources of service management best practices include the following:

- Proprietary knowledge/internal experience
  - This is often deeply embedded in an organization. Although this is valuable, it is very difficult to share with another organization. It is also often undocumented, held as knowledge by the individual.
  - Proprietary knowledge is specific to the organization and can be so customized as to be ineffective in another organization, unless it requires the same conditions.
  - The sharing of this knowledge may be constrained by ownership, and it may be subject to legal or financial negotiations.
- Standards/industry practices
  - This is preferable to organizations when compared to proprietary knowledge. Standards and commonly used industry practices are captured, documented, and made available publicly.
  - Standards also have the advantage of being verified in a variety of situations and environments, rather than a single organization's experience. The standards are vetted and reviewed by a wide range of partners, competitors, and suppliers.
  - Commonly used standards include the following: ITIL, Lean, Six Sigma, COBIT, CMMI, Prince2, PMBOK, ISO 9000, ISO/IEC 20000, and ISO/IEC 27001.

- Training and education/academic research
  - Information and education on publicly available standards and research let organizations educate their staff in a consistent manner. It is easier for organizations to acquire knowledge through the marketplace, because levels of skill and qualification can be standardized.

Using standards and publicly available knowledge enables organizations to build on their proprietary knowledge and follow best practices for their organizational requirements in service management.

These standards have to be filtered through the constraints that affect all organizations, such as regulatory requirements, compliance, and financial concerns.

Why Is ITIL So Successful?

For a while after its origins in the 1980s, ITIL was the best-kept secret in the IT sector; however, the framework has become the recognized approach for service management excellence.

The main reason for its widespread adoption is that it is based on a practical approach to service management, utilizing what works in real organizations. The guiding principle behind the framework is to ensure that all efforts have a common goal: to deliver IT services that support the requirements of the business by delivering value to the organization.

This section explores the key factors for ITIL's success:

Vendor Neutrality   The ITIL framework is not based on a specific technology platform or industry type. It is not tied to any specific vendors; it is owned by the U.K. government and has no associations to any commercial proprietary practices or solutions. As a consequence, the guidance it provides for service management is applicable across any industry sector or enterprise. This allows its guidance to be globally adopted by any organization.

Nonprescriptive   From the beginning of its development, ITIL has recommended the approach of "adopt and adapt" to the guidance it offers. The true benefit of its application is in the adaptation to meet the specific requirements for value creation in an individual organization. The guidance contains time-tested, robust, and mature practices that can be utilized by any service organization. It is relevant to public and private sectors, internal and external service providers, and organizations of any size. It is not dependent on the technological environment, and it provides pragmatic guidance applicable and adaptable to any situation.

Best Practice   ITIL delivers the accumulated knowledge and guidance from the best sources of service management practices across the world.

The strength of the ITIL framework, and a key to its success, is that it describes practices that enable organizations to deliver benefits, return on investment, and value on investment through a sustained approach. The following are some of the factors that motivate organizations to adopt the framework:

- Creation of value for customers through the services provided
- The emphasis on integration with the business, ensuring that the business strategy and customer requirements are reflected in the service management strategy
- The ability to measure, monitor, and optimize IT services and the performance of service providers
- Management of the investment for IT services and budgetary controls
- Risk management in alignment with the business
- Knowledge management across the service management enterprise
- The delivery of services effectively and efficiently, through the management of the resources and capabilities required
- The adoption of a standard approach to service management across the organization
- A change of culture as part of the approach to service management, developing and maturing the processes to deliver effective IT services
- Improvement in the interaction and relationship between the service provider and their customers
- The ability to coordinate the delivery of goods and services and to be able to optimize and reduce costs

Services, Customers, and Stakeholders

To understand the service lifecycle, it is necessary to start with the concept of a *service*. The framework defines a service thusly:

> Services are a means of delivering value to customers, by facilitating the outcomes customers want to achieve, without the ownership of specific costs and risks.

Before exploring the concept further, it is important to ensure that you clearly understand this simple statement. Think of it in terms of an actual service, such as email. Email provides the ability to create a written communication in an electronic format, which is a desirable outcome for a business. But the user of the email service does not want to understand or manage the complexity of the infrastructure that supports the email service (network, server, client and application software, user accounts, and so on). The customer recognizes that the service has a cost and that this cost covers the "hidden" elements of the provision, but the ownership of these costs and associated risks in delivery are managed by the service provider, not the customer.

The services facilitate the desired outcomes by enhancing the performance of the tasks associated with the delivery of service, and reducing the effect of constraints, such as technology limitations, funding, or regulation. By enhancing performance and reducing constraint, the desired *outcome* is more likely to be achieved. This is applicable whether the service is enhancing the performance of a task required by the business or whether it is performing the task itself.

This is a recurring pattern in the delivery of a wide range of services. Understanding these patterns of service provision enables us to manage the delivery more effectively, in terms of complexity, cost, flexibility, and variety. Simply put, it means you can apply the same strategic approach to the management of a wide variety of services and make only minor adjustments to meet the specific requirements of each business. This is the core of ITIL's approach to service management.

ITIL defines the term *outcome* thus:

> The result of carrying out an activity, following a process, or delivering an IT service etc. The term is used to refer to intended results, as well as to actual results.

By focusing on the desired outcome from a customer perspective and managing services according to the delivery of the outcome, you are able to work closer with your organization, achieving IT and business integration, rather than IT and business alignment. It is only when you fully understand the required outcomes that you can deliver your services effectively.

ITIL defines an *IT service* thusly:

> A service provided by an IT service provider. An IT service is made up of a combination of information technology, people and processes. A customer-facing IT service directly supports the business processes of one or more customers and its service level targets should be defined in a service level agreement. Other IT services, called supporting services, are not directly used by the business but are required by the service provider to deliver customer-facing services.

Customer satisfaction with the services you provide is an important aspect of the delivery. Satisfaction with a service will consist of a number of factors, including the cost and value of the service. Customers do not want to have accountability for or ownership of the associated costs and risks, but the costs and risks must still be managed. Service costs will be reflected in financial terms such as return on investment (ROI) and total cost of ownership (TCO). Customers will be exposed only to the overall costs of the service provision but will use this as part of the basis for judging the value of the service being provided and the outcomes that are achieved.

Identifying Types of Service

Services can be grouped together to the value they provide for the customers.

Core Services   These are services that deliver the basic outcomes required by one or more customers. They are services that provide the value the customer wants and for which they are willing to pay. It is usually this set of core services that provides the capability for the business-critical functions to take place. An example that is often considered to be a core service is email. We will continue this example in the other service groups.

Enabling Services   These are services that are needed to ensure that the core service can be delivered successfully. These services may not be immediately visible to the customer and may not even be perceived as services in their own right. But without them, the core services cannot be delivered. Using our email core service example, the supporting services would cover the infrastructure and network to enable the service to work effectively.

Enhancing Services   These are additional services that enhance the core service, making it more attractive or appealing to the customer. They are not essential to the delivery of the core services but are extra factors that make the offerings more attractive to the customer. Using our core service email example, an enhancing service associated to the core might be the ability to access the email service remotely, through a web-based portal or the use of smart phone access to email. It is not an essential element of the core service functionality but adds something that provides value and customer satisfaction.

Understanding the Customer, Internal and External

Although it may not be relevant in your particular organization, for a great percentage of businesses, there are two types of customers. ITIL differentiates between internal and external customers, because there is a difference between those customers who work within the same organization and those working for a separate organization.

Internal Customers   These are people who work in the same organization as the service provider. For example, the HR department is an internal customer of the IT department because it uses IT services. It is likely that the service provider is funded through the internal accounting system, rather than as a revenue stream, although obviously this is entirely dependent on the financial strategy within the organization. Funding internally can sometimes cause challenges in managing the budget for IT services, because it may be hard to demonstrate the direct benefit to the business in terms of revenue.

External Customers   These are people who are not employed by the organization or are employed by a separate legal entity. External customers pay for services under agreement through a legally binding contract. In this situation, funding is direct, rather than through the internal accounting systems, and is managed through the specified contractual obligations.

There is often a requirement for internal IT service providers to deal directly with external customers through online services that are part of a standard offering. Organizations need to ensure that the strategies they adopt for IT service provision reflect these requirements and understand the implications for funding and commitment to customers.

Whatever the customer relationship, either internal or external, it is important to ensure that the service is delivered according to the agreed service definition, under the service level agreements in place.

Differentiating Between Internal and External Services

Just as there are internal and external customers, ITIL identifies internal and external services, as Figure 1.2 illustrates.

FIGURE 1.2   Internal and external services

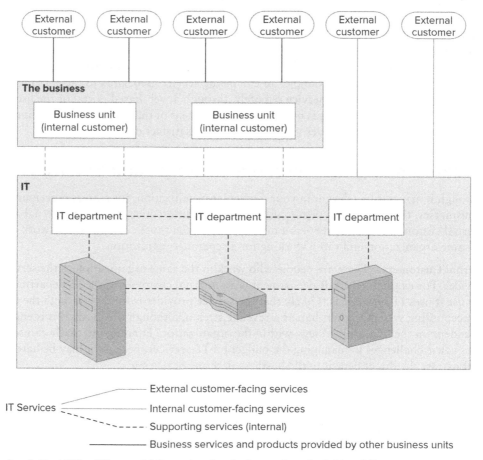

Based on Cabinet Office ITIL material. Reproduced under license from the Cabinet Office.

Internal services are delivered between departments or business units within the same organization. As you would expect, external services are those delivered to an external customer.

As you can see in Figure 1.2, some services are provided internally, and others externally, but all are being provided by the same service provider.

There are sound reasons for differentiating between these two types of service. Remember, the definition of *service* includes the phrase "facilitating outcomes customers want to achieve." You need to be able to differentiate between services that support an internal activity and those that deliver business outcomes. It is often the case that an internal service needs to be linked to an external service before you can fully appreciate its contribution to a business outcome. This will have an impact on the funding and management of the services.

As we have identified, an IT service is a service that is provided to one or more customers by an IT service provider. Services are made up of the combination of technology, people, and processes and are based on the use of information technology and support the customer's business processes.

Table 1.1 shows the differentiation between internal and external services via an extract in the ITIL Service Strategy publication (specifically, Table 3.4, "Types of IT Service").

TABLE 1.1 Extract from Table 3.4 "Types of IT service"

Type of service	Definition	Description
Supporting service, sometimes called an infrastructure service, although they are often broader than just infrastructure	A service that is not directly used by the business, but is required by the IT service provider so they can provide other IT services – for example, directory services, naming services, the network or communication services.	Supporting services are defined to allow IT teams to identify the interdependencies between IT components. They will also show how these components are used to deliver internal and external customer-facing services. Supporting services enable IT processes and services, but are not directly visible to the customer. Some IT teams view recipients of supporting services as 'customers'. Although this promotes good service quality, it is also misleading. Supporting services only exist to be combined with other supporting services to produce customer-facing services. If they cannot, they are of no value and their existence should be questioned. There can be no service level agreements for supporting services as they are all internal to the same department. Instead, the performance of supporting services should be managed using operational level agreements.

TABLE 1.1   Extract from Table 3.4 "Types of IT service" *(continued)*

Type of service	Definition	Description
		It should be noted that the diagram only refers to services originating inside the organization. In some cases supporting services are sourced from outside the organization. In these cases they are managed in the same way as other supporting services, but using underpinning contracts rather than operational level agreements.
Internal customer-facing service	An IT service that directly supports a business process managed by another business unit – for example, sales reporting service, enterprise resource management.	An internal customer-facing service is identified and defined by the business. If it cannot be perceived by the business as a service, then it is probably a supporting service.
		Internal customer-facing services rely on an integrated set of supporting services, although these are often not seen or understood by the customer or user.
		Internal customer-facing services are managed according to service level agreements.
External customer-facing service	An IT service that is directly provided by IT to an external customer – for example, internet access at an airport.	An external customer-facing service is available to external customers and is offered to meet business objectives defined in the organization's strategy.
		An external customer-facing IT service is also a business service in its own right, since it is used to conduct the business of the organization with external customers.
		Depending on the strategy of the organization, the service is either provided free of charge (many government agencies provide services to the public for no fee), or it is billed directly to the person or organization using the service. In other cases, the service may be provided free to the customer, but paid for by a third party, such as an advertiser or sponsor. These services are managed using a contract – even a simple online agreement constitutes a contract of sale and purchase with terms and conditions.

Who Are the Stakeholders in Service Management?

ITIL classifies stakeholders as those individuals or groups that have an interest in an organization, service, or project and are potentially interested or engaged in the activities, resources, targets, or deliverables from service management.

There may be many different stakeholders in a service provider organization, including the functions, groups, and teams that deliver a service. There are also other stakeholders external to the service provider organization; they include the following types:

Customers These are the individuals or groups that buy goods or services. They are responsible for agreeing on and defining the targets in the service level agreements with the IT service provider. They are the people within the organization who have financial authority over the services provided by the IT service provider and may be the key signatories for the service level agreement.

As you have already seen in this section, customers may be internal to the organization or external, dependent on whether they work within the organization or outside of it.

In organizations where the business model is to directly cross charge for IT services, it is easy to understand the concept of the customer. It becomes more complicated when the IT funding is managed through the accounting system and there is no direct connection between the IT services received and the cost for them. The definition of a customer implies that customers have financial authority over the agreements associated to the service. Often one of the most challenging elements of the process service level management is identifying and working with the appropriate customers. Service level management is discussed in Chapter 5, "Service Level Management: Aligning IT with Business Requirements."

Users This term is used to refer to those individuals or groups that use the service on a day-to-day basis. They are distinct from customers, because they have no overall authority over the service, and customers may not use the service directly.

A key challenge for service management is to ensure that the users are well informed about the items that concern them. An example is keeping users informed of the progress of incidents. Another challenge is to ensure that users are adequately informed of the agreements that have been made in service level management. This can be achieved by using the service catalog, which provides information about the operational services. This will be discussed in Chapter 6, "The Other Service Design Processes."

Suppliers Suppliers are classed as third parties who have responsibility for the supply of goods or services that are required to deliver IT services. There are many examples of suppliers, such as hardware or software vendors, network providers, and so on.

The engagement of suppliers is now a critical part of most IT service providers organizations, making sure that they perform according to the specification of the contract. This is managed through the supplier management process, which will be discussed in Chapter 6, "The Other Service Design Processes."

Understanding the Concepts of Service Management and IT Service Management

This section explores the key concepts of service management and IT service management.

Service Management

In today's business environment, IT has become considered a "utility" for a successful organization; in much the same way as you expect water to flow from a tap, your users expect their IT services to "flow" from your screens and devices. The technology has now improved to the point where this expectation is not only realistic but also achievable. The management of the technology to deliver the service is crucial to the success of your organization's required business outcomes. But the technology is not the sole element that makes up the services, which is why *service management* is more than technology management.

ITIL provides this definition for the concept of *service management*:

> A set of specialized organizational capabilities for providing value to customers in the form of services.

This is the definition provided for a *service provider*:

> An organization supplying services to one or more internal or external customers.

The organization of the *resources* and *capabilities* and their use in delivering valuable services is the core of service management. Resources and capabilities are important concepts in the way service management delivers value to customers. They are fully defined in Chapter 2, "Understanding Service Strategy." An IT service provider must understand the needs and requirements of the business and meet them in a cost-effective and efficient manner through the management of the resources and capabilities. The more mature the service management capability and organization, the greater the ability to deliver high-quality services.

Service management also provides a professional approach through the use of a wide body of knowledge, experience, and skills captured from a global community of organizations and individuals in all industry sectors. Within this there are formal schemes available for the education and training of staff so that organizations wanting to adopt this approach are able to benefit from industry-wide best practices.

The concept of service management did not originate with IT but with traditional service businesses, such as banks, hotels, and airlines. As IT organizations have adopted a service-oriented approach to the management of IT infrastructure, applications, and processes, the practice of service management has grown. Increasingly, the support for business operations and the solutions to business problems are delivered in the form of services. As outsourcing and shared service solutions have increased in popularity with organizations, so have the number of IT service provider organizations, including internal IT service providers. This has brought new challenges in the management of services across a broad range of providers but has improved the best practices applied through service management.

IT Service Management

Now let's consider the role that IT has in service management, by looking at the definition for *IT service management (ITSM) and IT service provider*.

> IT service management (ITSM): The implementation and management of quality IT services that meet the needs of the business. IT service management is performed by IT service providers through an appropriate mix of people, process and information technology.

> IT service provider: A service provider that provides IT services to internal or external customers.

Every IT department should consider itself an IT service provider and adopt the principles and practices of service management to deliver IT services.

ITSM should be carried out efficiently and effectively, managing IT provision by understanding the business perspective of the value that IT brings.

This requires a good relationship between the IT service provider and its customers, achievable by the customer receiving the services it requires at an affordable cost and acceptable level of quality and performance. The IT service provider needs to work out how to provide services that achieve the balance of these three areas, while communicating effectively with the customer if there are any constraints that may prevent successful delivery.

ITSM recommends that this relationship and the service requirements of business need, cost, and performance are documented in a *service level agreement (SLA)*. The SLA should describe the service, the targets for performance, and the responsibilities of the customer and the IT service provider. An agreement may cover many IT services or customers. We will cover the details of service level agreements in Chapter 5.

IT Service Provider Types

ITIL suggests that there are three main types of service provider. The different types will share most aspects of service management, but other aspects such as the contracts, revenue, and strategy, as well as the customer types, will vary and take on different meanings according to the service provider type. This is how ITIL defines the three provider types:

Type I: Internal Service Provider   The internal service provider is located within the business unit it supports. There may be several Type I service providers within a single organization. An example of this is the support offered to the individual faculties of a university or within an organization with multiple sites with local support teams.

Type II: Shared Services Unit   This is an internal service provider that provides shared IT services to more than one business unit. An example of this is the centralized IT department for a large multidivisional organization.

Type III: External Service Provider   This type of provider provides IT services to external customers. An example of this is an outsourcing partner, who would deliver their services to customers outside of the provider organization.

You will often find that ITSM concepts are described according to only one of these service provider types, and there may be an inference that only one service provider type exists in an organization.

Reality is much more complicated, and there may be a mix of provider types at work in your own organization. There is guidance in the ITIL Service Strategy core publication on how to manage these complex relationships. For your foundation course, we do not cover the details of this management, but it is covered in the next level of qualification, as part of the intermediate courses.

Understanding Processes and Functions

It is important to differentiate between processes and functions. This section explores the concepts of processes and functions, as well as the definitions provided by the framework for each.

Processes in the Service Lifecycle

ITIL provides defines a *process* thusly:

> A process is a structured set of activities designed to accomplish a specific objective. A process takes one or more defined inputs and turns them into defined outputs.

Processes are a vital component in the service management approach. The ITIL framework is based on processes, because the mechanisms used to ensure services are delivered according to a controlled set of activities, enabling the delivery of a specific outcome.

Within a process, we are able to define actions, dependencies, and sequence. A process that is well defined and managed can improve productivity across the organization or function, carrying out the activity identified as part of the process.

The Process Model

Figure 1.3 illustrates the process model. This is a key figure in your understanding of the service lifecycle because each process you consider should follow this model.

FIGURE 1.3   Process model

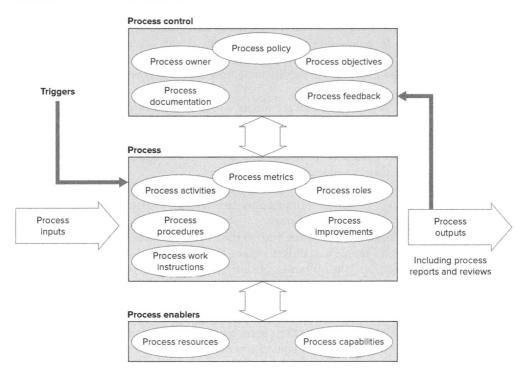

Based on Cabinet Office ITIL material. Reproduced under license from the Cabinet Office.

In the process model you can see three distinct sections. The upper section of Figure 1.3 shows the required controls for the process to take place.

A process is organized around a set of objectives, which drive the main outputs from the process. The objectives will include the process measurements (metrics) and other outputs, such as the required performance reports and process improvement actions.

In the central section of Figure 1.3, you can see the input, output, and activities. The output produced by the process should meet the requirements as specified by the business objectives. The business objectives will set out the standard or "norm" that is required for the output. Once the output has been confirmed as achieving this requirement, the process can be declared as effective. It can then be repeated, measured, and therefore managed to achieve the desired outcomes. If the activities are carried out utilizing the minimum resources, we can also declare the process to be efficient.

The inputs to the process are the data or information that is used by the process, and this may, of course, be the output from another process.

There will be a trigger for the initiation of the process or an activity within the process. There are many different mechanisms that can act as triggers, such as the arrival of an input or other event or an output from another process. This might be a failure report triggering the event management or incident management process.

Within the process, it is possible to establish the roles, responsibilities, tools, and management controls that are required in order to deliver the outputs to the required norm. The process may also define other elements, such as any required activities, work instructions, standards, and policies that are required to ensure the process will be carried out successfully.

Once a process has been defined and the inputs, outputs, and controls have been agreed on, it should be documented and controlled. The process can be repeated and managed once the controls are established, and metrics and measures can be incorporated into the controls. These measures and metrics will then be able to provide feedback and improvement in the form of regular management reports.

Supporting the process are the enablers: the resources and capabilities. We will cover these enablers in Chapter 2, "Understanding Service Strategy," as part of the key concepts covered by the service strategy lifecycle stage.

There are many examples of processes both in the IT environment and outside of IT.

Consider something as simple as making a cake. The inputs are the ingredients, the activities are the method, and the output is, of course, the cake.

Decisions need to be made on the type of ingredients based on the required 'outcome' or how many slices of cake are required. It must also satisfy the stakeholders in terms of quality.

In order to bake the cake, the correct resources and capabilities must be employed: the right number of cooks with the correct equipment and with the right skills, for baking.

The trigger for the process is the need for the cake, perhaps a special occasion like a birthday.

When this is translated into the IT environment, remember all of these factors must be considered in order to deliver a successful process.

Fixing a failed item of infrastructure requires the correct resources, capabilities, inputs and activities in order to deliver the required outcome.

Process Characteristics

Some common characteristics apply to all processes:

Measurability It is important to ensure that all processes can be measured in a relevant manner. Processes are based on the performance of activities to deliver a specific output, so the measurement should be performance based.

Different perspectives for the activities will require different measurement. For example, managers will typically be more interested in the measurement of cost, quality, and other variables of the performance, while those engaged in carrying out the performance are likely to be more concerned with duration and productivity.

Specific Results Processes exist to deliver a specific result, or else they should not be taking place. This result must be individually accountable and identifiable for it to have any measurable worth or value.

Customers/Stakeholders   Every process should deliver its primary result for the benefit of a customer or stakeholder. The process should meet the expectation of the recipient, regardless of whether they are an internal or external customer or IT or business stakeholder.

Responds to a Trigger   It makes no difference if the process is repeated or continual; the actions should be traceable to a specific trigger.

Organizing for Service Management

Obviously there is no single approach that can be adopted by all organizations for the structure of the service provider. The individual organization will have to tailor the structure and resources applied to service management according to constraints of cost, size, and needs of the business. However, there is a requirement to have a basic functional capability, no matter what size or other organizational constraints you have.

Functions

A *function* is defined by ITIL as a team or group of people and the other resources or tools that are used to carry out a process or process activities.

Commonly, in larger organizations, functions are broken down and carried out by individuals, groups, or teams with specific or specialist skills appropriate to the tasks. An obvious example of this is the service desk. In smaller organizations, there may be fewer specialist groups or teams, and one team may carry out a number of functions; for example, the service desk is incorporated into the wider technical support team.

It is important to define the roles and responsibilities required to carry out the processes and activities for each service lifecycle stage. Within the functions, you need to ensure you allocate the appropriate roles to individuals and that the structure of our teams, groups, or functions are managed to meet the service management requirements.

ITIL provides a set of defined roles:

Group   A number of people who are performing similar activities. Groups are not normally viewed as formal structures but are used to ensure processes are carried out in the same way across a number of different areas. An example is a group of people engaged in problem or incident management.

Team   A more formal structure for those working together with a common objective. Teams are very useful for collaboration and can be located in the same place or multiple locations. Examples are as diverse as a project team, incident resolution teams, or application development teams.

Departments   Formal organizational structures within an organization. There is usually a hierarchical structure that allows for the day-to-day management of staff in the department.

Division   A number of departments that have been grouped together, often self-contained within an organization.

Chapter 10, "Delivering the Service: The Service Operation Lifecycle Stage," explores the detail of the basic functions that ITIL identifies as part of the service lifecycle. Briefly, these functions are as follows:

Service Desk   Single point of contact for users into the IT service provider

Technical Management   Expertise and management of the technological infrastructure

Application Management   Expertise and management of the applications

IT Operations Management   Day-to-day management of the infrastructure and applications, including operation control and facilities management

 These functions are described in the Service Operation core publication, but all the service lifecycle stages make use of them.

Service Automation

Now that we've covered the function as a group or team, we'll cover the tools that can be applied to assist with service management.

Automation can be extremely beneficial to the delivery of services and improve the performance of processes and service assets. This can be applied in all areas, for example, management, organization, people, process, knowledge, and information. Applications are a means of automation in their own right, but even these can be enhanced by additional technology where they need to be shared across people and process assets. There has been such an increase in the capability of technologies (examples such as artificial intelligence, machine learning, and the massive increase in rich media technology), which has increased the potential of software-based service tools to handle a wider variety of tasks.

Improving the automated capability of your service provision offers advantages in several areas:

Capacity Management   Automation for capacity management enables a more rapid response to demand variations without human intervention and allows ease of management for a 24-hour service without an increase in staffing costs.

Measurement   Automation allows for a consistent measurement and identification of improvement, without the human variable. This can also show where the human element of knowledge, skills, and experience are providing benefits.

Optimization   More efficient optimization activities are often outside the human capability for processing data and scheduling and routing.

Knowledge Capture   System-driven knowledge management reduces the reliance on individual knowledge and the difficulties of sharing proprietary knowledge.

Internal IT service providers often find it challenging to address the funding requirements for introducing suitable automation, but when applied appropriately, there should be benefits. Reducing costs and risks by managing complexity in a consistent manner will improve the quality of service.

There are a number of areas throughout service management where automation can provide significant benefit:

- Design and modeling. Modeling tools can assist with projection and forecasting.

- Service catalog. Implementing an automated service catalog can enable the capture of demand for services, by recording interactions from the business.

- Pattern recognition and analysis. Understanding patterns of business activity allows you to manage demand.

- Classification, prioritization, and routing. Incident management can benefit from an automated approach based on the targets in service level agreements.

- Detection and monitoring. Service quality and speed to restore service can be improved through automated tools for availability management.

- Routine service requests can also be handled with some level of automation.

To ensure that automation fulfills the promises of benefit realization, it is necessary to do some preparation, or there may be more problems created than are solved. First simplify the service processes prior to automation. This will help reduce the variations in the process, which may impede successful automation.

Simplification should ensure that you retain the outcome of the process; it is important to make sure that there are no necessary steps or information removed from the process during this activity.

Then you need to clarify the exact steps that are to be undertaken and automated. This includes inputs, dependencies, and interactions that are critical for the process to succeed. Once this has been established, the automation should be tested, and then if corrections are required, they can be applied.

Self-service technology can be extremely beneficial, but it does need to ensure that the users have the best possible experience, with the minimum requirement for interaction with the system.

The only tasks and interactions that should be automated, or considered for automation, are those that have a recognizable recurring pattern and clear inputs, activities, resources, and outputs.

By utilizing the data and information you capture from automation, you can perform service analysis to understand where enhancements can be achieved. In this way, you will be able to improve service quality.

Introducing the Service Lifecycle

In Figure 1.4 you can see the ITIL core, which represents the five ITIL service lifecycle publications. The publications explore the processes and concepts for each lifecycle stage and how they interact with each other. Each lifecycle stage feeds into the others, with the stage of continual service improvement interacting with all of the others. Each of the publications provides guidance on a particular aspect of service management and builds to form an integrated approach.

FIGURE 1.4 The ITIL service lifecycle

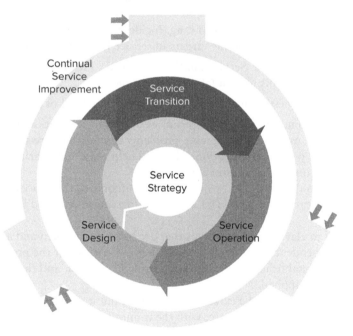

Based on Cabinet Office ITIL material. Reproduced under license from the Cabinet Office.

The following are the five ITIL publications:

Service Strategy This covers the core of the lifecycle, setting the strategic approach for service management activities.

Service Design This provides guidance on the design and development of services according to the requirements of the customer and the strategic approach.

Service Transition This provides guidance on the transition of new or changed services into the live environment, including the development and improvement of capabilities.

Service Operation This covers the management of the day-to-day delivery of services, including optimizing effectiveness and efficiency.

Continual Service Improvement   This provides guidance on the maintenance of value creation and continual alignment to changing business needs.

We review each stage of the service lifecycle in the following chapters.

In each chapter, we explore aspects of the concepts and processes in each lifecycle stage:

- Chapters 2 and 3: Service Strategy
- Chapters 4, 5, 6, and 7: Service Design
- Chapters 8 and 9: Service Transition
- Chapters 10, 11, and 12: Service Operation
- Chapter 13: Continual Service Improvement

Each chapter considers the capabilities that have a direct effect on the service provider's performance and delivers structure to the service management enterprise by describing principles and processes for best practices.

ITIL guidance can and should be adapted to support your specific organizational environment and strategy. The core publications are designed to provide a flexible approach that can be incorporated into any size or type of environment.

To assist with the adaptation and tailoring your approach to its use, the core is supported by complementary publications. These are often specific to a particular industry sector and help with the provision of context when utilizing the generic guidance. Complementary publications are available from a variety of sources, including online resources and documentation.

Summary

This chapter set out the basic concepts that support service management. It provided an initial introduction to the ITIL terminology, the service lifecycle, and the process model. The remaining chapters will follow the service lifecycle and cover each of the stages of the lifecycle in turn. We will explore each in more detail and review the processes that make up the lifecycle stages.

In this chapter, you studied the following concepts:

- Best practices in the public domain
- Why ITIL is successful
- Internal and external customers
- Internal and external services
- Stakeholders in service management
- The ITIL process model and the characteristics of processes
- Processes and functions
- Service automation
- The structure of the service lifecycle

Exam Essentials

Understand that ITIL is a source of best practices.   Best practices are available in a variety of sources, and ITIL is one of them. ITIL should be used in association with other best-practice approaches. Standards and industry practices should be used to complement proprietary knowledge to achieve best practices for your organizational requirements.

Understand why ITIL is successful.   The guidance that exists in the framework is based on a pragmatic approach of "adopt and adapt." The key factors that make it successful are the nonprescriptive, vendor-neutral best practices that form the core service lifecycle publications.

Be able to recall the definitions of the key terms used in this chapter.   The most important terms to remember are service, IT service, outcome, service management, IT service management, and IT service provider.

Understand that services may be grouped together.   Services are grouped into core (business-critical services), enabling (services that support the delivery of core services), and enhancing (services that add value to the core services).

Understand the different types of customer that ITIL defines.   Internal customers are based in the same organization as the service provider. External customers are based outside of the organization of the service provider.

Be able to differentiate between the three service provider types.   The three types are Type I (internal, within individual business units), Type II (shared, providing services shared across a number of business units), and Type III (external, providing services to external customers).

Understand the difference between the stakeholder types.   The stakeholder types are customers who are individuals or groups that buy goods or services, users who use the services on a daily basis, and suppliers who are third parties who provide services that support or enable IT services.

Be able to name the characteristics of processes.   The characteristics of processes are that they are measureable, respond to a trigger, deliver a specific result, and deliver to a customer or stakeholder.

Understand that automation is used to help improve efficiency and effectiveness. Although it is not explicitly referred to in every process or lifecycle stage, automation and the use of technology are key enablers for process enhancement and improvements.

Be able to name the core stages of the service lifecycle.   The core lifecycle stages are service strategy, service design, service transition, service operation, and continual service improvement.

Understand that the ITIL core publications are supported by complementary guidance.   This guidance may be industry-specific or provide context to the adoption of service management best practices.

Review Questions

You can find the answers in Appendix A.

1. Which of the following is *not* a recognized source of IT best practices according to ITIL?
    A. Proprietary knowledge
    B. Industry standards
    C. Training
    D. Auditors

2. Which of the following is a reason an organization might want to adopt ITIL best practices?
    A. Advice on the technical specification of infrastructure
    B. Advice on business strategy
    C. Development of programming techniques
    D. Management of IT services and budgetary controls

3. Which of the following is the correct description of a service?
    A. Restores normal operations as soon as possible
    B. Delivers value to customers, without ownership of specific costs and risks
    C. Investigates the underlying cause of issues
    D. Monitors targets according to contractual obligations

4. What is this? "The result of carrying out an activity, following a process, or delivering an IT service."
    A. A procedure
    B. A work instruction
    C. An outcome
    D. An input

5. What is an IT service made up of?
    A. A combination of information technology, people, and processes
    B. A combination of best practices, information technology, and outcomes
    C. A combination of best practices, outcomes, and inputs
    D. A combination of controls, outcomes, and inputs

6. Which of these is *not* a recognized type of service according to ITIL?
    A. Core service
    B. Supplier service
    C. Enabling service
    D. Enhancing service

7.   Which of these statements is/are correct?

1. Internal services are delivered between departments or business units within the same organization.

2. External services are those delivered to an external customer.

A.   1 only

B.   2 only

C.   Both

D.   Neither

8.   Which of these statements describes an IT service provider?

A.   A third-party service provider delivering components of services

B.   A business unit responsible for IT processes

C.   A function that provides controls for IT infrastructure

D.   A service provider that provides IT services to internal or external customers

9.   How many service provider types does ITIL identify?

A.   1

B.   2

C.   3

D.   4

10.   Which of these is *not* a characteristic of a process?

A.   Delivers functions

B.   Responds to a trigger

C.   Delivers a specific result

D.   Is measurable

Chapter

2

Understanding Service Strategy

THE FOLLOWING ITIL FOUNDATION EXAM TOPICS ARE COVERED IN THIS CHAPTER:

✓ **Account for the purpose, objectives and scope of service strategy**

✓ **Briefly explain what value service strategy provides to the business**

✓ **Generic concepts and definitions:**

- Utility and warranty
- Assets, resources and capabilities
- Governance
- Risk management
- Patterns of business activity

✓ **Describe value creation through services**

This chapter explores the service strategy lifecycle stage. This is often referred to as the core of the service lifecycle, and it sets the strategic approach for the whole of the lifecycle, leading into the operational environment.

The concepts that are explored in this chapter set the policies for the whole service lifecycle and cover important aspects relating to how IT service management provides value to customers.

The service strategy lifecycle stage also includes the policies for governance and risk management that will apply to the whole service lifecycle.

Understanding the Service Strategy Stage

This section explores the service strategy lifecycle stage, covering the key concepts and policies defined as part of this stage of the lifecycle.

Purpose and Objectives of Service Strategy

Service strategy is the core stage of the service lifecycle. As its title suggests, the purpose is to define the strategic approach for service management across the whole lifecycle.

This includes understanding the business perspective, position, future plans, and activity patterns that a service provider needs in order to be able to deliver services that meet the business needs. By understanding the business outcomes, we will be able to guide the focus for the whole service lifecycle.

The objectives of service strategy include the following:

- Providing an understanding of what strategy is
- Identifying the services and the customers who use them
- Understanding how to define value creation and delivery
- Providing the means to identify opportunities to provide services and how to make the best of them
- Delivering a comprehensive and clear service provision model, in which we identify how the services will be funded and presented, to whom they will be delivered, and the purpose that they will serve

- Understanding the organizational capability that will be required to deliver services according to the strategy
- Coordinating and documenting the use of service assets for providing services and how they can be used, including optimizing their performance
- Defining the processes and services that will deliver the strategic plans for IT service management and the level of investment that will be required
- Understanding the levels of demand and how to establish a relationship between the service provider and the customer

The service strategy lifecycle stage provides guidance on understanding the most important practices that need to be employed to define and carry out a service strategy in a service provider organization.

Setting the Scope for Service Strategy

By defining the generic principles and process for service management, you can apply them to ensure the consistent management of IT services.

The definition is applicable for use by both internal and external service providers, and the Service Strategy publication provides guidance for both profit and nonprofit service providers for the consistent management of services.

Two aspects are covered by the guidance in service strategy:

- Defining a strategy that gives a service provider guidance and recommendations about delivering services to meet a customer's business outcomes
- Defining a strategy for managing those services

What Value Does Service Strategy Provide to the Business?

Adopting appropriate best practices as recommended in the ITIL publications can have significant benefits. Implementing standard and consistent approaches for service strategy will provide the following:

- The ability to link the activities carried out by the service provider to the business-critical outcomes that are required by internal or external customers. This will ensure that the service providers are seen to be contributing to the overall organizational value, not just being associated to cost generation.
- The ability to understand the type and levels of service that will support the customers and their success and then to organize them in order to deliver those services. This will be managed by a process of defining strategies and services to ensure a repeatable, consistent approach to delivering valuable services to stakeholders.
- The ability to respond to business change, quickly and efficiently, improving the competitive capability of the organization over time.

- Guidance for creating and maintaining a service portfolio, which shows the overall capability of the service provision to deliver a positive return on investment for the business.

- Support for the transparent communication between the service provider and the customer, ensuring both parties have a consistent understanding of the requirements and their mode of delivery.

- The ability to understand how to organize so that the required services can be delivered in an effective and efficient manner.

Demonstrating the Value of Services

A simple view of the value of a service could be identified as the level to which the service meets the expectation of the customer. For example, a measure of this can be how much the customer is prepared to pay for the service, rather than the actual cost of the service or any specific attribute of the service.

It is difficult to compare services and products, because, unlike products, services do not display much basic and essential value. A service demonstrates its value through what it enables a customer to do. The service provider does not determine the value of a service; the person who receives the service determines it. It will be based on their perception, what the service allows them to do, and what benefit they receive by using the service.

The following are the characteristics of value:

Value Is Defined by Customers   A service provider may promote their service, but the customer will make the final decision of its value.

Affordable Mix of Features   Customers will choose the service that provides the best combination of features, at a price that is reasonable.

Achievement of Objectives   The service may not be valued in commercial terms; it may be measured against the capability to deliver against a specific objective. Many organizations, particularly those in the public sector, or nonprofit organizations, will not have a profit-related measurement framework.

Value Changes Over Time and Circumstance   It is important to recognize that what is valuable to a customer today may not be valuable in the future when business circumstances or market situations have changed.

There is a basic calculation of value for most organizations; a service will be seen to be valuable when the value achieved is higher than the cost of purchasing the service.

To properly understand the value of a service, the IT service provider requires three pieces of information:

The Services IT Provided   If IT is perceived only as managing the infrastructure equipment (servers, networks, PCs, and so on), then the customer's perception of value will be difficult to associate to business outcomes and activities. To determine the value of a service, a customer must be able to link it to something measurable in terms of value to them. Information captured as part of the service portfolio and service catalog will help the customer understand the specific value provided by a service.

What the Services Achieved   It is important for the customer to understand what they were able to do as a result of receiving the service and how important that was for them.

What the Services Cost (or the Price of the Service)   The cost or the price for the service is a major piece of information that the service provider needs to deliver so that the customer can calculate the value. It is the service provider's responsibility to make this available to the customer.

So, you now understand that the customer is key in deciding the value of a service. But what other factors influence a customer's understanding of value? See Figure 2.1 for an illustration.

FIGURE 2.1   Components of value

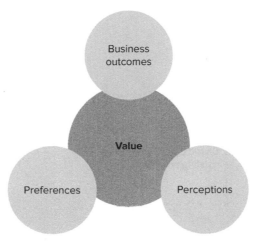

Based on Cabinet Office ITIL material. Reproduced under license from the Cabinet Office.

ITIL identifies three areas that will be used by customers in their understanding of value: the business outcomes achieved, the customer's preferences, and the customer's perception of what was delivered. The combination of these three elements will support the value statement. We covered the association of business outcomes with value already, so we will now cover the perceptions and preferences.

Perceptions are influenced by many different factors, including the attributes of a service or the experience of the customer with other similar services or a competitor's experiences. They may also be affected by the organization's culture or image; perhaps they are seen as a risk-taking market leader or a solid and mature reliable company. These perceptions will affect the customer preferences.

Service providers need to understand these factors and provide customers with information that helps influence perceptions and respond to preferences.

Figure 2.2 illustrates how this translates to the economic value of a service as determined by the customer.

FIGURE 2.2   How customers perceive value

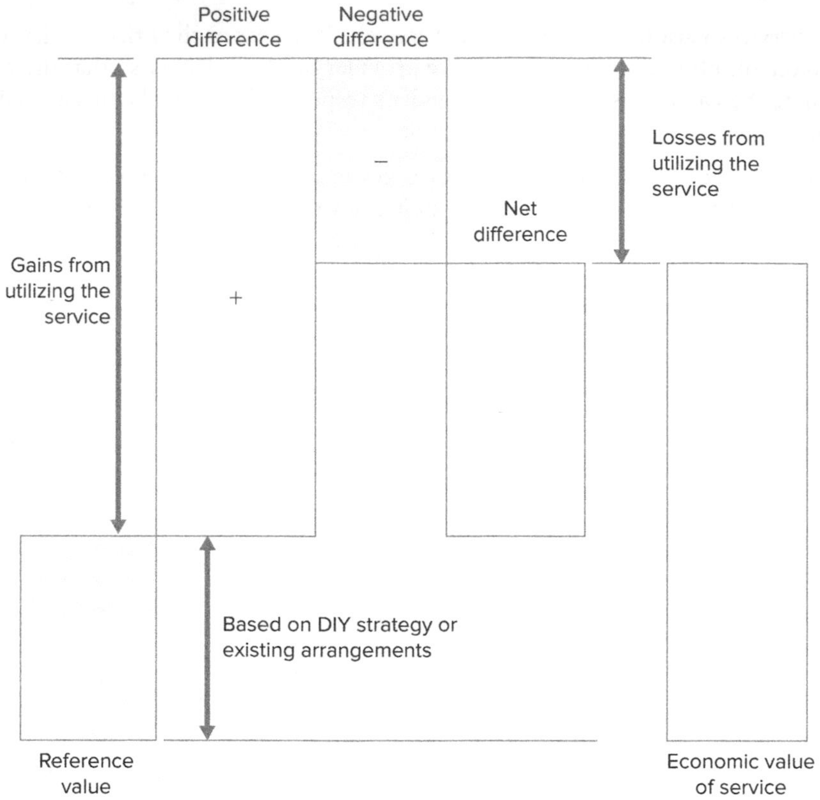

Based on Cabinet Office ITIL material. Reproduced under license from the Cabinet Office.

Figure 2.2 is based on research completed by Tom Nagle and Reed Holden in 2002. The starting point for customer perception in the diagram is the reference value. This could be based on a number of factors, for example, what the customer has heard about the service or a previous experience with the service or a similar service. It is important for the service provider to understand this reference point, either through consultation with the customer or through appropriate research in the marketplace.

The positive difference shown in Figure 2.2 is based on the customer's perception of the additional benefits or gains delivered by the service provider.

The negative difference is the perception of the customer of what they would lose if they invested in the service; this could be quality issues or unexpected costs. Understanding the potential negatives, and then matching the features of the service to these, is a way of influencing a customer's perceptions.

The net difference shown in Figure 2.2 is the perception of the customer of the actual value of the service, once the negatives have been discounted. This could be better or worse than the reference we began with, and it will be this final perception that will support the decision the customer makes about the service.

The economic value represents the overall value of the service, according to the customer's perception. It includes the "value calculation" shown in Figure 2.2 and is measured by the customer in terms of the ability of the service to meet the required outcomes.

It is important to recognize this strategic approach so you fulfill required outcomes for the business and not just deliver a set of services that you, as a service provider, believe the customer needs. This shift in strategic focus is one of the many cultural changes that ITIL promotes to address the common lack of connection between businesses and their IT departments.

Understanding Key Concepts of Service Strategy

This section covers the importance of value creation.

Utility and Warranty in Value Creation

As we discussed earlier, when considering the value of services, you should be concerned with delivering business outcomes and achieving business objectives. You can create this value by looking at two primary elements of a service: *utility* (fit for purpose) and *warranty* (fit for use). These work together to deliver the desired outcomes that allow customers to assess value.

Utility is what the service does, and warranty is how it is delivered, as you can see in Figure 2.3.

FIGURE 2.3 Services are designed, built, and delivered with both utility and warranty

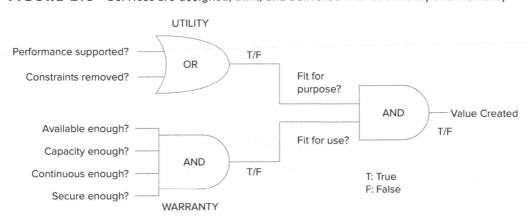

Based on Cabinet Office ITIL material. Reproduced under license from the Cabinet Office.

Utility   Utility is the functionality offered by a product or a service to meet a specific customer need. Often summarized as "what the service does," this is where you understand if the service is able to meet the required outcomes. This is also commonly known as "fit for purpose." This aspect of service value refers to tasks associated to achieving outcomes.

Warranty   Warranty provides the assurance that a product or service will meet the agreed requirements. This may be captured as part of a formal agreement, such as a service level agreement or contract. It refers to the ability of the service to be available when needed, have sufficient capacity to meet the requirements, and be reliable in terms of both security and continuity. This is often summarized as "how the service is delivered" and commonly referred to as "fit for use."

Value in Practice

Looking at any service-based industry can show an example of utility and warranty in a non-IT situation. For example, in a restaurant, no matter what the quality of the service required (fine dining or fast-food), there are basic requirements in terms of premises, furniture, kitchen, funding, food, staff, and so on. These are the utility aspects of providing the service.

The warranty aspects depend on the type of service being provided. For a fast-food experience, you would expect the restaurant to be available 24 hours in the day, whereas a fine-dining restaurant may have exclusive opening times. Fast-food is all about high turnover and high capacity, but once a fine-dining restaurant is fully booked, they are OK with ensuring their customers are not rushed, because it adds to the exclusivity and appeal. Security and continuity are managed appropriately to the dining experience. Fast-food restaurants often have special counters that allow them to keep finances away from the high volumes of customers, whereas a fine-dining experience has an exclusivity approach with staff on hand to ensure security. Continuity of service for both types of establishment has to be managed according to the requirements of their customers. Fast-food is dependent on high turnover, fine dining specializes in high quality, but both provide a valuable service.

The different types of service (fast-food or fine dining) have very different costs associated to them, but the customer has the ability to choose the most appropriate for their budget and their needs.

Assets, Resources, and Capabilities

All processes need to have the appropriate resources and capabilities in order to be successful.

Assets   Resources and capabilities are classed as assets of an organization. All interactions between the service provider and customer are based on the use of assets, both those of the service provider and the customer. Because many customers use the services provided to deliver services or products to their own customers, customer assets from the service provider perspective may be considered to be service assets by the customer.

However the assets are perceived, the performances of all assets are part of defining the value of a service.

ITIL provides us with these definitions for assets:

> Asset: Any resource or capability.
>
> Customer asset: Any resource or capability used by a customer to achieve a business outcome.
>
> Service asset: Any resource or capability used by a service provider to deliver services to a customer.
>
> There are two types of asset used by both service providers and customers: resources and capabilities. They are used to create value in the form of goods and services.

Resources   *Resources* are the direct inputs for the production of services. These cover everything from money, infrastructure items, applications, people, and anything that could be used to assist in the delivery of a service. They are often considered to be assets of an organization, and many will be classified under capital expenditure as a physical asset.

Capabilities   *Capabilities* are the assets that represent the organization's ability to do something to achieve value, such as the ability to coordinate, control, and deploy resources in the form of a service. Typically these are knowledge or information based and include experience, which is embedded in the organization.

Figure 2.4 shows some examples.

FIGURE 2.4   Examples of capabilities and resources

Capabilities	Resources
Management	Financial capital
Organization	Infrastructure
Processes	Applications
Knowledge	Information
People (experience, skills and relationships)	People (number of employees)

Based on Cabinet Office ITIL material. Reproduced under license from the Cabinet Office.

Capabilities cannot produce value by themselves; they need appropriate and sufficient resources. Equally, sufficient resources cannot provide value without the appropriate capability to make use of them to deliver value. It is the combination of resources and capabilities that enables a process to take place in order to deliver successful service management.

Governance and Its Place in the Lifecycle

ITIL defines *governance* as:

> Ensures that policies and strategy are actually implemented, and that required processes are correctly followed. Governance includes defining roles and responsibilities, measuring and reporting, and taking actions to resolve any issues identified.

Governance is an area where IT and the business meet, and the two should operate together according to a common direction, policies, and rules for both parties to achieve the organizational goals.

It is often the case that service management initiatives are unsuccessful when they ignore the corporate governance approach and attempt to impose their own structures. Service management must include the standards and policies of corporate governance, which may require adaptation of best-practice approaches for the individual circumstance.

It is important to have a consistent approach for management at all levels of the organization. This begins with setting a clear strategy and defining the policies that drive the way it will be achieved. Policies also provide structure and boundaries, which will control the way that the organization carries out its operational approach. Governance also provides the controls for the strategy itself, in terms of evaluation, monitoring, and direction for the strategic goal of the organization.

There is an international standard for corporate governance of IT, designated ISO/IEC 38500. Information on this standard is available from the International Standards Organization (www.iso.org).

The role of governance is often the driver for improvement activity, so as well as being important in the role for strategic policy setting, it also plays a significant role in continual service improvement (CSI). CSI will have an effect on service strategy, as it will on the whole of the lifecycle, and as a result, governance provides structure across the whole of the service lifecycle.

Management of Risk in Service Management

In terms of risk management, the Service Strategy publication does not provide a comprehensive organization-wide approach but considers the basic risk management that is required by a project implementing an IT service management approach.

However, it is important to understand that any risk management approach that is adopted for IT should be complementary to the approach in place for the organization as a whole. The corporate approach to risk identification, assessment, management, and mitigation must be enhanced by the IT service provider, not be in conflict with it.

Identifying Risks

This is where the risk is identified and named, which does not mean you have to immediately explain or quantify the risk, but it should be possible to capture what may impact the project or strategy that is under consideration.

Each identified or suspected risk should be documented, and the potential consequences of the risk captured should be part of the record. A commonly used mechanism for capture is a risk register. This is a centralized record of the risks that need to be managed. It will be managed through the continual service improvement lifecycle stage.

Analysis of Risks

After the initial identification and capture of potential consequence, it is possible to begin analyzing the risk. This is where we consider what the impact will be if the risk becomes a reality and the consequence takes place.

The majority of risk management methods use both a numeric and quality calibration and description for the risks. It allows you to define the consequences in words, as well as an associated numeric value, so that a clear understanding can be achieved. The quantitative value is used to calculate a ranking for the risk, while the qualitative statements and descriptions are used for the definition of how to deal with or manage the risk.

Risk management has its basis in probability approaches and theories and can be an extremely mathematical discipline. Risk is the likelihood or potential for something to happen. It is important to ensure that common sense is also applied. A risk that has been identified with 100 percent probability is not a risk; it is a certainty. This should be classified as an issue and be recorded and managed accordingly. Similarly, a risk with a 0 percent probability can be removed from the risk register.

Managing Risks

As part of the documentation for risk management, each risk should be associated with an individual action plan, which incorporates the initial documentation with any outcomes from the analysis. These individual plans should be collated to form an overall risk management plan. This should be reviewed regularly to ensure that the individual risks are being managed appropriately and any actions that have been taken are delivering the expected results.

Throughout a project, there may be variations in the level of risk associated with an activity, and the management of individual risk may be such that it is completely mitigated and now has a 0 percent probability of happening. Alternatively, a risk considered to be low or unlikely at the start of a program may become high or more likely as circumstances change. It is important to continue to review the risk management plan and also to identify any new risks that may arise.

This should be part of the best-practice approach for any project management method and should also be part of the normal risk management approach adopted for operational management.

Risk management is a repetitive activity, and this should become part of the accepted culture of any program or initiative.

Understanding Patterns of Business Activity

Because services are there to enable a business activity and the business activity then generates the business outcome, it is necessary to understand any patterns in the business activity so that you can deliver services that meet the required outcomes. From your own experience in your organization, you will recognize that activities tend to form patterns if they are repeated frequently enough. These interactions form something recognizable and therefore potentially predictable. The more you can predict the likely patterns of business activity, the better you can be prepared to ensure the levels of capacity and availability meet the requirements of the customer outcome. In this way, you will increase the levels of satisfaction with your services and be seen to deliver value.

Business activity covers the use of customer assets such as people, processes, and applications, as well as the interactions between customers, suppliers, partners, and other stakeholders. Capturing and analyzing patterns of business activity are key factors in determining strategies that allow you to deliver services to meet customer demands.

Once a *pattern of business activity (PBA)* has been identified, you should attempt to understand the profile of the PBA and document it. It is recommended that the following items should be captured:

Classification   This identifies the type of PBA and may reference its origins (user or automated), the type and impact of the outcomes that are supported, and the workload associated.

Attributes   This includes frequency, volume, location, and duration.

Requirements   This includes performance, security, availability, privacy, and tolerance for delays. Some of these could be classified as the warranty considerations.

Service Asset Requirements   This is used by design teams to capture and understand what is required to support a specific PBA, in terms of resource and capability. This level of detail is important in the understanding of meeting the requirements for demand, as long as the actual requirements remain within a given forecast.

Figure 2.5 gives some examples.

FIGURE 2.5   Examples of patterns of business activity

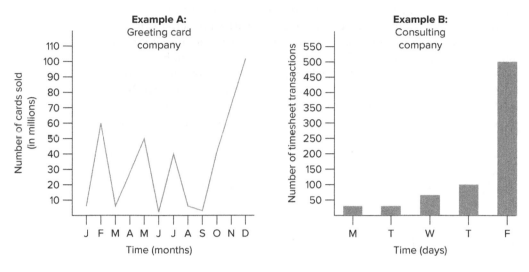

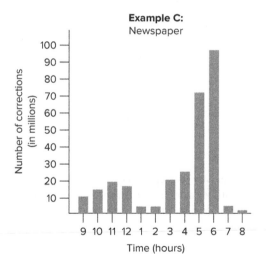

Based on Cabinet Office ITIL material. Reproduced under license from the Cabinet Office.

Figure 2.5 shows an example of three PBAs from three separate organizational models. In the first, you can see an annual approach to pattern recognition. The greetings card company shown in example A will have customers buying according to major holidays or events. The IT service provider must recognize the impact of this activity on IT system usage and provide sufficient capability to enable the business to meet its peaks. Decisions must be made about carrying spare capacity at nonpeak times or how the workload will be balanced at peak times, for a cost-effective provision of service.

In the second example, you can see a weekly pattern of activity, for the use of time-sheet recording. This is obviously an important system, because it directly relates to the billing of external customers for services, so ensuring this can be managed and provided cost-effectively is important. It may be possible in this instance to work with the business to encourage different behaviors from its staff to enable a smoother PBA for the system, perhaps encouraging a daily entry of time allocated. In this way, you can meet the business outcome, but with the cooperation of the business in keeping the need for spare capacity manageable.

In the third example, you have a daily pattern to review. The workload of the business will not alter, because it is concerned with a print deadline. This is a pattern that will require the resources required to be available to match the requirement.

Summary

This chapter explored the purpose, objectives, scope, and value of the service strategy phase of the service lifecycle. This included how the phase creates value for the business and the value of services across the service lifecycle.

We covered the following key concepts:

- Utility and warranty and value creation
- Assets, resources, and capabilities
- Governance
- Risk management
- Patterns of business activity (PBA)

You learned how these concepts are used in the service strategy lifecycle stage and how they relate to the rest of the service lifecycle. The policies and controls that are identified and put in place in the service strategy lifecycle stage have an effect on all of the other lifecycle stages.

Exam Essentials

Be able to differentiate between the purpose, objectives, and scope for the service strategy phase of the lifecycle.   The purpose is to provide the strategy for the service lifecycle. The objectives include the definition of the strategy and governance control. The scope covers defining a strategy to meet a customer's business outcomes and defining a strategy for managing those services.

Understand the terms *utility* and *warranty*.   *Utility* ensures that the service is fit for the purpose, and *warranty* ensures that the service is fit for use. Both of these should be ensured to deliver value to customers.

Be able to differentiate between resources and capabilities.   Resources are items that could be used to assist in the delivery of a service, such as financial capital. Capabilities are the assets that represent the organization's ability to do something to achieve value, such as processes.

Understand the role of governance in the service lifecycle.   Governance is a key part of service management throughout the lifecycle. It provides structure and standardization for the management of services and unites the IT service provider approach with that of the organization.

Understand the role of risk management in the service lifecycle.   Risk management is the approach adopted to identify, document, analyze, and mitigate against the likelihood of potential impact to a project or service. Developing a consistent corporate approach to risk management will ensure a repeatable and manageable process.

Understand the importance of patterns of business activity in the management of services.   Patterns of business activity (PBA) are important in understanding the strategic and tactical approaches you take to the management of resources and capabilities. You need to be aware how you are going to meet the requirements of the business, and capturing, recording, and utilizing PBA will enable you to manage your service provision more efficiently and cost-effectively.

Review Questions

You can find the answers in Appendix A.

1. What is the purpose of the service strategy lifecycle stage?

   A. Identify the processes in use for the service lifecycle.

   B. Create a database of services for the service lifecycle.

   C. Define the strategic approach for service management across the service lifecycle.

   D. Define the objectives for all roles and responsibilities across the service lifecycle.

2. Which two statements reflect the guidance found in the Service Strategy publication?

   1. Defining a strategy that allows a service provider the guidance and recommendations to deliver services to meet a customer's business outcomes.

   2. Conducting customer satisfaction surveys as required on a periodic basis.

   3. Defining a strategy for managing services that meet customers' business outcomes.

   4. Measuring and identifying the value created by continual improvement initiatives.

   A. 1 and 2

   B. 1 and 3

   C. 2 and 3

   D. 2 and 4

3. Who defines the value of a service?

   A. Service strategy process manager

   B. Service strategy process owner

   C. Customer

   D. Business relationship manager

4. To properly understand the value of a service, the IT service provider requires three pieces of information. Which of these is *not* one of the pieces of information?

   A. The services IT provided

   B. What the services achieved

   C. Who designed the services

   D. How much the services cost

5. ITIL identifies three areas that will be used by customers in their understanding of value. Which of these is not one of them?

   A. The business outcomes achieved

   B. The customer's preferences

   C. The customer's perception

   D. The service provider's preferences

6. What is the meaning of "utility of a service"?

    A. The service is "fit for use."

    B. The service meets the requirements for facilities management.

    C. The service delivers the functionality required to meet a business outcome.

    D. The service is capable of supporting the business strategy.

7. Which one of these four assets can be classed as both a resource and a capability?

    A. People

    B. Financial capital

    C. Organization

    D. Knowledge

8. Which of these statements about governance is true?

    1. Ensures that policies and strategy are actually implemented

    2. Ensures that required processes are correctly followed

    3. Ensures that the CAB assesses all changes

    A. 1, 2, and 3

    B. 2 and 3

    C. 1 only

    D. 1 and 2

9. The risk management approach consists of three stages. Which of these is not a stage identified in the ITIL guidance?

    A. Analyze risks

    B. Calibrate risks

    C. Manage risks

    D. Identify risks

10. ITIL recommends that you understand and document the profile of patterns of business activity (PBA). Which of these represents the four things that you should capture about each PBA profile?

    A. Classification, attributes, requirements, and service asset requirements

    B. Attributes, service asset serial numbers, prioritization, and requirements

    C. Management information, prioritization, service asset serial numbers, and configuration baselines

    D. Classification, prioritization, requirements, and service asset requirements

Chapter

3

Service Strategy Processes

THE FOLLOWING ITIL FOUNDATION EXAM OBJECTIVES ARE COVERED IN THIS CHAPTER:

✓ **Generic concepts and definitions:**

- Service portfolio
- Business case

✓ **State the purpose, objectives and scope for:**

- Service portfolio management
- The service portfolio
- Financial management for IT services
- Business case
- Business relationship management

In this chapter, we will cover some of the processes of the service strategy phase of the lifecycle. Service portfolio management provides an important source of information for managing services across the lifecycle. Financial management consists of understanding the costs for IT services, including being able to justify the expenditure of those services. Business relationship management is crucial to ensuring an integrated approach to the delivery of services to meet organizational needs.

We will review the purpose, objectives, and scope for each of the processes and consider their importance in the service strategy lifecycle stage.

Understanding Service Portfolio Management

We will begin this chapter by covering the *service portfolio management* process, which allows you to gain an understanding of the complete portfolio of services provided across the lifecycle.

In the Foundation exam syllabus, this process is covered only by the requirement to understand the purpose, scope, and objectives of the process. More information about this process is available in the lifecycle core publication of Service Strategy, and further education on the process can be found in the ITIL qualification scheme.

In the Foundation exam syllabus, the service portfolio management process is covered only by the requirement to understand its purpose, scope, and objectives. More information about this process is available in the service lifecycle core publication Service Strategy (published by TSO), and further education on the process can be found in the ITIL qualification scheme.

Purpose of SPM

The purpose of this process is to ensure that you have the appropriate mix of services delivered by the service provider to meet the requirements of the customer. The process enables you to track important information about your services, including the investment that has been made and the interaction with other services.

The information captured in the *service portfolio* also ensures that you clearly define the services and link them to the business outcomes they support. Once you do this, you provide the capability for alignment across the whole of the lifecycle through design, transition, and operation in order to ensure value is delivered to customers.

Objectives of SPM

The following are the objectives of service portfolio management:

- Provide a process that allows an organization to manage its overall service provision. As part of this process, you are able to develop mechanisms that allow you to investigate and decide on the services to provide to your customers, based on the analysis of the potential benefits and acceptable levels of risk.

- Maintain the definitive managed portfolio of services provided by the service provider. Each service should be identified, along with the business need and outcome it supports.

- Provide an information source that allows the organization to understand and evaluate how the IT services provided enable them to achieve their desired outcomes. It will also be a mechanism for tracking how IT can respond to organizational changes in an internal or external environment.

- Provide control over which services are offered, to whom, with what level of investment, and under what conditions.

- Track the organizational spend on IT services throughout their lifecycle, allowing for regular reviews of the strategy to ensure that the appropriate investment is being made for the chosen strategic approach.

- Provide information to enable decision making regarding the viability of services and when they should be retired.

Scope of SPM

Service portfolio management has a very broad scope, because it covers all the services a service provider delivers, as well as those that it is planning to deliver and those that have been retired from live operation.

Because the primary concern of the service portfolio management process is to understand if the services being provided are delivering value, the process should cover the ability to track investment and expenditure on services. This can then be compared to the desired business outcomes.

Internal and external service providers may have a different approach from the way they connect services to business outcomes. For an internal service provider, it will be necessary to work closely with the business units in the organization to compare the outcomes with the investment. External service providers are more likely to have this information captured as part of the agreement or contract that defines the relationship with the business. The services they provide are also more likely to be directly associated to revenue generation or support revenue generation services.

Service portfolio management should be responsible for evaluating the value of the services provided throughout the whole of their lifecycle. It is also important to be able to compare the merits of the existing services against those that are being planned or the benefits they provide in replacing retired services. In this way, you can be certain that the services provided meet the required business outcomes.

The Service Portfolio

We will now review the service portfolio, which is the output from the process. Figure 3.1 gives an overview.

FIGURE 3.1   The service portfolio

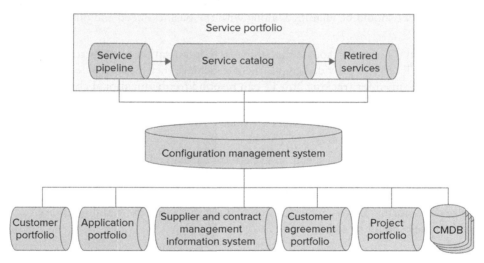

Based on Cabinet Office ITIL material. Reproduced under license from the Cabinet Office.

The *service portfolio* is the complete set of services managed by a service provider. This includes the contractual and financial commitments across internal, external, or third-party providers; new service development activity; and improvement initiatives. All services should be included, whether they are visible, customer-facing services or the enhancing, enabling services that support them.

The service portfolio consists of three sections: the pipeline section, which contains information about the services that are in a pre-operational state; the service catalog section, which is the customer-facing section of the service portfolio that shows details of live operational services; and the retired section, which contains details of the services that have been retired.

The service portfolio also covers the services that are currently only in a conceptual stage—potentially the services that would be developed if there were no limit on budget, resources, or capabilities. This will be maintained in the pipeline section of the service portfolio. It may seem strange to document what you currently cannot achieve, but by doing so, you will be able to allow for better assessment of your existing delivery and determine whether you are allocating resources and capabilities efficiently.

From the service portfolio, you can see the allocation of all the resources in use across the whole service lifecycle. Each stage of the lifecycle will be making demands on available resources and capabilities, and the service portfolio allows you to see those allocations and resolve any potential conflicts according to the importance of the business outcomes.

Any new project or development should have an approved financial plan and allocated budget, demonstrating the cost recovery or return on investment, and this will be captured in the service portfolio. By ensuring you have the right mix of services across the pipeline and catalog, you can make sure you have the correct funding for all of the IT service provider activities across the service lifecycle. A balanced approach to the introduction of new services and development of services, compared to the maintenance of live services, will ensure that you can manage any conflict in resource allocation.

As you will see in Chapter 6, the service catalog is the only part of the service portfolio that is customer-facing, although the other information the service portfolio contains may be used as part of customer-facing reports, presentations, and business cases. The live operational services, as captured in the service catalog, are the only services that will be expected to demonstrate cost recovery or profitability.

Understanding the Financial Management Process

Organizations have to be able to manage their finances, but it is a complex process used across an entire organization. It is normally owned by a very senior executive and managed as a separate business function. It is an extremely important area that allows organizations to manage resources and ensure that their objectives are being achieved.

The IT service provider, as part of the overall organization, must be involved in the financial management process. It is important to make sure that all financial practices are aligned; even though a separate process may be used, it should follow the overall organizational principles and requirements.

Purpose of Financial Management

To design, develop, and deliver the services that meet the organizational requirements, you must secure an appropriate level of funding. This is the main purpose of financial management for IT services. At the same time, the financial management process should act as a gatekeeper for the expenditure on IT services to ensure that the service provider is not over-extended financially for the services that the service provider is required to deliver. Obviously, this will require a balance between the cost and quality of the service, in line with the balance of supply and demand between the service provider and their customers.

Cost and quality are key factors in the provision of services, and the only way you can allocate and understand the cost of service provision is through sound financial practices.

Objectives of Financial Management

The following are the objectives of the financial management process:

- Defining and maintaining a financial framework that allows the service provider to identify, manage, and communicate the actual cost of service delivery.

- Understanding and evaluating the financial impact and implications of any new or changed organizational strategies on the service provider.

- Securing the funding that is required for providing the services. This will require significant input from the business and will naturally depend on the overall approach to financial management and cross charging within the organization.

- Working with the service asset and configuration management process (covered in Chapter 9) to ensure service and customer assets are being properly maintained and all associated costs are recorded.

- Performing basic financial accounting in respect of the relationship between expenses and income and ensuring they are balanced according to the overall organizational requirements.

- Reporting on and managing expenditure for service provision, on behalf of the stakeholders.

- Management and execution of the organization's policies and practices relating to financial controls.

- Ensuring that financial controls and accounting practices are applied to the creation, delivery, and support of services.

- Understanding the future financial requirements of the organization and providing financial forecasts for the service commitments and any required compliance for legislative and regulatory controls.

- If appropriate, defining a framework that allows for recovering the costs of service provision from the customer.

Scope of Financial Management

Financial management is normally a well-recognized activity in any organization, but the specific requirement to manage funding related to the provision of IT services may not be so well established.

It is important to understand the strategic approach that is adopted in relation to IT service provision. How will it be managed; is it internally or externally sourced? If it's internal, is there a requirement to cross charge for services, or is there some other mechanism of cost recovery in place?

In the majority of organizations, there will be qualified accountants in charge of the corporate finances, usually as part of the finance department. They will set the policies, standards, and accounting practices for the business. The strategy relating to IT funding will be part of the overall accounting approach, but the specifics may be managed locally as part of the IT department.

Those engaged in financial management for IT services must ensure that the practices are consistent with existing corporate controls and that reporting and accounting activities meet with the governance standards as defined for the whole organization. This will also assist with general understanding by the various business units of how IT is funded. Communication and the reporting of internal funding practices across an organization are extremely important for enabling a true understanding of the costs of IT services.

Using a service management approach to delivering services should mean that the accounting for IT services is more effective, detailed, and efficient than it would be otherwise. For an internal service provider, this will enable a translation of information between service provider and business.

Financial management consists of three main processes:

Budgeting   This is the process of predicting and controlling the income and expenditure of money within an organization. Budgeting consists of a periodic cycle (usually annual) of negotiation to set budgets and the monthly monitoring of the same.

Accounting   This is the process that enables the IT organization to account fully for the way that its money has been spent. It should enable a cost breakdown by customer, service, activity, or other factor to demonstrate the allocation of funds. It will normally require some form of accounting system (ledgers, charts of accounts, journal, and so on) and should be managed and overseen by someone with an accountancy qualification or skills.

Charging   This is the process required to bill customers for the use of the services and will be applicable only where the organizational accounting model requires it to take place. It requires sound accounting practices and supporting systems so that any cross charging is accurate and traceable.

Table 3.1 shows the cycles associated with financial management.

TABLE 3.1   Budgeting, IT accounting, and charging cycles

Frequency	Budgeting	IT accounting	Charging
Planning (annual)	Agree overall expenditure	Establish standard unit costs for each IT resource	Establish pricing policy and publish price list
Operational (monthly)	Take actions to manage budget exceptions or changed costs	Monitor expenditure by cost center	Compile and issue bills

The two cycles are as follows:

- Planning (annual), where cost projections and workload forecasting form a basis for cost calculations and price setting
- Operational (monthly or quarterly), where costs are monitored and checked against budgets, bills are issued, and revenue is collected

Preparing and Using a Business Case

One of the key benefits of having an established financial management process is the ability to capture and understand costs and use this information to create justification for expenditure in the form of a business case.

A *business case* should be a tool for decision planning and support, allowing you to predict the likely consequences of a business decision. This outcome may be either quantitative or qualitative; for example, financial analysis is a common feature of a business case.

In Table 3.2, you can see an example of a basic structure for a business case.

TABLE 3.2   Structure of a business case

A. Introduction	Presents the business objectives addressed by the service.
B. Methods and assumptions	Defines the boundaries of the business case, such as time period and which organizational context is being used to define costs and benefits.
C. Business impacts	The financial and nonfinancial results anticipated for the service or service management initiative. Please bear in mind that many nonfinancial results can also be expressed in financial terms. For example, an increase in staff morale can result in lower staff turnover and therefore less expenditure on hiring and training.
D. Risks and contingencies	The probability that alternative results will emerge.
E. Recommendations	The specific actions recommended.

Two main considerations for any business case are business objectives and business impact.

Business Objectives

Obviously business objectives will vary from organization to organization. However, they should form a key part of any business case. It is only by examining and understanding the business objectives that you can properly appreciate the impact to the business of the proposal under consideration in the business case. Objectives should start broadly:

- Commercial provider organizations usually have objectives that are the organization's overall objectives in terms of financial and organizational performance.

- Where the service provider is internal, the objectives are likely to be linked to business units, which in turn are linked to the overall organizational objectives.

- Business objectives for nonprofit organizations are more complex but are usually associated with the users or members who benefit from the organization's goals, as well as the standard financial objectives.

Business Impact

There is a strong relationship between the business objective and the business impact, as shown in the following figures. Figure 3.2 illustrates one aspect of this, and Figure 3.3 shows the converse.

FIGURE 3.2 A single business impact can affect multiple business objectives.

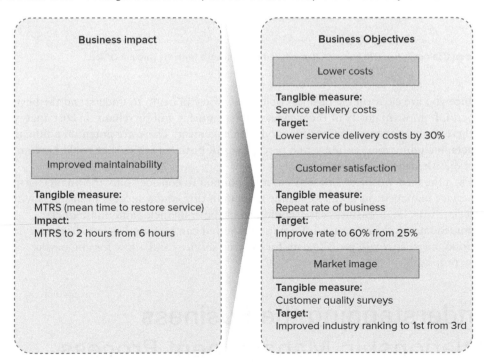

Based on Cabinet Office ITIL material. Reproduced under license from the Cabinet Office.

FIGURE 3.3   Multiple business impacts can affect a single business objective.

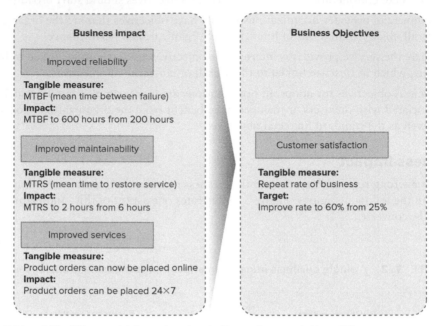

Based on Cabinet Office ITIL material. Reproduced under license from the Cabinet Office.

Once you are clear on the business objectives, you can begin to understand the business impact. Often the majority of the business case argument will be reliant on cost analysis, but there are other considerations for service management. There are potential nonfinancial impacts, including market image and perceptions of business ethics that could have an effect on sales or customer satisfaction.

When the term *business case* is used, it is common to consider only the financial aspects, but service management needs to include more than this, and a successful business will appreciate this. So, a business case should include both financial and nonfinancial recommendations. Much of the information required can be found as part of the service portfolio, because it will provide data for existing services and allow for comparing a new proposal.

Understanding the Business Relationship Management Process

Business relationship management has matured as a process over time, because initially it was simply a role fulfilled to ensure the business had a named contact within the IT service provider. But now, as part of a mature service management approach, we recognize the need for the process of business relationship management as a strategic process in its own right, not just as a role supporting service level management at an executive level.

The process of business relationship management provides a connection between organizational executives and the strategic management of the service provider.

 In the Foundation exam syllabus, this process is covered only by the requirement to understand the purpose, scope, and objectives of the process. More information about this process is available in the lifecycle core publication of Service Strategy, and further education on the process can be found in the ITIL qualification scheme.

Purpose of the BPM Process

This process has a very important part to play in the alignment of the IT service provider and the customer.

The purpose of the process is twofold:

- Establish a relationship between the service provider and the customer, and maintain this by continuing to review the business and customer needs. This relationship is extremely important for building a rapport between the service provider and the customer.

- Identify customer needs and ensure that the service provider can meet those needs, both now and in the future. Business relationship management is the process that ensures the service provider is able to understand the changing needs of the business over time. The relationship also allows the customer to articulate the value of the services to the service provider.

One of the most important concepts in this relationship is that of expectation—the customer's expectation of the service provider's capabilities and the service provider's expectation of the customer's needs. It is critical that the expectation of the customer does not exceed what they are prepared to pay for, and business relationship management is instrumental in managing this communication.

Objectives of the BPM Process

The objectives of business relationship management are as follows:

- Ensure that the service provider has a clear understanding of the customer's perspective of the service so that you are able to prioritize the services and assets accordingly.

- Ensure that customer satisfaction remains high, which will demonstrate that the service is achieving the needs of the customer.

- Establish and maintain a relationship between the customer and service provider that enables understanding of the business drivers and the customer.

- Ensure that the organization and the service provider communicate effectively so that the service provider will be aware of any changes to the customer environment. Changes to the customer environment may have an impact on the services provided.

- Identify technology changes or trends that may have an impact on the type, level, or utilization of the service provided.

- Ensure that the service provider is able to articulate the business requirements for new or changed services and that services continue to meet the needs of the business and continue to deliver value.

- Provide mediation where there is conflict on the use of services between business units. This may be a conflict of resource allocation, or perhaps the requirement to utilize or change functionality differs for specific departments.

- Establish a formal procedure for managing complaints and escalations with the customer. This is a common requirement for governance standards, because it demonstrates a commitment to customer satisfaction and improvement.

Scope of the BPM Process

The scope of business relationship management will vary depending on the nature and culture of the organization. If the organization works with an internal service provider, it is likely that the business relationship management will be carried out between senior management representatives in both the IT department and business units. Often in larger organizations, you will be able to find dedicated business relationship managers (BRMs), but in smaller organizations the role can be combined with other managerial responsibility. The BRM will work with the customer representatives to understand the objectives of the business and ensure that the services provided are in alignment and supportive of those objectives.

If an external service provider supports the organization, you will commonly find that a dedicated account manager carries out the process, with an individual allocated to a customer or group of smaller customers with similar requirements. As the external service provider relationship with the business is captured in a contract, the focus will be on achieving the contractual obligations and customer satisfaction with the service value.

One of the major requirements for business relationship management is to focus on understanding how the services you provide meet the requirements of your customers. The process needs to ensure that you can communicate effectively with your customers so that you can understand their needs. The following are some of the key areas you should consider:

- Business outcomes, so that you understand what the customer wants to achieve.

- How the customer uses your services and which services are being offered to them.

- How you manage the services that are being offered, in terms of responsibility for the provision, the service levels you deliver, and the quality of service that is being achieved. You should also consider any changes that may be required in response to business and IT plans.

- As IT service providers, it is vital that you keep track of technology trends and advances that may impact your service delivery. All too often, customers will hear about new technologies but not understand the impact of them, so it is the responsibility of business relationship management to ensure that you communicate and advise on the best use of technology to deliver service value.

- You need to measure the levels of customer satisfaction and respond to any drop in satisfaction with suitable action plans. The BRM will be a key figure in the communication and management of any such plans.

- How you can optimize the service you provide for the future.

- The business relationship management process should be concerned with the way that the service provider is represented to the customer. This may mean engaging with the business to ensure that commitments from both sides have been fulfilled.

To successfully carry out the process of business relationship management and so that all of the previous factors can be considered, it is necessary to work with other service management processes and functions. For example, the ability to associate business outcomes with services is part of service portfolio management; service level management provides information about service levels and their achievement; and service asset and configuration management maps customers and service owners to the infrastructure, applications, and services.

This interaction between the processes of business relationship management and service-level management will require clear boundaries, relationships, and responsibilities to be identified between business relationship management and other service management processes, because there is a strong potential for confusion. Business relationship management should focus on the relationship between the customer and service provider, as well as the achievement of customer satisfaction, but the other service management processes should focus on the services themselves and how well they meet the agreed requirements.

Business relationship management does not ignore the services, but it should be focused on the high-level perspective of whether the service is meeting the business needs, rather than on specific targets for delivery. Equally, the other service management processes do not ignore this aspect of customer satisfaction, but they should be focused on the quality of the services and how customer expectations can be met.

An example of this is the difference between the service level management and business relationship management processes. They both have regular interaction with customers and are concerned with the ongoing review and management of service and service quality. But each has a different purpose, and the nature of the interface with the customer differs in content and responsibility.

This is clearly shown in Table 3.3, which is an extract from the core publication Service Strategy.

TABLE 3.3 Differences between business relationship management and service level management

	Business relationship management	**Service level management**
Purpose	To establish and maintain a business relationship between the service provider and the customer based on understanding the customer and its business needs. To identify customer needs (utility and warranty) and ensure that the service provider is able to meet these needs.	To negotiate service level agreements (warranty terms) with customers and ensure that all service management processes, operational-level agreements, and underpinning contracts are appropriate for the agreed service-level targets.
Focus	Strategic and tactical—the focus is on the overall relationship between the service provider and their customer, as well as which services the service provider will deliver to meet customer needs.	Tactical and operational—the focus is on reaching agreement on the level of service that will be delivered for new and existing services and whether the service provider was able to meet those agreements.
Primary measure	Customer satisfaction, also an improvement in the customer's intention to better use and pay for the service. Another metric is whether customers are willing to recommend the service to other (potential) customers.	Achieving agreed levels of service (which leads to customer satisfaction).

Business relationship management is also concerned with the design of services, which makes BRMs the ideal contact for strategic communication with customers for all departments in the service provider. There is a potential connection for business relationship management with application development, as well as other development and design areas.

There are many connections and similarities between business relationship management and service level management and other service management processes, and the roles are often combined. But as you can see from Table 3.4, there are distinct differences in the activities for the processes, and there needs to be a clear understanding that when carrying out business relationship management, an individual needs to be aware when they are working on a strategic business relationship and when they are working tactically. For example, making long-term plans and managing a business relationship at a very senior level are part of a strategic approach, whereas working with services on an operational basis will be part of a tactical approach.

TABLE 3.4 Business relationship management process and other service management processes

Scenario	Primary process being executed	Other processes involved
Developing high-level customer requirements for a proposed new service	Business relationship management	Service portfolio management
Building a business case for a proposed new service	Business relationship management	Service portfolio management
Confirming customers' detailed functionality requirements for a new service	Design coordination	Business relationship management
Confirming a customer requirement for service availability for a new service	SLM	Business relationship management, availability management
Establishing patterns of business activity	Demand management	Business relationship management
Evaluating a business case for new service request from the customer and deciding go/no go	Service portfolio management	Business relationship management, financial management for IT services
Reporting service performance against service level	SLM	Business relationship management

Summary

In this chapter, you explored how the service management processes in the service strategy phase of the lifecycle contribute to the whole service lifecycle.

You learned about the processes in the service strategy stage, considering the purpose, objectives, and scope for the following processes:

- Service portfolio management
- Financial management (including the use and value of the business case)
- Business relationship management

Each of these processes is important in managing the strategic approach to the service lifecycle. The service portfolio provides information that is used throughout the service lifecycle, and the financial management process is used to manage costs and budgets for all the lifecycle stages.

Business relationship management is a key process in the management of services, because it provides the high-level, strategic interface to the customers who pay for the services provided by the IT service provider.

Exam Essentials

Recall the purpose of the service portfolio management process.   The process ensures you have an appropriate mix of services being delivered and developed for your customers.

Identify the various components of the service portfolio.   The service portfolio comprises the service pipeline, which shows services prior to live operation; the service catalog, which shows the customer-facing view of the live operational services; and the retired services, which shows information about decommissioned services.

Identify the three main areas of the financial management process.   The three main areas are budgeting, which is planning for expenditure; IT accounting, which is where you account for the expenditure on IT services; and charging, which is where the customer is charged for the IT services if this is appropriate. Financial management is crucial for calculating value for services.

Understand the purpose of a business case.   A business case is a tool for decision making. Much of the information required will be part of the service portfolio and part of the financial management reports and outputs.

Understand the purpose of business relationship management.   This is the process that connects the customer and the service provider at a strategic level.

Be able to differentiate between business relationship management and the other service management processes, especially service level management.   Remember, business relationship management is concerned with a strategic relationship with the customer, whereas other processes are more tactically based.

Review Questions

You can find the answers in Appendix A.

1. What is the purpose of the service portfolio management process?
    A. To capture details of live operational services only
    B. To ensure you have an appropriate mix of services to meet the requirements of customers
    C. To ensure all services are documented according to the requirements of the business
    D. To capture details of retired services only

2. Which of these statements represents an objective of service portfolio management?
    A. Deliver authorized change requests.
    B. Maintain records of all service components and their relationships.
    C. Maintain the definitive managed portfolio of services provided by the service provider.
    D. Provide accurate information about the service level achievements for core services.

3. Which of these is *not* part of the scope of service portfolio management?
    A. All the services a service provider currently delivers
    B. All the projects the customer is planning to deliver
    C. All the services a service provider is planning to deliver
    D. All the services a service provider has retired from live operation

4. Which of these statements about service portfolio management is/are correct?
    1. Service portfolio management should be responsible for monitoring the performance of the services according to the service level agreements.
    2. Service portfolio management should be responsible for evaluating the value of the services provided throughout the whole of their lifecycle.
    3. Service portfolio management should be able to compare the merits of the existing services against those that are being planned.
    4. Service portfolio management should compare the results of continual service improvement initiatives to decide whether to improve services.

    A. 1, 2, and 4
    B. 1, 2, and 3
    C. 2 and 4
    D. 2 and 3

5. Which of these is *not* part of the structure of the service portfolio?
    A. Service register
    B. Service pipeline
    C. Service catalog
    D. Retired services

6. What is the purpose of financial management?

  A. To agree to the business requirements for managing the finance systems

  B. To agree to the operating policies for the finance systems

  C. To secure to the appropriate software programs for financial systems

  D. To secure to the appropriate funding for IT services

7. Which of these is *not* part of the scope of financial management?

  A. Budgeting

  B. Consolidating

  C. Accounting

  D. Charging

8. Which of these is/are recommended elements of a business case?

  1. Introduction

  2. Methods and assumptions

  3. Business impacts

  4. Risks and contingencies

  5. Recommendations

  A. 1, 2, 3, 4, and 5

  B. 2, 3, 4, and 5

  C. 1, 2, 3, and 4

  D. 1, 3, and 5

9. Which of these is a purpose of business relationship management (BRM)?

  A. Manage the services provided to a customer

  B. Establish a mechanism for recording service requests from the customer

  C. Establish a relationship between the service provider and the customer

  D. Manage the funding for services provided to a customer

10. Which of these statements about business relationship management (BRM) is *most* correct?

  A. BRM focuses on the relationship with users through the service desk.

  B. BRM monitors the service targets for all services.

  C. BRM reviews all service changes.

  D. BRM focuses on a high-level relationship with customers.

Chapter

4

Understanding Service Design

THE FOLLOWING ITIL FOUNDATION EXAM OBJECTIVES ARE COVERED IN THIS CHAPTER:

✓ **2-5. Account for the purpose, objectives and scope of service design**

✓ **2-6. Briefly explain what value service design provides to the business**

✓ **Unit 3: Generic concepts and definitions:**

- 3-14. Service design package

✓ **4-3. Understand the importance of people, processes, products and partners for service management**

✓ **4-4. Understand the five major aspects of service design**

- Service solutions for new or changed services
- Management information systems and tools
- Technology architectures and management architectures
- The processes required
- Measurement methods and metrics

The success or failure of a service is largely dependent on its design. As a result, the ITIL framework spends a lot of time looking at this key lifecycle stage, so we will be spending the next few chapters covering service design and its processes.

This stage starts with a customer requirement for a new or changed service and finishes when a service that matches that need is ready to be handed over to the transition phase (together with the service design package that documents all aspects of the design). It is the aim of the transition stage to build and test the service and deploy it successfully into the operational environment, where it becomes the responsibility of the operation stage.

Poor design may mean that the service never delivers the value envisaged in the strategy stage. In Chapter 2, "Understanding Service Strategy," we discussed the need for services to provide utility and warranty in order to deliver value. If a service is unable to deliver the level of service required consistently (because of poor availability, capacity issues, insufficient security, or a lack of service continuity), it will have failed to deliver the warranty required. It has often been an issue that design projects concentrate on delivering the utility of a new service but spend too little time ensuring that warranty is also delivered. It is the combination of these two aspects that deliver value (as we discussed when we covered the service strategy stage of the lifecycle in Chapter 2). Designing a service without considering what service levels it will need to meet will result in a service that fails to meet the customer's requirements or requires expensive amendments once it is in operation.

Understanding the Purpose, Objectives, and Scope for Service Design

Service design is involved in planning both new services and changes to existing services, ensuring that the new or changed service fulfills the service strategy by delivering the business objectives. It touches all areas of IT because each area will have a role in delivering and supporting the eventual service. It includes the design of both services and the service management processes, which will ensure that the service continues to provide value.

Successful design depends on taking the time to plan ahead. This is often seen as wasted time, with the service provider anxious to press ahead with the design. In fact, nothing could be further from the truth; insufficient planning leads to costly rework and delay later. Part of the planning phase is identifying and managing risks to ensure a successful outcome.

The Purpose of Service Design

The purpose of service design is to deliver a new service or a change to an existing service that is capable of delivering the strategic outcome required. This involves not only the technology used to deliver the service but the processes and policies needed to ensure that the technical solution delivers the intended value. It considers what will be required by the transition phase to implement the service in the operational environment, how the service will perform, and what will be required to support it. Service design must ensure that the service runs within the allocated budget and delivers a level of service that meets or exceeds the customer requirement.

The Objectives of Service Design

In an ideal world, services would be designed so well that they would require little or no improvement later. Although this is not realistic, service design should aim to deliver a service that will require very little improvement later. This is not to say that there is no role for continual service improvement; every design effort should apply lessons learned from previous design projects because these lessons can improve the eventual output. The business requirement may also change, requiring improvements to the original design.

Service design activities may be undertaken on a regular basis or as the result of identifying a new or changed business requirement.

The Scope of Service Design

ITIL service design considers not only the current requirement; it extrapolates from this to identify possible future needs and ensures that the service being designed will be able to be developed to meet these requirements too. It ensures that the design fits the requirements, and tries to take advantage of technical developments to deliver an innovative service.

It is essential that the service is aligned with the business need, so service design describes how to identify these requirements and ensure that the service delivers what the customer requires. It considers the functional requirements that must be delivered as well as the required service levels. It ensures that any design constraints are identified and adhered to.

The processes included within service design are as follows:

- Design coordination
- Service catalog management
- Service level management
- Availability management
- Capacity management
- IT service continuity management
- Information security management
- Supplier management

We will be examining these processes in later chapters. It is important to remember that these processes are considered during the design stage, but many of their activities also take place during other lifecycle stages. Service level management, for example, has to be considered during design to ensure the service is designed to meet the service level requirements. Once the service is operational, however, service level management is involved in monitoring, reporting, and improving the level of service being delivered and works closely with continual service improvement to implement any service improvement plans.

All processes across the lifecycle must be linked; it is important to understand how these various processes interact so that an amendment to one process does not have unintended consequences on another.

The Value Service Design Provides to the Business

As we mentioned, good service design delivers high-performing services that match the business requirement and are delivered at an affordable cost. Following the service design guidelines in the ITIL framework will have a number of positive outcomes for the business.

Foremost among these is a lower total cost of ownership across the lifetime of the service, because all aspects of the design, processes, and technology have been considered and designed to work together, therefore minimizing later rework. Good design will also consider the corporate strategy and existing architecture, as well as any design constraints, to ensure that the service operates within these parameters.

By ensuring that the warranty aspects of the service are included during the design stages, the service design delivers a reliable, effective service that meets the customer requirement. The service will be designed to meet the agreed service level requirements and will ensure the required capacity, availability, and service continuity requirements are met cost-effectively.

Service design considers not only how the service will perform in the live operational environment; it also considers the most effective way of enabling the transition from design to live, ensuring that all the required information for this transition stage is captured in a *service design package (SDP)*.

Service design will consider what metrics and controls may be required for good governance and ensure that these are part of the design. Ensuring that the design gathers the appropriate metrics will assist in the continual service improvement of the service in the future. It will also consider what processes are required and ensure that these are designed to be both effective and efficient.

Finally, service design will consider particular strategic requirements, such as using cloud technologies or delivering services with the lowest possible carbon footprint, ensuring that the design is aligned with these business requirements.

Describing the Service

ITIL recommends producing a key output from the service design stage—a service design package (SDP). The service design package consists of one or more documents, produced during the service design stage, that describe all aspects of the service, throughout its lifecycle. It contains all the necessary information that will be used to transition and operate the service. It is passed forward to the transition stage so that those transitioning the service have a clear understanding of the requirements that need to be verified in testing.

Typical contents of an SDP include the following:

- Original agreed business requirements for the service
- How the service will be used
- Key contacts and stakeholders
- Functional requirements
- Management requirements
- Service level requirements
- Technical design of the new or changed service including hardware, software, networks, environments, data, applications, technology, tools, and documentation
- Sourcing strategy
- New or changed processes required to support the service
- Organizational readiness assessment
- Service lifecycle plan, including the timescales and phasing, for the transition, operation, and subsequent improvement of the new service
- Service program, service transition plan
- Service operational acceptance plan
- Service acceptance criteria (SAC)

A large amount of information is gathered during the design stage, often as part of a formal project management methodology; the production of the SDP ensures that all the relevant information is captured when the project ends and is passed on to those who will be transitioning, managing, and improving the new or changed service.

Four Key Elements of Service Design

Service design, as described within the ITIL framework, takes a holistic view of what is required to design and deliver a service. A frequent error in service design is that this view, encompassing all aspects, is replaced with a narrow, technical view of the design. Such a design may work well in theory but fail to deliver in practice because of the lack of attention given to changes to processes that may be required, the skills required for users and those providing support of the service, or the poor choice of third-party suppliers.

Successful service design must therefore consider the four key elements, sometimes known as the four p's:

- People
- Processes
- Products
- Partners

People

The best technical design will fail if the people who need to use it or support it are not adequately prepared. The people element of service design ensures that the human aspect is not forgotten. In Chapter 2, we covered resources and capabilities; Figure 2.4 describing resources and capabilities showed "people" as both a resource (you need the right number of people) and a capability (you need the right people, with the right skills). Service designers must consider how many people will be required to support the new service (resource) and what skill set they will require to do so effectively (capability). Training in the specific processes required to support the service will also be necessary. The people who will be using the service will also need training in its use in order to gain the full benefit of the service.

If existing staff members are to be used, a training needs analysis will be required, and adequate time and money need to be budgeted for training. A communications plan that ensures the right information is given to the right people at the right time by the most appropriate method will also be needed in order to ensure that the staff members understand what is required of them. If new staff members are to be recruited, consideration must be given to drawing up job descriptions, assessing job grades, and defining the required skills and experience that candidates must have. An induction into the organization will also be required. Recruiting staff can be time-consuming, so it is essential that adequate time is allocated to this task if the delivery of the service is not to be delayed.

Processes

The second element to be considered is that of processes. In addition to the service design processes described in the ITIL framework, the new service may require additional processes to be designed, such as an authorization or procurement process. Some IT service providers may ignore the need to design either of these groups of processes in order to shorten the "speed to market" time; this is a false economy. Failure to consider the future capacity requirements of the service—for example, because the design appears to be adequate—could cause problems later when the service is unable to support increased demand without a major redesign. If the new service becomes business-critical, failure to design sufficient resilience may mean that poor availability impacts the business.

As part of service design, processes should be documented, together with the interfaces between them and other processes. All existing processes across the lifecycle should be assessed to identify whether any changes to them are required to enable this new or changed service to become operational and be supportable. Each process should be examined to ensure that the activities described are measurable so that they can be assessed for effectiveness and efficiency and be improved as required.

Products

Products are not only the services that result from the service design stage itself but also the technology and tools that are chosen to assist in the design or to support the service later. So, for example, the service design may be for an online shopping service, and the other products may include a credit-card processing application, an automatic stock reordering service when stock levels reach a threshold, monitoring tools to alert the service provider if user response time exceeds a set time, and so on.

Partners

Partners are those specialist suppliers—usually external third-party suppliers, manufacturers, and vendors—that provide part of the overall service. Ensuring the correct supplier is chosen is essential, because failure by a supplier may cause the IT service provider to breach an agreed service level (we examine the importance of supplier performance in achieving service level targets in more detail in Chapter 5). External suppliers are managed through the supplier management process, which ensures that the necessary contracts are put in place and monitors the delivery by the supplier against the contract terms. Supplier management is covered in Chapter 6.

Building the Service

Figure 4.1 shows how a service consists of constituent parts, all of which have to be considered during the design stage.

FIGURE 4.1   Service composition

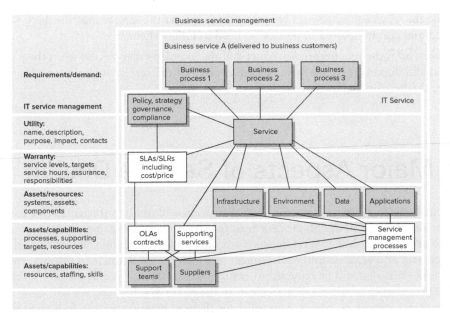

Based on Cabinet Office ITIL® material. Reproduced under license from the Cabinet Office.

Services are composed of the following:

- The business processes that the IT service is going to support need to be understood if the design is to deliver what is required.

- The designer must ensure that the service being designed fulfills all the utility requirements—removing constraints or enhancing performance—in addition to abiding by any governance or reporting requirements and ensuring the service is in line with the organization's strategic goals.

- As we discuss in Chapter 5, "Service Level Management: Aligning IT with Business Requirements," the service level requirements for the new or changed service must be understood, and the necessary service level agreements and supporting agreements with support teams and suppliers need to be put in place.

- The designer must specify all the technical components of the service, using the configuration management system to show how these are linked to provide the service. The CMS is described in Chapter 9. The environmental aspects of the technical design must be documented, so that the operations management function understands what is required in terms of power, air conditioning, and so on.

- The applications that will provide the functional requirements of the business process and the data they require will also form part of the overall design specification.

- It is essential to understand what other services support the new or changed service; defining these dependencies will be done using the CMS, and service level management and supplier management will ensure that these supporting services deliver the level of service required.

- Finally, the service management processes that support the service must be documented and communicated to those who need to follow them.

Only when *all* these requirements are met and the interdependencies between them are understood and documented can there be confidence that the service will work as designed and deliver the benefits required.

Five Major Aspects of Service Design

As mentioned, concentrating on just the service solution will not be sufficient; other aspects need to be considered. The design process must take a holistic approach to designing new or changed services, because success depends not only on the technical solution but also the management and architectural environment in which that solution is to operate, the processes and skills that will be required to ensure it runs effectively, and the metrics that need to be provided to monitor and manage it. In the next two chapters, we will cover the service design processes; however, in order for them to be effective, the following five essential elements of design must be considered.

Five Key Aspects

You may find it helps to remember these by using the acronym STAMP:

Service solutions

Tools and systems for management information

Architectures

Measurement systems

Processes

Service Solutions

The first aspect is the solution itself; in other words, the new functionality offered by a new application or other service. The requirements will have been defined in the service portfolio; it is the job of service design to deliver a solution that meets these requirements within any technical or financial constraints that exist. The solution must conform to corporate rules and must work with the existing services. The supporting services must be able to deliver to the level required; if this is not possible, the overall design will need to be altered. Figure 4.2 shows typical design constraints.

FIGURE 4.2 Design constraints driven by strategy

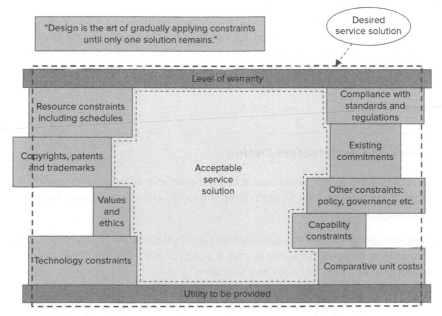

Based on Cabinet Office ITIL material. Reproduced under license from the Cabinet Office.

It is likely that a structured design approach will be used to deliver the service solution, ensuring that it meets the required utility, warranty, and service levels and that it is delivered on time and within budget. As the service lifecycle progresses, requirements may change, so the approach must be not only structured but also flexible enough to meet the developing requirements.

Management Information Systems and Tools

Management information tools and systems are used to support and automate processes. They are usually part of a bigger framework of policies, processes, functions, standards, guidelines, and tools in use within the organizations. Organizations may have (for example) a quality management system, an information security management system, and the service management system. The second aspect to be considered when designing a service, therefore, concerns ensuring that the new or changed service will integrate with existing management information systems, such as the service knowledge information system (SKMS). The SKMS holds details about the service within the service portfolio and service catalog. These management information systems need to be examined to ensure that they are able to provide the information required to manage the service effectively. These management information systems must also be compatible with the rest of the management information framework in use within the organization, such as its quality and security management systems.

Architectures

The organization will have existing systems, and the new or changed service will need to be compatible with them. This is another aspect to be considered during design. There will be an existing architectural platform as well as agreed technical standards, and they will need to be evaluated to see whether they can support the new service. If not, then either the architectures or management systems will need to be amended or the design of the new service will need to be revised.

Architecture and Architecture Design

Architecture is defined as the fundamental organization of a system, embodied in its components, their relationships to each other and to the environment, and the principles guiding its design and evolution.

Architecture design comprises the development and maintenance of IT policies, strategies, architectures, designs, documents, plans, and processes for the deployment, operation, and improvement of IT services and solutions.

Measurement Systems

The next aspect of service design is that of measurement. The design needs to ensure that what is being measured meets the requirement. The current metrics that are gathered must be sufficient to enable the service to be assessed for efficiency and effectiveness. If not, then the measurement methods will need to be improved, or the service metric requirement will need to be altered.

Processes

Each new or changed service will require processes. These processes may be existing processes or specific to the service. Any processes, roles, responsibilities, and skills that will be required by the new or changed service need to be considered. New processes will need to be designed, and existing processes need to be checked to see whether they require any improvement in order to support the new service. If they cannot be improved, the design of the service will need to be amended. Be aware that the processes being evaluated here are not only the processes under service design, but all IT and service management processes throughout the lifecycle. Process models can be used to clarify the processes. Remember the generic requirements of every process that we discussed in Chapter 1; in particular, all processes should have defined inputs, outputs, and triggers.

Summary

Good design requires that the service level requirements are thoroughly understood, and any gap between these requirements and what is possible using current resources and capabilities needs to be identified. The cost of closing this gap must be understood, and staff members in all the IT functions should be made aware of the planned service so that they can prepare to support it. Those involved in transition should plan how this should be done well in advance.

In this chapter, we covered where service design fits in the lifecycle, as well as its purpose, objectives, and scope. We considered the value good service design brings to the business and looked at the key output from this lifecycle stage, the service design package. We also covered the four key elements of successful design—having the right processes, having the required number of suitably skilled people, using the best products, and having appropriate agreements with suppliers. Finally, we considered the five aspects of the service design stage, not just the solution itself, but the processes and management information systems to support it, the architecture to host it, and the metrics to measure it.

In the following chapter, we will cover some of the service design processes in more detail, but it is important to remember these other aspects of the service design stage.

Exam Essentials

Understand the purpose, objectives, and scope of the service design lifecycle stage. Service design must consider how the service will be run and managed when it is operational. It is important to remember also that service design includes the design of both new and changed services.

Understand why good service design is so valuable to the business. It is essential that the new or changed design works efficiently and fulfills the business requirements in terms of capacity, continuity, availability, and security, in addition to delivering new functionality. Good service design considers how the service will be delivered and ensures that all aspects have been considered.

Be able to explain the contents and purpose of the key output of this lifecycle stage, the service design package. You should understand who creates it, who uses it, and why it is helpful, and you should be able to list some of its contents.

Understand the four p's: people, processes, products, and partners. Be able to explain why each of these matters to successful service design, considering not only the technical solution (products) but also the other organizations (partners) who will be involved in providing the service and the contractual relationships that will be required with them. Understand the need for new or changed processes in order for the new service to work and for the right number of trained people to both use the new service in the business and support it in the IT department.

Understand the five key aspects of service design. These can be remembered easily by thinking of the acronym STAMP. The five aspects are the Solution that has been designed that fulfills the business requirement and enables the business process to take place; the management information systems and Tools that ensure that the right information is available when required to support the service; the technical Architecture that underpins the solution; the Measurements that will be taken to ensure the service is operating as it should, and the new and changed Processes that will need to be developed, both business processes and service management processes.

Review Questions

You can find the answers in Appendix A.

1. Service design delivers a new service or a change to an existing service. Which of the following are included in the service design?

    1. Technology
    2. Processes
    3. Budget
    4. Policies

    A. All of the above

    B. 1, 2, and 3

    C. 2, 3, and 4

    D. 2 and 4

2. Which of these statements *best* represents the objective of service design?

    A. Service design should design services that cannot be improved.

    B. Service design should design services that meet the requirements of the service provider.

    C. Service design should design services that require little improvement, except to meet ongoing business requirements.

    D. Service design should design services that deliver the expectations of the service provider in terms of service requirements.

3. Service design provides value to the business in many different ways. Which of the following is *not* recognized as value from service design?

    A. Lower total cost of ownership.

    B. Efficient assessment of changes to business strategy.

    C. Services meet the customer expectations for warranty requirements.

    D. Designs will include governance requirements.

4. "Documents defining all aspects of an IT service and its requirements through each stage of its lifecycle." This is a description of what?

    A. A service definition package

    B. A service transition document

    C. A service core package

    D. A service design package

5. Service design has four major areas that need to be considered in order to deliver an holistic design. Which of these are the four areas?

   A. Process, plan, performance, partners

   B. Partners, plans, people, performance

   C. People, process, products, partners

   D. Products, plans, performance, process

6. A service consists of constituent parts, all of which must be considered as part of the design. Which of these are identified as part of service composition?

   1. Utility

   2. Warranty

   3. Resources

   4. Capabilities

   A. 3 and 4

   B. All of the above

   C. 1, 2, and 4

   D. 1 and 2

7. Service design is subject to a number of constraints that impact the ability to design the solution. Which one of these is *not* recognized as a constraint?

   A. Finance

   B. Regulatory framework

   C. Technology

   D. Service solution

8. Which of the following would be considered as suitable contents for a service design package? Select the best option.

   1. Organizational readiness assessment

   2. Organizational business strategy

   3. Service lifecycle plan

   4. Service transition plan

   5. Service operational acceptance plan

   6. Service acceptance criteria (SAC)

   A. 1, 2, and 6

   B. 1, 3, 5, and 6

   C. 1, 3, 4, 5, and 6

   D. 2, 5, and 6

9. Which of these statements is the *best* definition of architecture?

   A. The fundamental organization of a system, embodied in its components, their relationships to each other and to the environment, and the principles guiding its design and evolution

   B. Document(s) defining all aspects of an IT service and its requirements through each stage of its lifecycle

   C. A formal plan of actions and timescales to implement cost-justified measures to improve the level of service that forms part of continual service improvement

   D. The record and capture of the structure of the infrastructure, components, and services and the relationships between them

10. Which of these represents the five major aspects considered by service design in the design of quality services?

   A. Solution, service design package, business strategy, measurement, and processes

   B. Solution, architecture, management systems, processes, and measurement

   C. Architecture, service design package, business strategy, service transition plan, and processes

   D. Service management systems, processes, measurement, business strategy, and service operational readiness plans

Chapter

5

Service Level Management: Aligning IT with Business Requirements

THE FOLLOWING ITIL FOUNDATION EXAM OBJECTIVES ARE COVERED IN THIS CHAPTER:

✓ **Unit 3: Generic concepts and definitions:**

- 3-11. Service level agreement (SLA)

- 3-12. Operational level agreement (OLA)

- 3-13. Underpinning contract

✓ **5-3. Explain the purpose, objectives, scope, basic concepts, process activities and interfaces for:**

- 5-31 Service level management (SLM)

- The following list must be covered:

  - Service based SLA

  - Multi-level SLAs

  - Service level requirements (SLRs)

  - SLA monitoring (SLAM) chart

  - Service review

  - Service improvement plan (SIP)

  - The relationship between SLM and BRM

This chapter covers the *service level management (SLM)* process. This is one of the process areas we cover in detail, so when you come to the exam, you can expect to have questions that ask you about the activities and concepts, as well as the purpose, of the process. This is an important area, because it is through service level management that the IT service provider ensures that the services offered are aligned to the business requirement. It is also through this process that the service provider and the customer deal with the possibility that the business cannot afford to have the standard of service provision it would like (high availability, unlimited capacity, immediate response to incidents, and so on). Through negotiation, the provider and the customer agree what is achievable and affordable. By monitoring and reviewing the performance against these targets, both parties are able to ensure that the service provided continues to meet the requirement. Where issues are identified, improvement plans are agreed on and implemented.

The Purpose, Objectives, and Scope of Service Level Management

Let's begin by looking at the purpose of the service level management process according the ITIL framework. ITIL states that the purpose of service level management is to ensure that all current and planned IT services are delivered to agreed achievable targets. The key words here are *agreed* and *targets*. Service level management is about discussing, negotiating and agreeing with the customer about what IT services should be provided and ensuring that objective measures are used to ascertain whether that service has been provided to the agreed level.

Service level management is therefore concerned with defining the services, documenting them in an agreement, and then ensuring that the targets are measured and met, taking action where necessary to improve the level of service delivered. These improvements will often be carried out as part of continual service improvement, which we will cover in more detail in Chapter 13, "Understanding Continual Service Improvement."

Note also that the definition of service level management talks about current and planned IT services. Service level management's purpose is to not only ensure that all IT services currently being delivered have a *service level agreement (SLA)* in place but also ensure that discussion and negotiation takes place regarding the requirements for planned services so that an SLA is agreed on and in place when the service becomes operational.

It is for this latter reason that service level management is one of the service design processes; services must be designed to deliver the levels of availability, capacity, and so on, that the customer requires and that service level management documents in the SLA. It is a frequent problem that the SLA is not considered until just before (or even after) the go-live date, when it is realized that the customer service level requirements are not met by the design. We discussed the concepts of utility and warranty in Chapter 2; service level management is concerned primarily with the warranty aspects of the service. The response time, capacity, availability, and so on, of the new service will be the subject of the SLA, and it is essential that the service is therefore designed to meet both utility and warranty requirements.

The objectives of service level management are not restricted to "define, document, agree, monitor, measure, report, and review" (how well the IT service is delivered) and undertaking improvement actions when necessary. It also includes working with business relationship management to build a good working relationship with the business customers. The regular meetings held with the business as part of service level management form the basis of a strong communications channel that strengthens the relationship between the customer and IT.

In Chapter 1, we covered how ITIL differentiates between customers and users. This distinction is important in service level management. Customers are usually senior people within the organization who specify the level of service required, take part in SLM negotiations, and sign the agreed SLA. Users are provided with the service but have no direct input into the service level to be provided.

It is an essential feature of service level management that the customer and IT agree on what constitutes an acceptable level of service. Therefore, one of the objectives of SLM is to develop appropriate targets for each IT service. These targets must be specific and measurable so that there is no debate whether they were achieved. The temptation to use expressions such as "as soon as possible" or "reasonable endeavors" should be resisted, because the customer and IT may disagree on what constitutes "as soon as possible" or what is "reasonable." By using such expressions in an SLA, it may be impossible for the IT service provider to fail, but this leads to cynicism from the customer and damages the relationship that the SLM aims to build. Where the IT service provider is an external company, the legal department will inevitably seek to reduce the possibility of the provider being sued for breach of contract, and these phrases may therefore be included; for an internal service provider, there is no such excuse. Using objective success criteria is essential if SLM is to achieve another of its objectives, that of ensuring that both the customer and IT have "clear and unambiguous expectations" regarding the level of service.

A further SLM objective is to ascertain the level of customer satisfaction with the service being provided and to take steps to increase it. There are challenges in this objective, because obtaining an accurate assessment of customer satisfaction is not straightforward. Customer satisfaction surveys may be completed only by a self-selecting minority. Those who are unhappy are more likely to complete such a survey than those who are content. Despite this tendency, the service level manager must still attempt to monitor customer satisfaction as accurately as possible, using whatever methods are appropriate; in addition to surveys, focus groups, and individual interviews, other methods can be employed.

The final objective that ITIL lists for service level management is that of improving the level of service, even when the targets are being met. Such improvements must be cost-effective, so an analysis of the return expected for any financial or resource investment must be carried out. SLM actively seeks out opportunities for such cost-effective improvements. Achieving this objective forms part of the continual service improvement that is an essential element in all ITIL processes.

The scope of service level management includes the performance of existing services being provided and the definition of required service levels for planned services. It forms a regular communication channel between the business and the IT service provider on all issues concerning the quality of service. SLM therefore has an important role to play in managing customers' expectations to ensure that the level of service they expect and the level of service they perceive they are receiving match. As stated earlier, SLM is concerned with ensuring that the warranty aspects of a service are provided to the expected level. The level of service expected for planned services is detailed in the service level requirements (*SLR*) specification, and the agreed service levels (following negotiation) are documented in the SLA. SLAs should be written to cover *all* operational services. Through this involvement in the design phase, SLM ensures that the planned services will deliver the warranty levels required by the business.

SLM does *not* include agreeing on the utility aspects.

Each IT service is composed of a number of elements provided by internal support teams or external third-party suppliers. An essential element of successful service level management is the negotiation and agreement with those who provide each element of the service, regarding the level of service that they provide. A failure by these providers will translate to a failure to meet the SLA. We will look at these agreements, called *operational-level agreements* (OLAs) in the case of internal teams and *underpinning contracts* in the case of external suppliers, later in this chapter.

Finally, SLM includes measuring and reporting on all service achievements compared to the agreed targets. The frequency, measurement method, and depth of reporting required is agreed as part of the SLA negotiations.

It is important to understand the relationship between service level management and business relationship management. SLM deals with issues around the quality of service being provided; a business relationship management's role is more strategic. The business relationship manager works closely with the business, understanding its current and future IT requirements. It is then the responsibility of the business relationship manager (BRM) to ensure that the service provider understands these needs and is able to meet them. SLM is concerned more about how to meet the targets by ensuring that agreements are in place with internal and external suppliers to provide elements of the service to the required standard.

Service level management cooperates with and complements business relationship management. Similarly, the improvement actions identified by SLM in a *service improvement plan (SIP)* are implemented in conjunction with continual service improvement; they are documented in the CSI register, where they are prioritized and reviewed.

Providers and Suppliers

It is important to understand the difference between providers and suppliers. Suppliers are external organizations that supply an element of the overall service. Customers may have little or no knowledge of the suppliers and the contracts that are held with them. The IT service provider will usually aim to provide a seamless service to the customer.

Providers fall into three categories; we examined the three types in Chapter 1. To recap, they can be embedded in a business unit (Type I), be shared across business units (Type II), or be external to the organization (Type III). Type III service providers will have an SLA with their external customers that will be a legal contract, because they are separate organizations.

The critical difference between suppliers and service providers is that suppliers provide only an element of the service and are not visible to the customer, whereas providers (including Type III providers) provide the whole service. A Type III provider would typically use a number of suppliers to provide elements of the service which they were providing, but the service level agreement is between the provider and the customer; the provider is responsible for ensuring that the supplier fulfills the contract that the provider has with them.

Capturing Service Level Requirements

Before detailed design work can commence, the service designers must have a good grasp of the *service level requirements (SLRs)*. These SLRs represent what is required by the customer for a particular aspect of the service, and they are therefore based on business objectives. If the business objective is to sell more products through the company website, for example, the SLRs will specify the number of simultaneous users the website must be able to handle, the speed of response, and so on.

The high-level SLRs will have been discussed during the strategy phase of the service lifecycle and will have been used as an input to the decision whether the service should be developed at all. Once the decision has been made and the service moves into the design phase, it is the responsibility of SLM to expand upon and clarify these and any additional requirements.

As stated previously, SLRs relate primarily to the warranty aspects of the service, defining the capacity, security, availability, and service continuity requirements. They must be delivered in conjunction with the utility aspects defined elsewhere, if the service is to deliver value. The SLRs are an essential element of the service design specification, and specific testing criteria must be developed to ensure that these aspects are delivered by the design.

One issue encountered by service level managers is that the customer has not considered the service level requirements and therefore does not know what is required. The customer may have detailed and documented functionality requirements (the "what") but has not defined the level of service required (the "how"). Service level managers will often draft an outline SLR as a starting point for negotiation. This can be a useful approach, focusing the customer's thoughts about what they really need, but it should be flexible enough to allow for requirements to be developed through discussion and negotiation. As stated previously, SLM must ensure that clear, objective targets are agreed; if the customer requires the new service to be faster than the existing one, how much faster does it have to be?

Determining what the customer wants is not the same as agreeing to deliver the service against the SLRs. It is essential that the service level manager confirms that all elements of the service can be delivered to meet the required targets. Considerable amount of negotiation may have to take place before the emergence of a set of SLRs that both the customer and the service provider are happy with.

Understanding the Service Level Agreement

In essence, the SLA describes the service and the quality measures by which the delivery of that service will be judged. It is also an opportunity to clarify what is and is not provided. In addition to the service provider responsibilities, any customer responsibilities are also stated here.

It is important that the SLA is an actual written agreement, not a vague "understanding." It should be signed by all parties to the agreement, including the service provider and the customer. Ensuring that the signatories have the authority to make the agreement is important; often the SLM will do all the preparatory work, but the IT director actually signs, showing that the commitment is that of the whole department.

The SLA should be written in plain language, with as few technical expressions as possible; where these are unavoidable, a glossary should be provided. It is crucial that the business users understand what the technical commitments actually mean. If the agreement is with an internal service provider, legal terminology is unnecessary and can cause confusion.

What Does an SLA Contain?

Let's examine the typical contents of an SLA.

The first essential element in a good SLA is a simple description of the purpose and scope of the document so that any reader is clear what the intention is. Typically this might consist of a statement such as "This document is the service level agreement between the IT department of Company A and the customer department of Company B for the provision of (specified) services within the head office and branch offices of Company B. Provision of services to overseas subsidiaries are excluded from this agreement." Even better is to also include a description, in business terms of the service, such as "The (specified) service tracks delivery of orders from the warehouse to the end customer using GPS data."

As with all important documents, it should be clear the period to which the agreement applies: "This agreement is valid from January 1, 2012, until December 31, 2012." Version numbers are also essential, if any changes are to be tracked. It is good practice to review and reissue SLAs annually, even if there have been no changes. This is to ensure that any changes that take place in the service or in the organization are picked up and included in the SLA. It is a good idea to define the SLA as a document configuration item, subject to change management.

It is important to make the distinction between the service and the support provided for that service and to specify the hours that each of these is available. For example, email may be available 24 hours a day, but support may be offered only between 9 A.M. and 5 P.M. A fault occurring at 6 p.m. will not be responded to until the following day. There should be no confusion regarding the support hours, because it will be these hours that are used to judge whether an incident response or fix met the target.

What level of availability and reliability has been agreed on? (We will be looking at availability management in more detail in Chapter 6.) Is the level of availability expressed in business terms, such as "no more than five breaks, with a total combined downtime of two hours in any month," or in a less meaningful 99.x percent?

The SLA should state what level of throughput is reasonable. If the business decides to employ temporary staff to clear a backlog of orders, resulting in twice as many transactions per hour, will the service still be guaranteed at the same response time?

The situation regarding any service continuity provision should be stated. This might be a target for the return of the service following a disaster or major disruption. However, if there is no such plan, this should be stated. "In the event of a major disruption, there is no guaranteed target for a return to normal service provision. Service will be restored as soon as possible." In this situation it is permissible to use the expression, "as soon as possible" as in the event of a major disruption, which has not been planned for, the IT department would do the best they could, but cannot give any guarantees.

Security aspects of the service should be stated in the SLA. What security is provided by the service provider in terms of data protection, encryption, and so on? What are the customer responsibilities for safeguarding passwords, or for ensuring unattended screens are always locked and so on.

The SLA should state the method used to calculate priority levels for incidents and state the target times for incidents to be resolved and requests to be fulfilled. It should be clear whether this target applies to all incidents and requests; some service providers are unwilling to make commitments that they may not achieve, so they commit to a very low service level. Stating in the SLA that the target is, for example, "90 percent of all priority-one faults will be resolved within two hours" means that exceptional circumstances leading to a short-term drop in service (such as a snowstorm preventing engineers from getting to work) will not cause an SLA breach, so the provider is willing to commit to a faster response.

Other possible SLA contents would include specifying agreed downtime for maintenance and critical business periods when changes would not be applied to the service.

If the service provider charges for providing services, the basis for charging should be stated clearly. Is it a charge per head or a charge for particular elements, such as per gigabyte of storage, and so on? Is there a rebate if service fails to reach the agreed standard?

Finally, the methods by which the service provision is to be judged should be stated. What reporting will be provided? How frequently will service review meetings be held? Who will attend?

Building the SLA

As stated earlier, every service provided consists of a number of elements. To make a commitment in an SLA, the service level manager must be confident that each part of that service will be delivered to the required standard. This is achieved by ensuring that agreements exist with the internal teams providing elements of the service and that the necessary contracts exist with third-party suppliers to underpin those aspects of the service provided by external bodies. Taken together, these agreements form the basis of what can be promised in the SLA. We are going to look at these different agreements in the following pages.

Let's look first at *operational-level agreements (OLAs)*. These are straightforward agreements between internal support departments or other internal departments who are supplying an element of the service. Typical commitments might include the hours during which support is provided, what level of on-call support is provided, what technology each team supports, and what is outside their area of expertise. Commitments to follow the agreed processes may also be included, such as a commitment to monitor the queue of incidents on the service management tool set at least hourly and to provide regular status updates on outstanding incidents.

 These agreements should be kept simple, because they are between colleagues, not different organizations. The temptation to add legal jargon should be resisted; because no team is going to sue the other, there is no need for such obfuscation. Technical language is allowable to describe areas of expertise, for example, but they should also be explained in a glossary if obscure or unclear. Targets should be challenging but achievable; setting unrealistic and therefore unattainable targets is pointless and will undermine the SLA.

OLAs describe the commitments for each IT team; sometimes other internal teams involved in providing the overall service may be included (such as office facilities, the training department, and so on). As you have seen, these agreements can be simple and are often not more than one or two pages. As with SLAs, the signatories must hold the authority to make the commitments contained within the agreement.

A useful tip when trying to understand what OLAs are required for a particular service is to use the RACI matrix described in Chapter 7. All those areas where responsibility was identified are potential areas for inclusion in an OLA.

As with SLAs, the work does not stop with signing the agreement; the monitoring and reporting of OLA performance against the agreed targets is an ongoing SLM responsibility. Any deviation from delivering against these targets must be identified and addressed if the customer SLA is to be delivered. Failure to deliver against an OLA may cause a breach in SLA targets. Simple reporting against OLA targets, showing a rolling 12-month trend, will identify any areas at risk of breach or any gradual but continual deterioration. The service level manager has to identify and act upon any such issues, taking these up with the relevant team manager, possibly as part of an overall service improvement plan (SIP).

It is recommended that OLAs be reviewed at least annually, or after any major reorganization, to ensure that they remain current; they may also be identified as *configuration items (CIs)*, subject to change management. Categorizing OLAs and other agreements as CIs ensures that the relationship between a service and its supporting agreements is clear and the impact of any changes is fully considered. For more details about configuration items and their relationship to change management, see Chapters 8 and 9.

The second set of agreements that need to be in place to support a service level agreement are the *underpinning contracts (UCs)*. These agreements are with the external organizations that provide elements of the overall service. Because these suppliers are external, these agreements will be contractual and therefore legally enforceable. As with OLAs, the service level manager must identify which third parties provide elements of the service provided in the SLA and ensure that the targets within the UC are at least as demanding as the resolution targets within the SLA. Working with the supplier management process, the SLM must ensure that sufficient monitoring and reporting are in place to confirm that the contracted service is being provided to the required level. Typical third-party suppliers might include Internet service providers, hardware and software maintainers, and so on. As stated earlier, the contractual nature of UCs will mean that the language used in these agreements will often be legalistic; however, it is important that the required service targets are clear and unambiguous.

Every commitment in the SLA should be supported by an underpinning agreement, either an OLA or a UC.

The underpinning contract may be referred to by the supplier as an SLA; however, we call it an underpinning contract to avoid confusion.

It is important to understand the difference between an underpinning contract (in which an underpinning *element* of the overall service is supplied by an external organization) and an SLA covering a complete service provided by a third party, such as an outsourcer (a Type III provider). *Both are contracts.*

Figure 5.1 shows the relationship between the various agreements.

FIGURE 5.1 The service relationships and dependencies

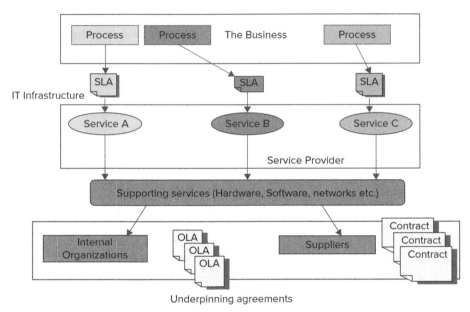

Based on Cabinet Office ITIL® material. Reproduced under license from the Cabinet Office.

Structuring the Agreement

An important decision taken during the planning phase of implementing SLM is to decide upon the most suitable SLA structure for the organization. There are three options specified by ITIL: customer-based, service-based, and multilevel, each with advantages and disadvantages:

- A service-based SLA is one in which each SLA refers to only one service. The service described is provided to all users of that service, so the requirements of all customer groups need to be ascertained. This option is useful for organization wide services such as email. There are disadvantages to this approach, however. The service provided across all locations may not be of equal quality, because of network issues, for example. Different departments may have differing requirements. This requirement can be addressed by agreeing on gold, silver, and bronze service levels within the SLA. Difficulties can also arise when trying to identify the appropriate signatory to the agreement, because the service is provided to many customer groups. An external service provider may also use this type of agreement for a standard service in their catalog.

- Another option is to have one agreement covering all the services provided to a single customer or customer group. This is called a customer-based SLA. For example, the human resources department would have a customer-based SLA, as would the finance department, and so on. This is straightforward from the customer point of view, because all the services they use are in a single agreement. It is also a fairly easy to identify the appropriate signatory. From the IT provider's viewpoint, however, customer-based agreements means that the same service may appear in multiple SLAs, which can be difficult to monitor.

By using a combination of service-based and customer-based SLAs, the service level manager can provide a simple framework, covering all services.

- The third option is a multilevel SLA. This option has three levels:

    - The corporate level contains information that is applicable to all users across the organization. This saves a lot of repetition of this information in every SLA and should not need frequent updating.

    - The customer level contains information that is applicable only to that particular customer, whatever service is being used.

    - The service level will contain information on a particular service as it is delivered to that particular customer. There may be several of these sections.

The multilevel SLA prevents unnecessary duplication of effort and can be a very effective approach. It does require that the SLM understands the relationships between the various services and customers (Figure 5.2).

FIGURE 5.2   Multilevel SLA structure

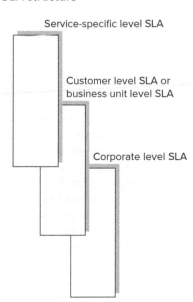

Service-specific level SLA

Customer level SLA or business unit level SLA

Corporate level SLA

Monitoring and Improving Service Delivery

As stated previously, the service level agreement should have clear, objective targets so that it can be determined by the business and the IT service provider whether the service was delivered as agreed on. To monitor this delivery, the service level manager must produce reports that show whether these targets were achieved. Agreeing on the format and frequency of the reporting should be included in the service level negotiations. It can be difficult to produce reports that match the customer perception of the service delivered; a 99.7 percent availability measurement may not match the perception of the service received if all the downtime was concentrated on one business area, for example. The SLM must strive to produce service metrics that describe, as closely as possible, the level of service experienced by the customer rather than technical measurements that mean little or nothing to the business.

It is important that the service management tool used by the IT service provider captures the required information accurately. The time an incident was logged, responded to, resolved, and closed must match what the customer experienced, or else they will become cynical and believe that the service provider is "twisting the figures." If the SLA contains commitments regarding response times, for example, the service provider must have the requisite monitoring tools in place to measure them.

Care should be taken in providing the optimal level of detail; too much information swamps the customer in reports, without indicating clearly whether a target has been met, but too high level a report may not give the detail required.

 **Real World Scenario**

Reporting and Customer Perception

A desktop support outsourcing company provided its customers with a large report each month, containing approximately 50 graphs. Each graph represented the performance against targets for a particular category of incident or service request. The level of detail provided actually obscured the situation; one graph showed that 100 percent of Type 20 requests were fulfilled within target but did not show that there had been only one of them. Another chart showed that only 85 percent of Type 30 had met their target, again not showing the number involved, which could have been several hundred. By producing this level of reporting, a superficial analysis appeared to show that the customer was receiving an acceptable service. This analysis did not match the customer perception, however, and engendered deep cynicism regarding the supplier. Not surprisingly, the contract was not renewed.

In the early days of a new service, reporting may need to be more frequent, possibly weekly. As the service stabilizes, these reports can be reduced to monthly. Very well-established services may be reported upon only quarterly. There is a danger in this, however, because any poor service may have persisted for many weeks before coming to the attention of the SLM. The reasons for the poor service may be hard to identify after such a long period, and poor practice may have become embedded and therefore hard to change.

The service reports should be reviewed to identify any service that is deteriorating gradually, although no targets have been breached as yet. The reason for the deterioration should be identified, and action should be taken to address the issue so that the service improves and the service level target is never breached. This demonstration of a proactive approach to service provision confirms to the customer the service provider's commitment to providing a quality service.

The use of a simple SLA monitoring chart or SLAM at the start of each report, summarizing achievements across all the services, should be considered. These are often colored to show all services that comfortably met their targets in green, those where the target was under threat but not actually breached in amber, and those that failed to meet the targets in red. This "traffic-light" system of red, amber, and green is sometimes referred to as a RAG report and is very effective in concentrating attention and discussion on the services that merit it, rather than plowing through all the reports equally.

Figure 5.3 shows a simple but effective RAG report, showing achievement against targets for six services over an eight-month period.

FIGURE 5.3 Service level achievement monitoring chart

	January	February	March	April	May	June	July	August
A								
B								
C								
D								
E								
F								

Target met   Target breached   Target threatened

Measuring customer satisfaction levels is also the responsibility of the service level manager. These measurements are more problematic than a straightforward pass or fail against a specific target. Ensuring that there is a reasonable response to surveys is challenging; those who are most unhappy are the most likely to complete a survey. Asking every customer to provide feedback every time they have a service provided can prove irritating, with the result that the customer marks everything as satisfactory to get rid of the survey.

Despite the issues surrounding surveys, measuring satisfaction is useful. For example, there may be dissatisfaction at some aspect of service provision, such as unhelpful IT staff, even though all other SLA targets have been met. This would otherwise not be apparent. Similarly, customer satisfaction may be high following a major incident, because the customer appreciated the effort put in by the IT staff to overcome it or were very happy with the level of information they were given during the outage, for example.

The SLM should agree with the customer regarding the target satisfaction score and monitor and measure achievement against this. Reasons for poor scores should be identified, and actions taken, as with any other target.

Reviewing the Service with the Customer

The service level manager should meet regularly with the various customers to review the delivery against the service level agreement. The temptation to avoid face-to-face meetings by sending copies of the service reports to the customer should be resisted. The regular service review meeting between the customer and the service level manager is an important opportunity to build a stronger relationship and to increase each party's understanding of the other. Regular meetings will ensure that successes as well as failures are discussed and that issues that could be destructive to the relationship are aired and dealt with.

As discussed with regard to service reporting, meetings should be held monthly or at least quarterly. It is a good idea to arrange these meetings in advance, for the whole year, so that there are no calendar conflicts later that could prevent the meetings from taking place. The meetings should have an agreed agenda, and minutes should be taken. Actions should be assigned to both the customer and the service level manager, and the progress against these should be checked at subsequent meetings.

A standard agenda might contain the following:

- Review of previous minutes and actions
- Review of any major incidents since the last meeting (what caused them, what was the impact, how were they handled, what has been done by IT to prevent recurrence)
- Review of service reports for previous month and for a rolling 12-month period
- Discussion of any issues arising from the reports and allocation of actions
- Review of service improvement plan progress against targets
- Discussion of future business developments
- Notification of any IT changes that may affect the service to be delivered

As a result of the discussions that take place at the service review, it may be decided by both parties that the current SLA targets are unsuitable or unachievable. If necessary, the SLA would then be renegotiated.

Taking Steps to Improve: The Service Improvement Plan

The issues identified at the service review may be addressed through actions allocated to individuals, as discussed earlier. Often the improvement needed is more fundamental than this and involves a number of actions by different groups or individuals. In this case, a formal *service improvement plan (SIP)* will be drawn up by the service level manager and agreed on at the service review.

The SIP will have an agreed desired outcome and timescale. Actions will be allocated, and progress will be checked. When complete, the results of the SIP will be reviewed to ascertain whether the plan has been successful and whether any further actions are required. The SLM should undertake the action plan in partnership with the CSI manager. The CSI approach, which we cover in detail in Chapter 13, should be the basis of an SIP: understanding the vision, baselining the current situation, setting measurable objectives, and reviewing the objectives to understand whether the plan has been effective. The plan should also be registered in the CSI register (the CSI register is discussed in more detail in Chapter 13).

When deciding whether an SIP is required, the SLM should consider the cost of any improvement actions and the business benefit to be achieved.

Interfacing with Other Service Management Processes

SLM interfaces with several other processes to ensure agreed service levels are being met:

- Problem management will address the causes of any failures and work to prevent their recurrence, thus improving the delivery of the service against targets.

- Availability management works to remove any single points of failure that could lead to downtime and addresses the causes of such downtime in order to deliver the highest possible level of availability to the customer.

- Capacity management plans ahead to ensure sufficient capacity is provided and therefore preventing service failures that would otherwise have occurred.

- Incident management focuses on resolving incidents and restoring service as quickly as possible. Performance against targets for incident resolution is usually a major area within an SLA.

- IT service continuity will plan to ensure that service continues to be provided despite major upheavals; where a break in service cannot be prevented, it will work to ensure that the service is restored in line with the business requirements.

- Information security ensures that the customer's data is protected and will work with the service level manager to educate the customers and users regarding their own responsibilities in this area.

- Supplier management ensures UCs are in place and are being fulfilled.

- Service catalog management provides information about services to support the SLA.

- Financial management provides cost information.

- Design coordination ensures the design meets the SLR.

- SLM works with CSI in designing and implementing the SIP.

- SLM works with business relationship management. However, as stated earlier, BRM is more concerned with strategy, identifying customer needs and ensuring the objectives are met.

Summary

This chapter covered the purpose, objectives, and scope of service level management and examined the basic concepts, the activities, and the interfaces involved in the process. We examined the differences between SLM and business relationship management and how these two processes relate to each other.

We examined the different types of service level agreement (the service-based, customer-based, and multilevel service level agreements) and covered when each of these would be used.

We examined the different types of agreement in service level management: the service level agreement (SLA), the operational-level agreement (OLA), and the underpinning contract (UC).

We looked at the role of service level requirements and targets and how SLM monitors service against these targets, specifically the use of the SLAM chart. We also considered the purpose of service reviews and service improvement plans.

Exam Essentials

Understand the purpose, objectives, and scope of service level management.   In particular, understand how SLM ensures that current IT services are delivered to agreed *specific and measurable* targets. Understand how the process also ensures that requirements for new services are understood and delivered.

Be able to explain the basic concepts of service level management.   These include the definition of service level requirements and the role of targets in assessing the level of service being delivered. Understand the difference between service providers and suppliers.

Understand the activities that are undertaken as part of the process.   These activities include the definition and documentation of service level targets that meet the business requirement and the negotiation with the business and with those internal groups and external suppliers that provide elements of the complete service to agree on targets that are both challenging and achievable.

Understand how SLM uses underpinning agreements to ensure that targets are achievable.   Be able to describe operational-level agreements and underpinning contracts. Understand when each is used and how these agreements support the service level commitments.

Understand the importance of the SLM activities of monitoring, measuring, and reviewing the service level achievements to ensure that targets are being met.   Be able to describe what an SLAM report is and the benefits of using a RAG report. Be able to explain the role of the service improvement plan when targets are missed.

Be able to list and describe the different SLA structures of service-based, customer-based, and multilevel SLAs.   Understand the advantages and disadvantages of each. Understand the purpose of the service review meeting.

Understand how service level management builds a relationship with the business units by understanding their requirements and how it delivers a service that meets these requirements.   Be able to explain the different roles of the service level manager and the business relationship manager in building a relationship between the IT service provider and the business. Understand how SLM tracks customer satisfaction levels and takes action to improve them.

Be able to describe the interface between SLM and other process areas.   Understand especially business relationship management, incident and request management, supplier management, and continual service improvement.

Review Questions

You can find the answers in Appendix A.

1. Which of these statements provides the *best* description of the purpose of service level management?

   A. Ensure that all current and planned IT services are delivered to agreed achievable targets

   B. Ensure there is a high-level relationship with customers to capture business demands

   C. Ensure users have a single point of contact for all operational issues

   D. Ensure there is a smooth transition of services to and from service providers

2. Which of these is an objective of service level management?

   A. Monitor changes throughout their lifecycle

   B. Define, document, agree, monitor, measure, report, and review services

   C. Respond to service requests and inquiries promptly

   D. Establish the root cause of incidents and problems efficiently and cost effectively

3. Which of these statements is correct about the scope of service level management (SLM)?

   1. The scope of SLM includes the performance of existing services being provided.

   2. The scope of SLM includes the definition of the components that make up the services and their relationships.

   3. The scope of SLM includes the definition of required service levels for planned services.

   4. The scope of SLM includes the definition of the type of changes for change management.

   A. 2 and 4

   B. 1, 2, 3, and 4

   C. 1 and 3

   D. 1, 2, and 3

4. Which of the following is a type of service provider as identified in the service design lifecycle stage?

   A. Embedded service provider

   B. Shared service unit provider

   C. External service provider

   D. Customer-based service provider

5. Service level requirements are related to which of the following?

   A. Utility

   B. Warranty

   C. Change records

   D. Configuration records

6. Which of the following would *not* be part of a service level agreement?

    A. Description of the service

    B. Service hours

    C. Definition of business strategy

    D. Service continuity arrangements

7. Which of the following agreements commonly supports the achievement of a service level agreement?

    1. Operational level agreement

    2. Strategic business plan

    3. Underpinning contract

    4. Internal finance agreement

    A. 1, 2, and 3

    B. 1, 2, and 4

    C. 1 and 3

    D. 2 and 4

8. Which of the following is the best description of an underpinning contract?

    A. An agreement between an IT service provider and another part of the same organization assisting in the provision of services

    B. An agreement between an IT service provider and customer relating to the delivery of services

    C. An agreement between different customers about the requirements of the service

    D. A contract between an IT service provider and an external third-party organization assisting in the delivery of services

9. Multilevel service level agreement structures can contain which of the following types of service level agreement?

    A. Service-based, customer-based, and corporate-based

    B. Service-based, technology-based, and customer-based

    C. Technology-based, supplier-based, and customer-based

    D. Technology-based, supplier-based, and user-based

10. Which of the following is a common color scheme applied to a service level management monitoring chart?

    A. Red, blue, green

    B. Red, amber, green

    C. Blue, green, black

    D. Black, amber, blue

Chapter 6

The Other Service Design Processes

THE FOLLOWING ITIL FOUNDATION EXAM OBJECTIVES ARE COVERED IN THIS CHAPTER:

✓ **Unit 3: Generic concepts and definitions:**

- 3-4. Service catalogue (both two-view and three-view types)
- 3-15. Availability

✓ **5-4. State the purpose, objectives and scope for:**

- 5-41 Service catalogue management
- 5-42 Availability management
  - Service availability
  - Component availability
  - Reliability
  - Maintainability
  - Serviceability
  - Vital business functions (VBF)
- 5-43 Information security management (ISM)
  - Information security policy
- 5-44 Supplier management
  - Supplier categories
- 5-45 Capacity management
  - Capacity plan
  - Business capacity management
  - Service capacity management
  - Component capacity management
- 5-46 IT service continuity management
  - Purpose of business impact analysis (BIA)
  - Risk assessment
- 5-47 Design coordination

We have covered the service level management process in some detail, but the remaining processes do not require such an in-depth consideration for the foundation syllabus. As a result, we will review only the purpose, objectives, and scope for each process, along with a review of the some of the basic process steps and concepts.

Service Catalog Management

This section covers the service catalog management process. We do not look in detail at this process, but it is important that you understand its purpose, objectives, and scope. In Chapter 3, we covered the service portfolio, which contains the service pipeline and retired services, in addition to the service catalog. Figure 6.1 shows these three elements and the changing status of the service as it moves from pipeline to catalog to retired services.

FIGURE 6.1 Service portfolio

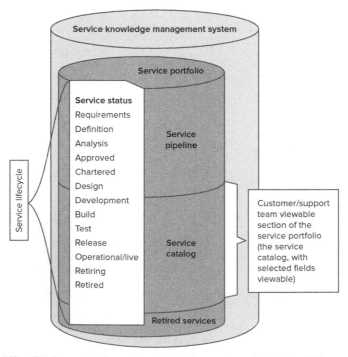

Based on Cabinet Office ITIL® material. Reproduced under license from the Cabinet Office.

Understanding the Service Catalog

A *service catalog* is defined in the ITIL glossary as follows:

> "A database or structured document with information about all live IT services, including those available for deployment. The service catalogue is part of the service portfolio and contains information about two types of IT service: customer-facing services that are visible to the business and supporting services required by the service provider to deliver customer-facing services."

Let's examine this definition in more detail:

A database or structured document The catalog gathers the service information and presents it in a form that is easy for the business to understand.

Information about all live IT services, including those available for deployment The catalog contains details of services that are available to the business; in this way, it differs from the other components of the service portfolio (the service pipeline and retired services). Gathering and maintaining that information is the job of service catalog management.

Information about two types of IT service The catalog provides the details that the customers require about the services available, namely, deliverables, prices, contact points, ordering, and request processes. There is another view of the service catalog—the view that is visible only to IT, showing the supporting services that must be in place if the customer services are to be delivered.

These different views of the catalog are similar to what one would expect to see for any other type of catalog. For example, a store catalog will show customers the items for sale, prices, colors, and specifications, and it will give a catalog reference for ordering. The store staff would have a different view of the same items, showing stock level, cost price, lead time, and supplier.

As shown in Figure 6.2, the structure should consider the different needs of different audiences, because not every service is of interest to every person and not every piece of information about a service is of interest to everyone. The customer does not need to see the technical aspects of service delivery, and the technicians do not need to see the business processes as a regular view.

FIGURE 6.2   A two-view service catalog

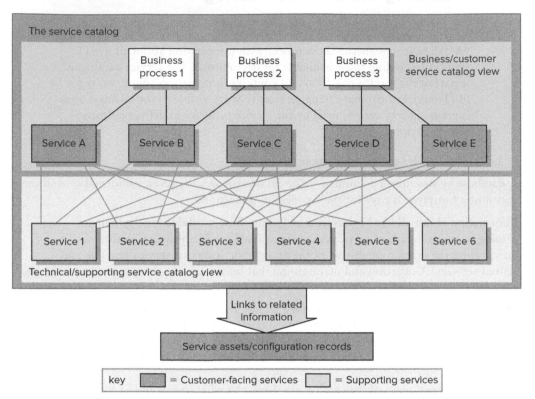

Based on Cabinet Office ITIL® material. Reproduced under license from the Cabinet Office.

Dependent on the nature of the business, the service provider may have both internal and external customers and different types of customers, who have different services available to them. Figure 6.3 shows a service catalog structure where the catalog defines services available to wholesale and retail customers.

This catalog has three views:

- The first two views show all the IT services delivered to wholesale or retail customers (customer-facing services), together with relationships to the customers they support.

- The third view shows all the supporting IT services, together with relationships to the customer-facing services they underpin. The technical information regarding components, CIs, and other supporting services required to support the provision of the service to the customers is also shown here.

FIGURE 6.3   A three-view service catalog

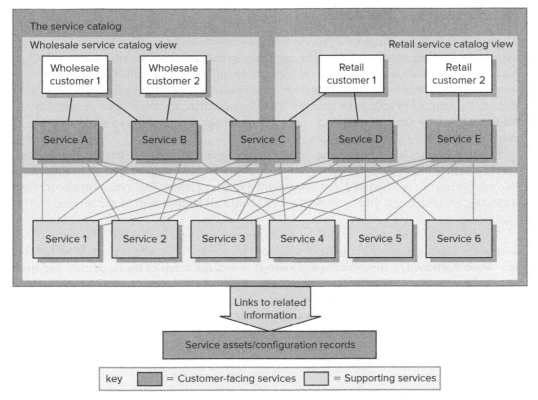

Based on Cabinet Office ITIL® material. Reproduced under license from the Cabinet Office.

Purpose of the Service Catalog Management Process

The purpose of the service catalog management process is to provide and maintain a single source of consistent information on all operational services and those being prepared to be run operationally and to ensure that it is readily available to those who are authorized to access it. The catalog will include services that are also being developed or enhanced for future transition into a live environment, from pipeline to operations to retirement. It is an essential resource for service management, so the production and maintenance of the information are extremely important.

The catalog will be used by customers and IT and for the basis for service level (ITIL core guidance does not hyphenate service level) management. Identifying and documenting all the services provided, together with their supporting services, are challenging tasks, but the advantages of having one agreed, definitive source for this information make the effort worthwhile.

Objectives of the Service Catalog Management Process

The service catalog management process has as its objective the production and maintenance of the service catalog. The information contained within the catalog must be accurate, so there should be a link to service transition. As service transition moves new services to the operational environment or retires other services, the service catalog will need to be updated to reflect the changes. To ensure consistency, the service description should remain the same as the service progresses through the portfolio to avoid any confusion with other, similar services.

Effective service asset and configuration management will ensure that the supporting services for each customer-facing service that is run, or is being prepared to run, in the live environment are identified and documented in the catalog. The details of the service, its status, its interfaces, and its dependencies should all be held within the service catalog.

A further objective of service catalog management is to ensure that the information within the catalog is made available in a suitable format to those who need it. Whether this is a Word document, a spreadsheet, or an intranet site, the needs of the customers and users should be considered. Appropriate controls should be put in place to control access to those approved to see that level of detail.

The service catalog information is used by other service management processes; an objective of service catalog management is to ensure that the information provided within it meets the requirements of all who access it. Working with service asset and configuration management, the dependencies within components can be identified and shown.

Scope of the Service Catalog Management Process

The scope of the service catalog management process includes all services that are being transitioned or have been transitioned to the live environment. The catalog may list services individually; more commonly, it describes service packages. A service package is an offering that combines two or more services to offer a solution to a specific customer need or business outcome. It may consist of a combination of core services, enabling services and enhancing services.

Included within the scope of this process is the definition of these services or service packages and the descriptions to be used for them within the catalog. Also included is the actual production and ongoing maintenance of the catalog, showing the dependencies between all services and supporting services. This information is obtained from the Configuration Management System. We shall be examining the CMS in Chapter 9.

Although the service catalog may describe the services that can be requested, the fulfillment of them is outside the scope of this process and belongs in request fulfillment or the overall change management process.

Availability Management

The availability of a service is critical to its value. No matter how clever it is or what functionality it offers (its utility), the service is of no value to the customer unless it delivers the warranty expected. Poor availability is a primary cause of customer dissatisfaction. Availability is one of the four warranty aspects that must be delivered if the service is to be fit for use. Targets for availability are often included in service level agreements, so the IT service provider must understand the factors to be considered when seeking to meet or exceed the availability target. This section covers how availability is measured; the purpose, objectives, and scope of availability management; and a number of key concepts.

Defining Availability

ITIL defines *availability* as the ability of an IT service or other configuration item to perform its agreed function when required. Any unplanned interruption to a service during its agreed service hours (also called the agreed *service time*, specified in the service level agreement) is defined as *downtime*. The availability measure is calculated by taking the downtime from the agreed service time as a percentage of the total agreed time.

It is important to note the inclusion of *when required* in the definition and the word *agreed* in the calculation. The service may be available when the customer does not require it; including this time in the calculation gives a false impression of the availability from the customer perspective. If customer perception does not match the reporting provided, the customer will become cynical and distrust the reports provided (see Chapter 5).

Calculating Availability: Two Examples

Example A: A service is available 24 hours a day, 7 days a week. One hour of downtime per week is calculated as follows:

> 168 hours − 1 hour downtime = 167/168 × 100 = 99.4% availability

Example B: If the service is available but used only 9 a.m. to 5 p.m., Monday to Friday (and these 40 hours are the service hours agreed in the SLA), then the same one hour of downtime results in a different figure:

> 40 hours − 1 hour downtime = 39/40 × 100 = 97.5% availability

$$\text{Availability (\%)} = \frac{\text{Agreed service time (AST)} - \text{downtime}}{\text{AST}} {}^{*}100$$

If the downtime occurred overnight, it would be included in the calculations in Example A but not those in Example B, because there was no agreed service after 5 p.m.

It is important therefore to agree on exactly what the agreed service hours are; they should be documented in the SLA. The basis for the calculation should be clear to the customer.

Keep in mind that the customer experiences the end-to-end service; the availability delivered depends on all links in the chain being operational when required. The customer will complain that a service is unavailable whether the fault is with the application, the network, or the hardware. The availability management process is therefore concerned with reducing service-affecting downtime wherever it occurs. Again, it should be clearly stated in the availability reports whether the calculations are based on the end-to-end service or just the application availability. It is therefore essential to understand the difference between service availability and component availability.

Purpose of Availability Management

The purpose of the availability management process is to take the necessary steps to deliver the availability requirements defined in the SLA. The process should consider both the current requirements and the future needs of the business. All actions taken to improve availability have an accompanying cost, so all improvements made must be assessed for cost-effectiveness.

Availability management considers all aspects of IT service provision to identify possible improvements to availability. Some improvements will be dependent on implementing new technology; others will result from more effective use of staff resources or streamlined processes. Availability management analyzes reasons for downtime and assesses the return on investment for improvements to ensure the most cost-effective measures are taken. The process ensures that the delivery of the agreed availability is prioritized across all phases of the lifecycle.

Objectives of Availability Management

The objectives of availability management include the following:

- Producing and maintaining a plan that details how the current and future availability requirements are to be met. This plan should consider requirements 12 to 24 months in advance to ensure that any necessary expenditure is agreed on in the annual budget negotiations and any new equipment is bought and installed before the availability is affected. The plan should be revised regularly to take account of any changes in the business.

- Providing advice throughout the service lifecycle on all availability-related issues to both the business and IT, ensuring that the impact of any decisions on availability is considered.

- Managing the delivery of services to meet the agreed targets. Where downtime has occurred, availability management will assist in resolving the underlying problem, utilizing the problem management process.

- Assessing all requests for change to ensure that any potential risk to availability has been considered. Any updates to the availability plan required as a result of changes will also be considered and implemented.

- Considering all possible proactive steps that could be taken to improve availability across the end-to-end service, assessing the risk and potential benefits of these improvements, and implementing them where justified.

- Implementing monitoring of availability to ensure that targets are being achieved.
- Optimizing all areas of IT service provision to deliver the required availability consistently to enable the business to use the services provided to achieve its objectives.

Scope of Availability Management

As discussed, the availability management process encompasses all phases of the service lifecycle. It is included in the design phase, because the most effective way to deliver availability is to ensure that availability considerations are designed in from the start. Once the service is operational, opportunities are continually sought to remove risks to availability and make the service more robust. These activities are part of proactive availability management. Throughout the live delivery of the service, availability management analyzes any downtime and implements measures to reduce the frequency and length of any future occurrences. These are the reactive activities of availability management. Changes to live services are assessed to understand any risks to the service, and measurements are put in place to ensure that downtime is measured accurately. This continues throughout the operation phase until the service is retired.

The scope of availability management includes all operational services and technology. Where SLAs are in place, there will be clear, agreed targets. There may be other services, however, where no formal SLA exists but where downtime has a significant business impact. Availability management should not exclude these services from consideration; it should strive to achieve high availability in line with the potential impact on the business of downtime. Service level management should work to negotiate SLAs for all such services in the future, because without them, it is the IT service provider who is assessing the level of availability required when this is a business decision. Availability management should be applied to all new IT services and for existing services where SLRs or SLAs have been established. Supporting services must be included, because the failures of these services impact the customer-facing services. Availability management may also work with supplier management to ensure that the level of service provided by partners does not threaten the overall service availability.

Every aspect of service provision comes within the scope of availability management; poor processes, untrained staff, or ineffective tools can all contribute to causing or unnecessarily prolonging downtime.

Understanding the Effect of Downtime on Vital Business Functions

Availability management must align its activities and priorities to the requirements of the business. This requires a firm understanding of the business processes and how they are underpinned by the IT service. Information regarding the future business plans and priorities and therefore the future requirements of the business with regard to availability is essential input to the availability plan. Only with this understanding of the business requirement can the service provider be sure that their efforts to improve availability are correctly targeted.

The response of the IT service provider to failure can improve the customer's perception of the service, despite the break in service. The service provider's actions can show an understanding of the impact of the downtime on the business processes, and an eagerness to overcome the issue and prevent recurrences can reassure the business that IT understands its needs.

Additionally, the process requires a strong technical understanding of the individual components that make up each service, their capabilities, and their current performance. Through this combination of business understanding and technical knowledge, the optimal design can be delivered to produce the required level of availability to meet current and future needs.

When designing a new service and discussing its availability requirements, the service provider and the business must focus on the criticality of the service to the business being able to achieve its aims. Expenditure to provide high availability across every aspect of a service is unlikely to be justified. The business process that the IT service supports may be a *vital business function (VBF)*, and identifying which services or parts of services are the most critical is therefore a business decision. For example, the ability for an Internet-based bookshop to be able to process credit card payments would be a vital business function. The ability to display a "customers who bought this book also bought these other books" feature is not vital. It may encourage some increased sales, but the purchaser is able to complete their purchase without it. Once these VBFs are understood, the design of the service to ensure the required availability can commence. Understanding the VBFs informs decisions regarding where expenditure to protect availability is justified.

It is a business, not an IT decision, what the appropriate availability target of a service should be. However, availability comes at a price, and the service provider must ensure that the customer understands the cost implications of too high a target. Customers may otherwise demand a very high availability target (99.99% or greater) and then find the service unaffordable.

Where very high availability is cost-justified, the design of the service will include highly reliable components, a resilient design, and minimal or no planed downtime.

Having considered the importance of availability to the business, in the following section we examine some of the key availability management activities and concepts that the IT service provider may employ to cut downtime and thus deliver the required availability to the business, enabling it to achieve its business objectives.

Improving Availability

Availability management is comprised of both reactive and proactive activities, as shown in Figure 6.4. The reactive activities include regular monitoring of service provision involving extensive data gathering and reporting of the performance of individual components and processes and the availability delivered by them. Event management is often used to monitor components because this speeds up the identification of any issues through the setting of alert thresholds. It may even be possible to restart the failing service automatically, possibly before the break has been noticed by the customers. (Event management is discussed in detail in Chapter 12.) Instances of downtime are investigated, and remedial actions are taken to prevent a recurrence. The proactive activities include identifying and managing risks to the availability of the service and implementing measures to protect against such an occurrence. Where protective measures have been put in place to provide resilience in the event of component failure, the measures require regular testing to ensure that they actually work as designed to protect the service availability. All new or changed services should be subject to continual service improvement; countermeasures should be implemented wherever they can be cost-justified. This cost justification requires an understanding of the vital business functions and the cost to the business of any downtime. It is ultimately a business, not a technical decision. Figure 6.4 also shows the availability management information system; this is the repository for all availability management reports, plans, risk registers, and so on, and it forms part of the service knowledge management system (SKMS).

FIGURE 6.4 The availability management process

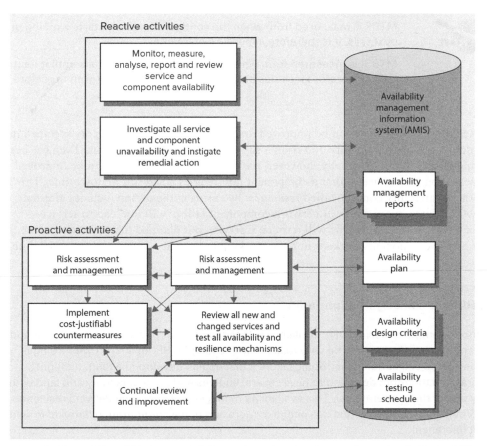

Based on Cabinet Office ITIL® material. Reproduced under license from the Cabinet Office.

Business continuity management and IT service continuity management are outside the scope of availability management. There is a strong relationship between availability management and these processes, however, because every action taken to mitigate a risk to availability or to provide resilience will support ITSCM.

The first availability concept we cover is *reliability*. This is defined by ITIL as "a measure of how long a service, component, or CI can perform its agreed function without interruption." We normally describe how reliable an item is by stating how frequently it can be expected to break down within a given time: "My car is very reliable. It has broken down only twice in five years." We measure reliability by calculating the *mean* (or average) *time between failures (MTBF)* or the *mean (or average) time between service incidents (MTBSI)*.

MTBF is measured from when the configuration item starts working until it next fails. It is therefore a measure of uptime.

MTBSI is measured from when a system or IT service fails until it next fails. It therefore includes both the MTBF and the time taken to restore the service.

Reliability of a service can be improved first by ensuring the components specified in the design are of good quality and from a supplier with a good reputation. Even the best components will fail eventually; however, the reliability of the service can be improved by designing the service so that a component failure does not result in downtime. This is another availability concept called *resilience*. By ensuring the design includes alternate network routes, for example, a network component failure will not lead to service downtime, because the traffic will reroute. Carrying out planned maintenance to ensure that all the components are kept in good working order will also help improve reliability.

Resilience Through Redundancy

A good example of designing in resilience is that of a modern passenger aircraft. Although the engines are designed to be very reliable, with a long MTBF, an aircraft with a single engine could still suffer catastrophic failure if that engine developed a fault midflight. Aircraft are therefore designed to have several engines and to be able to fly and land with only one of these operational. This availability management approach delivers resilience by providing redundancy (the use of one or more additional configuration items to provide fault tolerance).

However reliable the equipment and resilient the design, not all downtime can be prevented. When a fault occurs and there is insufficient resilience in the design to prevent it from affecting the service, the length of the downtime that results can be affected by how quickly the fault can be overcome. This is called *maintainability* and is measured as the *mean time to restore service (MTRS)*. It may be more cost-effective to concentrate resilience measures for those items that have a long service restoration time. To calculate MTRS, divide the total downtime by the total number of failures.

Calculating MTRS

A service suffers four failures in a month. The duration of each was 1 hour, 2 hours, 1.2 hours, and 1.8 hours, resulting in a total downtime of 6 hours.

MTRS = 6 ÷ 4 = 1.5 hours

$$\text{Maintainability (MTRS in hours)} = \frac{\text{Total downtime in hours}}{\text{Number of service breaks}}$$

Simple measures can be taken to reduce MTRS, such as having common spares available on site, and these measures can have a significant impact on availability.

ITIL recommends the use of MTRS, rather than Mean Time to Repair (MTTR), because this may or may not include the restoration of the service following the repair. From the customer perspective, downtime includes all the time between the fault occurring and the service being fully able to be used again. MTRS measures this complete time and is therefore a more meaningful measurement.

These concepts are illustrated in Figure 6.5, which shows what ITIL calls the *expanded incident lifecycle*. This shows periods of uptime, with incidents causing periods of downtime. MTRS is shown as the average of the downtime. MTBF is shown as the average of the uptime.

Each incident needs to be detected, diagnosed, and repaired, and the data needs to be recovered and the service restored. Any method of shortening any of these steps—speeding up detection through event management or speeding up diagnosis by the use of a knowledge base, for example—will shorten the downtime and improve availability. The figure also shows another concept, that of MTBSI; this calculates the average time from the start of one incident to the start of the next. Understanding MTBSI is not required for the examination.

FIGURE 6.5   The expanded incident lifecycle

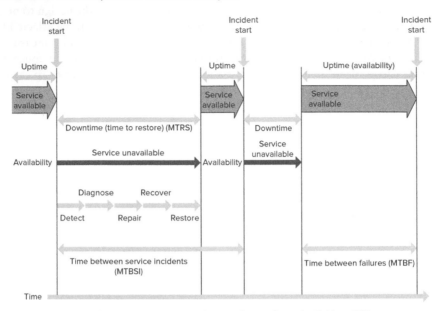

Based on Cabinet Office ITIL® material. Reproduced under license from the Cabinet Office.

Serviceability

Serviceability is defined as the ability of a third-party supplier to meet the terms of its contract. This contract will include agreed levels of availability, reliability, and/or maintainability for a supporting service or component.

Availability Concepts: Reliability and Serviceability

A large bakery had used a machine for making bread rolls for 15 years without any downtime. This machine was responsible for the production of all the bread rolls for a major fast-food company and was therefore very important to the business. The long period without failure showed that the machine was very *reliable*, possibly because of a *resilient* design. One day it failed. Because it had never failed before, there was consternation; there was no procedure in place for such an occurrence. Eventually a manual was located, which was in German. After tracking down the manufacturer in Germany (this was in the days before Google), a call was placed with them to send an engineer. He arrived the following day (exactly two days since the fault occurred) and fixed the machine in 15 minutes. The mean time to repair was therefore short (15 minutes), but the mean time to restore service was 2 days and 15 minutes, which had a major impact on the ability of the company to satisfy its external customer, the fast-food chain. The weakness here was in the *serviceability* of the machine; there was no contract in place to ensure a response and fix in an appropriate time.

Information Security Management

Another of the key warranty aspects of a service is security, and it is this aspect that we will discuss in this section. A service that is insecure will not deliver value to the customer and indeed may not be used by them at all.

ITIL defines information security as "the management process within the corporate governance framework, which provides the strategic direction for security activities and ensures objectives are achieved."

Central to *information security management (ISM)* is the identification and mitigation of risks to the security of the organization's information. The ISM process ensures that all security aspects are considered and managed throughout the service lifecycle.

> *Information* includes data stores, databases, and metadata (metadata is the term applied to a set of data describing and giving information about other data).

Organizations operate under an overall corporate governance framework, and information security management forms part of this framework. As with wide governance, ISM provides guidance as to what is required, ensuring risks are managed and the objectives of the organization are achieved.

Purpose, Objectives, and Scope of Information Security Management

The purpose of the information security management process is to ensure that IT security meets the requirements of the overall business security. It is responsible for making sure that the information, data, and IT services used by the organization are protected to the appropriate level. Information must be kept confidential, that is, made available only to those with the appropriate access rights. The data must be protected from any corruption or unauthorized alteration so that its integrity is assured. Finally, the information must be available to authorized users when required through robust systems that are resistant to failure. By ensuring these aspects—confidentiality, integrity, and availability—ISM enables the business to meet its objectives.

Where information is transmitted between partner organizations, ISM must ensure that this exchange is protected so that the information can be trusted.

ITIL defines the objective of *information security management (ISM)* as "to protect the interests of those relying on information, and the systems and communications that deliver the information, from harm resulting from failures of confidentiality, integrity, and availability."

The scope of ISM includes all aspects of information security that are important to the business. It is the responsibility of the business to define what requires protection and how strong this protection should be. Risks to security must be recognized, and appropriate countermeasures should be implemented. These may include physical (restricting access to secure areas through swipe cards) as well as technical aspects (password policies, use of biometrics, and so on). Information security is an integral part of corporate governance.

Producing an Information Security Policy

The information security management process is responsible for producing and maintaining an information security policy. This document should be made available to all IT staff, customers, and users. It is also part of ISM to ensure that the policy is being carried out, for example, by performing spot checks.

To produce such a policy, the IT security manager must have a thorough understanding of all security issues within the organization. This must include an understanding of the overall business security policy and requirements, its current and future plans, how these might impact security, and any risks to security (either business risks or IT risks), including how these risks are being managed. Any particular legal or regulatory requirements should also be included. For example, an organization that handles online credit-card payments will be subject to particular regulations to ensure that the transactions are adequately protected.

Information security management activities should be focused on and driven by an overall information security policy and a set of underpinning specific security policies. The information security policy should have the full support of top executive IT management and ideally the support and commitment of top executive business management. The policy should cover all areas of security and be appropriate to meet the needs of the business; specifically, it should include the following:

- Use and misuse of IT assets policy
- An access control policy
- A password control policy
- An email policy
- An Internet policy
- An antivirus policy
- An information classification policy
- A document classification policy
- A remote access policy
- A policy with regard to supplier access to IT service, information, and components
- A copyright infringement policy for electronic material
- An asset disposal policy
- A records retention policy

In most cases, these policies should be widely available to all customers and users, and their compliance should be referred to in all SLRs, SLAs, OLAs, underpinning contracts, and agreements. They are stored in the security management information system (SMIS), as shown in Figure 6.6. The SMIS forms part of the overall service knowledge management system (SKMS).

FIGURE 6.6   The information security management process

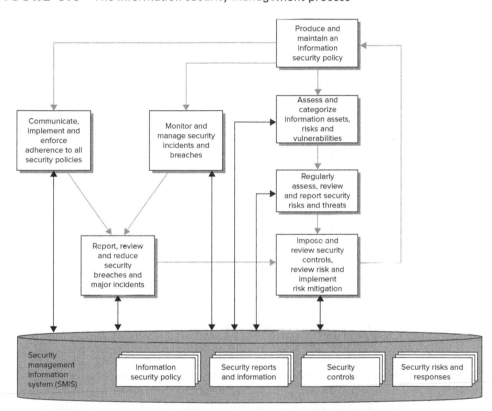

Based on Cabinet Office ITIL® material. Reproduced under license from the Cabinet Office.

Educating Staff About Security

The information security management process includes producing the information security policy and publicizing its contents. The process also involves working with the business to understand current and future needs in this area. Implementing appropriate protective measures and controls to manage the identified risks and ensuring that these measures are documented and maintained are ongoing aspects of this process.

The information security manager must ensure that controls are in place to manage the access to secure systems by third-party suppliers and ensure that faulty or obsolete hardware is not scrapped without removing the data held within it. Staff members must be made aware of their responsibilities with regard to protecting data (carrying data on unencrypted flash drives, sharing passwords, and so on); where a breach does occur, this should be used as an opportunity to reevaluate the existing policy for effectiveness.

For security to be effective, it must not be considered as an additional aspect but as integral to the design and operation of all services and across all ITSM processes. Security is an ongoing process; the information security manager should be constantly reviewing possible threats and taking the necessary steps to protect the organization's data. More security breaches occur as a result of lack of awareness than by deliberate action. The information security manager must continually emphasize the importance of adhering to the policy and be proactively seeking to improve security and reduce risk.

The information security policies should be authorized by senior management as they form an important part of overall governance. These business managers should emphasize the importance of adhering to the policies and ensure that all staff members are aware of what the policies are. Publicizing the policies through presentations, notices, posters, and so on, will help get the message across. There should be no scope for a staff member to argue that they did not know what the policy was. Should deliberate flouting of the policies take place, it is essential that these are taken seriously, with appropriate disciplinary measures enacted.

The nature of security threats changes with new technology; many organizations now have policies on downloading music or access to Facebook that would not have been necessary a few years ago. It is essential that the security policies keep in step with the new threats. All security policies should therefore be formally reviewed—and when necessary revised—at least every 12 months.

Supplier Management

In Chapter 5, we examined the contribution to the service made by external suppliers. The agreements that govern what level of service is provided by these third-party suppliers are called *underpinning contracts*. As we saw in that discussion, failure by a supplier may result in an impact on the service that the service provider delivers to their customer.

Large service providers may have dozens or even hundreds of supplier contracts. The elements of the service that these contracts provide are often critical to the overall service delivery. It is essential, therefore, that the service provider obtains the level of service specified in the underpinning contract and is sure that the contracts it has with its suppliers represent "value for money."

ITIL defines *supplier management* as the process responsible for obtaining value for money from suppliers, ensuring that all contracts and agreements with suppliers support the needs of the business and that all suppliers meet their contractual commitments.

The supplier management process describes best practices in managing suppliers to ensure that the services they provide meet expectations. It is included in the design phase of the service lifecycle, because it is important that this aspect is considered while the service is being designed. The type of supplier relationship will be part of the strategy phase, and a close relationship with suppliers will be required for a successful service transition. Once the service is operational, the day-to-day delivery against the contract must be monitored and managed, and should there be any issues, the improvement plan will be the responsibility of continual service improvement.

The Purpose and Objectives of Supplier Management

The purpose of supplier management is to ensure that suppliers provide value for money. By managing suppliers, the service provider can ensure the best delivery of service to their customer. Managing suppliers ensures that the necessary contracts are in place and enforced.

Ensuring that suppliers deliver the service paid for is a key objective of this process. It also ensures that the cost of the contract is controlled, by using objective selection criteria when choosing these suppliers.

Care must be taken to ensure that the terms of the contract are in alignment with the business requirement and underpin the service level targets.

 Real World Scenario

Supplier Management in Action

An internal service provider had agreed on an SLA target of an eight-hour fix for hardware faults. The contract with its supplier specified a 12-hour fix. To ensure that the SLA targets were met, the service provider had to send his own staff to swap out faulty equipment within the eight-hour target. This equipment then was repaired by the supplier. This arrangement meant that the service provider was paying for a service that did not match the business requirement and therefore had to duplicate the service he was paying for, by using his own staff. When the contract came up for renewal, the supplier manager suggested one of three alternatives:

- Renegotiate the SLA with the customer to be a 12-hour fix, thus aligning the business requirement with the contract and removing the need for the service provider's own staff to swap out the equipment.

- Renegotiate the contract with the supplier to be an eight-hour fix, again aligning the business requirement with the contract and removing the need for the service provider's own staff to swap out the equipment.

- Renegotiate or replace the contract with a much cheaper service, where faulty equipment is picked up weekly, repaired, and returned. Once the equipment was swapped out, it made little sense to have the supplier on a 12-hour fix, because the business requirement for an 8-hour fix had already been met.

Supplier management is involved in selecting suppliers and agreeing to the terms of the contracts. It is also responsible for the ongoing relationship with suppliers, including monitoring and managing their performance through regular reviews. These reviews are very similar to SLA reviews, but in supplier management the service provider is the customer.

Supplier management will draw up a supplier policy and keep all the information regarding suppliers and contracts in a supplier and contract management information system (SCMIS). The SCMIS forms part of the overall service knowledge management system.

What Is Covered by Supplier Management?

Supplier management's scope includes all the suppliers and contracts that are required in order to deliver the service to the provider's customer. It is important to identify which suppliers are particularly critical in delivering the service and ensure that they receive the appropriate attention. Some such suppliers will provide a critical element, such as network connectivity. Other suppliers may not appear to be as critical, but they may provide elements of several services, so the combined impact of poor service across several services could be extremely detrimental.

Many suppliers can be managed at the operational level, with service reports and reviews to ensure that they are delivering to the contract. Key suppliers will work closely with the business and the service provider, understanding and supporting the business and service strategy. We will look in more depth at different categories of supplier later.

As shown in Figure 6.7, the process includes categorizing suppliers and assessing and managing any risks that are identified. (The decision to award a contract to a new, untried supplier may result in a risk that the supplier may not be able to fulfill the contract, for example.) The selection of suppliers, following an objective assessment, and the negotiation of the contract are also included.

During the lifetime of the contract, supplier management will manage the supplier performance and any disputes that arise and will renew or terminate the contract at the end of its term, as appropriate. Where improvements need to be made, supplier management will identify them and ensure that they are entered in the continual service improvement register. (For more details on the CSI register, see Chapter 13.)

As part of the overall process, supplier management will draw up standard terms and conditions and contract templates. There will also be a supplier policy document that is produced and maintained as part of this process. Supplier management information is kept in the SCMIS. Throughout the process, the supplier manager will work within the overall financial and procurement framework in place within the organization.

Supplier Categorization

As discussed, some suppliers are more important than others. Some offer a specialized service and would be hard to replace. In some cases, the technical strategy of the service provider is largely dependent on the technical developments delivered by a particular supplier. Other suppliers provide standard services and could be replaced with little or no impact on the business, should another supplier offering better value be found.

FIGURE 6.7   The supplier management process

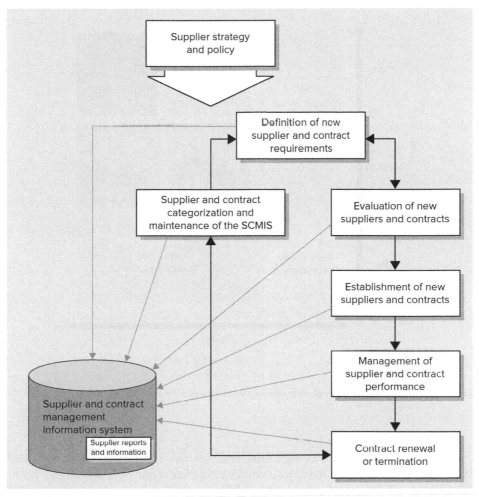

Based on Cabinet Office ITIL® material. Reproduced under license from the Cabinet Office.

It is an essential part of supplier management to devise a method of categorizing suppliers so that the appropriate time and attention is allocated to each—key suppliers are prioritized over less important ones. One of the best ways of categorizing suppliers is based on assessing the risk and impact from using the supplier and the value and importance of its services to the business. As shown in Figure 6.8, this assessment results in suppliers being assessed as strategic, tactical, operational, or commodity suppliers.

FIGURE 6.8 Supplier categorization

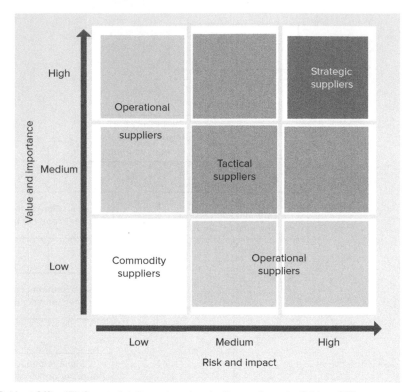

Based on Cabinet Office ITIL® material. Reproduced under license from the Cabinet Office.

■ Suppliers who are assessed as high value and high risk are strategic suppliers. The relationship between the business and a strategic supplier is one of "partnering." Both parties share confidential information to enable long-term cooperation to take place. These relationships are key to achieving the business objectives and, as such, will be managed by senior levels of management through regular meetings, strategy discussions, and improvement plans. An example of a strategic supplier may be one that is providing cutting-edge technology to provide its customer with a competitive advantage. For the customer to develop the new product, the supplier may need to provide information that it would normally keep confidential, such as the strategy for developing the technology. The customer similarly shares information regarding their strategy and plans. This cooperation enables the customer to benefit from new products before they are announced, and the supplier benefits from having a real case study of the new technology in use to use as marketing material when the product is launched.

- Suppliers assessed as medium value and medium risk are tactical suppliers. The relationship with them, although not as critical as with strategic suppliers, involves significant commercial activity. Middle-level managers will be responsible for managing these relationships through regular service reviews. Examples of this kind of supplier might include a server hardware maintenance organization.

- Operational suppliers are managed by junior managers through regular reviews. Failure by these suppliers would have relatively low impact. An example of such a supplier might be a PC or printer repair service.

- Low-value, low-risk suppliers of standard services, which can be easily sourced elsewhere, are commodity suppliers (for example, paper or toner suppliers). These require little management; a supplier that fails to meet the contract will be replaced by another that can.

From this, you can see that supplier management must have a clear understanding of how each supplier's services underpin both the SLA and the overall business objectives. Sufficient time and attention must be given to the more important suppliers, with little time wasted on the least important. With many organizations outsourcing elements of their service provision, the role of managing suppliers effectively has never been more essential.

Capacity Management

One of the responsibilities of the service provider is to ensure that the service is able to cope with the demands put upon it. If the design is not able to cope, the service will fail to meet the performance specified in the SLA. In addition, the service must be designed to meet not only the requirements for today; it must anticipate future requirements and be able to meet them, too. Overspecifying the design would ensure that it could meet future demands; however, this may result in wasted expenditure if the actual demand does not come close to the capabilities of the design.

ITIL states that *capacity management* is responsible for ensuring that the capacity of IT services and the IT infrastructure is able to meet agreed current and future capacity and performance needs in a cost-effective and timely manner. The capacity management process has therefore to understand the likely changes in capacity requirements and ensure that the design and ongoing management of the service meet this demand. Delivering sufficient capacity is a key warranty aspect of a service that needs to be delivered if the benefits of the service are to be realized.

Capacity management is considered throughout the lifecycle; as part of strategy, the likely capacity requirements for a new service are considered as part of the service evaluation to ensure that the service is meeting a real need. In design, the service is engineered to cope with that demand and to be flexible enough to be able to adjust to meet changing capacity requirements. Transition ensures that the service, when implemented, is delivering according to its specification. The operational phase of the lifecycle ensures that day-to-day adjustments that are necessary to meet changes in requirements are implemented. Finally, as part of continual service improvement, capacity-related issues are addressed, and adjustments are made to ensure the most cost-effective and reliable delivery of the service is achieved.

Delivering What Is Required, When It Is Required

The purpose of the capacity management process is to understand the current and future capacity needs of the service and to ensure that the service and its supporting services are able to deliver to this level. The actual capacity requirements will have been agreed upon as part of service level management; capacity management must not only meet these but also ensure that the future needs of the business, which may change over time, are also met. An essential objective is to deliver any increased capacity in time so that the business is not impacted.

The objectives of capacity management are met by the development of a detailed plan that states the current business requirement, the expected future requirement, and the actions that will be taken to meet these requirements. This plan should be reviewed and updated at regular intervals (at least annually) to ensure that changes in business requirements are considered. Similarly, any requests to change the current configuration will be considered by capacity management to ensure that they are in line with expectations or, if not, that the capacity plan is amended to suit the changed requirement. Those responsible for capacity management will review any issues that arise and help resolve any incidents or problems that are the result of insufficient capacity. This helps ensure that the service meets its objectives.

As part of the ongoing management of capacity and its continual improvement, any proactive measures that may improve performance at a reasonable cost are identified and acted upon. Advice and guidance on capacity and performance-related issues is provided, and assistance is given to service operations with performance and capacity-related incidents and problems.

What Should Capacity Management Include?

The capacity management process has responsibility for ensuring sufficient capacity at all times, including both planning for short-term fluctuations, such as that caused by seasonal variations, and ensuring that the required capacity is there for longer-term business expansion. Changes in demand may sometimes actually be reductions in that demand, and this is also within the scope of the process. Capacity management should ensure that as demand for the service falls, the capacity provided for that service is also reduced to ensure unnecessary expenditure is avoided.

The process includes all aspects of service provision and therefore may involve the technical, applications, and operations management functions. Other aspects of capacity, such as staff resources, are also considered.

🌐 Real World Scenario

Capacity Management in Action

A retail organization that was struggling to maintain its market position decided to expand its online and telephone-ordering service through a major marketing campaign. As part of this initiative, the telephone-ordering service hours were planned to be extended to 24 hours, 7 days a week. The business was considering what this would mean in terms of increased call-center staff, warehouse staff, and stock levels. The IT director was tasked with ensuring that the IT services would support this business initiative.

The IT director called together his managers involved in the capacity management process. Those in the technical management function had to ensure that the infrastructure would be able to cope with the expected increased demand. This included ensuring the telecoms infrastructure capacity required for the extra call-center staff and the voice traffic that the staff would generate in addition to the increase in data traffic. The website's capacity to handle increased traffic and the ability of the applications to handle a high volume of orders, credit-card processing, and so on, were investigated by the technical and applications management functions. The technical solutions that were recommended as a result meant more equipment would be purchased. The operations management function investigated the impact on operational processes, such as increased time needed to carry out backups and the impact of 24/7 operations on planned maintenance. Included was the impact on the UPS, air conditioning, and so on, of the extra equipment. Finally, the service desk manager calculated what increase in staff would be required to move to a 24/7 support operation and an increased user population during peak hours. This was calculated as requiring two new service desk analysts, and the building services department was asked to provide the extra office space for the new staff.

As this example illustrates, an increase in capacity requirements may have repercussions across the infrastructure and on the IT staff resources required to manage it. Although staffing is a line management responsibility, the calculation of resource requirements in this area is also part of the overall capacity management process.

Capacity management also involves monitoring "patterns of business activity" to understand how well the infrastructure is meeting the demands upon it and making adjustments as required to ensure that the demand is met. Proactive improvements to capacity may also be implemented, where justified, and any incidents caused by capacity issues need to be investigated.

Capacity management may also recommend demand management techniques to smooth out excessive peaks in demand.

Real World Scenario

Managing Capacity by Managing Demand

Like many countries, a certain European country requires that taxpayers complete a tax return online by a particular date. This is enforced by an automatic fine for late submissions. Inevitably, most taxpayers leave this until the last minute, with a huge demand for the system being generated in the last few days before the deadline. This demand profile means that the systems are overengineered to cope with a short-term spike in demand, and yet there is still a real risk of insufficient capacity in the last few days.

Providing even more capacity is not a good option to deal with this situation, because the design is overspecified for the level of demand across most of the year. Instead, an element of demand management is introduced. In addition to the 100-euro fine for late submission, an incentive is introduced; for every day before the deadline that the tax return is submitted, there is a one-euro reduction on the tax bill. This motivates people to submit well before the deadline, reducing the maximum capacity required and avoiding any capacity-related incidents.

The Capacity Management Subprocesses

To draw up the capacity plan, you must understand the future requirements of the business. Business capacity management is therefore a subprocess of the overall capacity management process. Its aim is to calculate what the business plans and forecast mean for the infrastructure. Business plans to expand (perhaps by buying smaller competitors) or launch a new service, offshore a call center, or outsource a function will all have an impact on capacity requirements. Capacity management has to understand this impact on the infrastructure and plan to meet the changed demand.

In addition to understanding overall business plans, capacity management must understand how the use of individual live services may vary over time. Service capacity management is the second of the capacity management subprocesses. The service level requirements for each of the live services must be understood, and monitoring needs to be implemented to check how well the service is performing. Thresholds can be set within the monitoring tools to enable any possible issues to be spotted and acted upon quickly. See Chapter 12, "The Other Service Operation Processes," for more information on event management and the use of monitoring tools and thresholds. Capacity management will take action to handle any issues that arise and will also consider any proactive steps that could be taken to improve performance. This may require working with the specialist staff members who carry out component capacity management.

🌐 Real World Scenario

Overlap with Business Capacity Management

Service capacity management focuses on delivering the required and agreed capacity for each service. Monitoring performance will help you understand any changing use of the service, which overlaps with and feeds into the business capacity subprocess. Even if overall capacity requirements are increasing, there may be a reduction in the demand for a particular service. For example, a car insurance company that was launched some years ago to sell insurance directly to the public, through large call centers, may find that although business is increasing, the use of the call center (and the IT services used by the call-center agents) is decreasing, being replaced by online sales. Monitoring the increase or decrease in the use of a service will help business capacity management to understand the likely requirements of the service in 12 to 18 months, which can be fed into the overall capacity plan.

The final subprocess of capacity management is component capacity management. This is the most technical aspect of capacity management and is likely to be carried out by the technical management staff, with day-to-day monitoring being the responsibility of the technical and operations management functions. It requires a detailed understanding of all the components that make up the end-to-end service and their individual capabilities. The current utilization of each of these components must be monitored, because insufficient capacity in a single component could cause a bottleneck and impact the whole service. This subprocess will use event management to track when thresholds are breached so that preemptive action can be taken to overcome the issue, before service is affected.

Figure 6.9 shows the three capacity management subprocesses and how each is involved in one or more of the capacity management processes steps of reviewing and improving current capacity, identifying changes to capacity requirements, and providing new capacity. The figure also shows the capacity plan, which we will discuss next.

Managing capacity requires the IT service provider to respond to changing circumstances because the expected capacity demands may prove to be an under or overestimation. This requires a number of key activities to be performed iteratively as part of the service operation stage of the lifecycle. Figure 6.10 shows this ongoing cycle. The first step involves monitoring capacity against thresholds and then analyzing the data this provides. Any necessary "tuning" adjustments, such as adding or removing resources in order to ensure that sufficient capacity is always available, are identified. These are then implemented, and the monitoring stage begins again. All of the information gathered from these activities is stored in the capacity management information system (CMIS). The CMIS forms part of the overall service knowledge management system (SKMS).

FIGURE 6.9 Capacity management overview with subprocesses

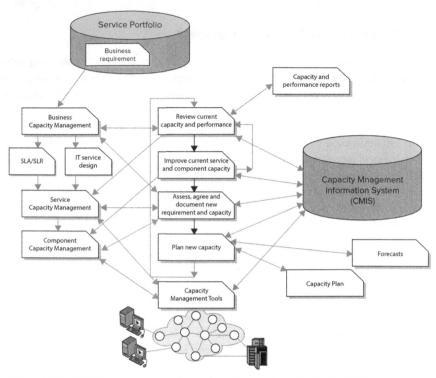

Based on Cabinet Office ITIL® material. Reproduced under license from the Cabinet Office.

FIGURE 6.10 Iterative activities in capacity management

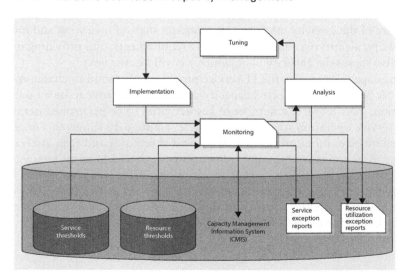

Based on Cabinet Office ITIL® material. Reproduced under license from the Cabinet Office.

Planning for the Future: The Capacity Plan and CMIS

Capacity management works with the business to understand its current and future business needs and investigates future technical developments that may be able to help provide capacity more cheaply; this information will be used to draw up the capacity plan.

The *capacity plan* is an important output from the capacity management process. It captures the current and future requirements and proposes how these should be met. Drawing up the plan requires a close relationship with the strategy phase of the lifecycle; the strategy needs to be based on a firm understanding of the current and future capabilities of the infrastructure, and the planners need input from the strategy discussions to understand what the future requirements will be.

The plan covers 12 to 18 months ahead so that any planned expenditure can be included in the negotiation of the annual IT budget. Planning this far ahead does mean assumptions have to be made, so the plan should be reviewed and reissued as actual requirements become clear. Reviews should take place at least annually and, additionally, after any major business change (decision to expand or divest, outsource, offshore, or otherwise change the IT requirements). Each review of the plan should include a reforecasting of requirements for the 12 to 18 months following the review.

The plan is a resource for the business and all IT departments, which will both contribute to it and refer to it when planning services. It should contain an introductory section explaining the current infrastructure and its performance and any capacity issues currently being experienced. It should be clear what is in scope and what is out of scope so that the reader understands any omissions and the reasons for them. Any assumptions made should also be stated.

The plan should consider a number of possible scenarios and explain why these have been chosen. These scenarios should be based on the information that has been gathered as part of the evaluation of business, service, and component capacity requirements as being reasonable possible outcomes. For example, the business may be planning to increase the workforce by at least 10 percent in six months, based on expected increased sales. The scenarios used might include not only one to meet the 10 percent increase but also one for a 5 percent increase and one for 12 percent so that if the business is less or more successful than it expects, there will be a plan for providing the required capacity.

The plan should examine the current capacity demands of each service, how these are met, and the forecast for future capacity requirements, based on the scenarios. This may be at a detailed level, considering storage, bandwidth, and so on. Options for meeting the new requirements should then be described, together with costs, risks, advantages, and disadvantages of each. Finally, the plan should recommend a particular approach. It is essential that changes are assessed for impact on the capacity plan and on the performance of all services and resources.

The capacity plan is stored in the capacity management information system (CMIS), together with reports of current performance and forecasts of future requirements.

Effective capacity management is essential if the service is going to be able to meet current and future demands. All three areas must be considered—business, service, and component capacity—to ensure that the process fulfills this requirement. Poor capacity management will have a serious effect on the ability of the business to achieve its objectives, either through a failure to deliver the service required or by making the service unnecessarily expensive by overproviding capacity.

IT Service Continuity Management

As discussed when talking about availability management, a service delivers value only when it is available for use. In addition to the activities carried out under the availability management process, there is a requirement on the IT service provider to ensure that the service is protected from catastrophic events that could prevent it from being delivered at all. Where these cannot be avoided, there is a requirement to have a plan to recover from any such disruption in a timescale and at a cost that meets the business requirement. Ensuring IT service continuity is an essential element of the warranty of the service.

It is important to understand that *IT service continuity management (ITSCM)* is responsible for the continuity of the IT services required by the business. The business itself should have a business continuity plan to ensure that any potential situations that would impact the ability of the business to function are identified and avoided. Where it is not possible to avoid such an event, the business continuity management process should have a plan, which is appropriate and affordable, to both minimize its impact and recover from it. Thus, ITSCM can be seen as one of a number of elements making up a business continuity plan (BCM), along with a human resources continuity plan, a financial management continuity plan, a building management continuity plan, and so on.

 **Real World Scenario**

ITSCM Without BCM

The internal IT service provider for a large insurance company in the United Kingdom had a well-developed IT service continuity plan. This plan was detailed and tested regularly, so staff members were aware of their roles should it ever have to be used.

The business did not have a business continuity plan, however. Despite being urged by the IT director to consider the impact of a disaster on its ability to operate, the business was reluctant to spend any time or money on something that might not happen. The business leaders also assumed that the IT plan would be sufficient on its own.

The IT plan was based upon the need to have critical systems available to staff from a remote recovery site within 12 hours of a disaster that rendered the data center inoperable. Suggested possible events that might have this effect were fire, floods, extreme weather, and so on. Any such event would have meant that the entire head office (where the data center was based) would also be out of commission. The head office employed 600 insurance clerks selling policies and settling claims.

If such an event had actually occurred, the IT plan would have meant the critical services would have been available within hours. However, the staff members who used these services would have nowhere from which to work, because there was no alternative office accommodation planned (because there was no BCM plan). Even if some accommodation had been found, the staff would have been unable to work, because their work was based on paper files, housed in filing cabinets in the head office. Those paper files would not have been available.

Thus, the IT service continuity plan would have been useful only in the very limited circumstances of a major event that affected the data center and no other parts of the building—an unlikely scenario!

A competitor insurance company, based a few blocks away, had a detailed business continuity plan in addition to an IT service continuity plan. Every document entering the building was scanned, and an electronic copy was stored off-site. This company could be secure in the knowledge that any major event affecting the data center would not prevent the business from being able to continue working.

IT service continuity management process supports the organization's business continuity management process. It is responsible for identifying and managing the risks to the IT services, agreeing with the business what the minimum requirement for the service would be in the event of a disaster, and ensuring that this agreed level can be provided.

A fundamental objective of the process is to reduce the chance of a disaster occurring at all by identifying the risks to IT services and implementing cost-effective countermeasures to reduce or remove the risk. Should a disaster occur despite these efforts, ITSCM ensures that there is a detailed, tested plan to recover the services to an agreed level within the agreed timescales. Dependent on the business requirement, the service restoration may need to take place within minutes, hours, or one or more days.

What Does ITSCM Aim to Achieve?

ITSCM should develop a number of plans to provide an acceptable level of IT services in the event of a major disruption. Several plans are required to fit the various scenarios involved. The scenarios catered for, and the decision as to what is an acceptable level of service, are arrived at in consultation with the overall business continuity management function.

The service continuity requirement may change over time as the business's use of and dependence upon the various IT services changes. It is essential that ITSCM carries out regular *business impact analysis (BIA)* to ensure that the plan still fits the requirement. Should the requirement have changed, the plan must also be changed.

Risks to the IT services may also change over time, so a program of risk assessment exercises must be undertaken to ensure that new risks are identified and mitigated; the level of acceptable risk needs to be agreed on with the business. Risk assessment may require the involvement of availability and information security management, because each of these processes involves identifying and managing particular risks.

The ITSCM manager will be a source of expertise on continuity issues and so may be consulted by the business or the rest of IT needing guidance. It is essential that all changes have been assessed to understand their impact on the ITSCM plans and procedures. An apparently straightforward change may remove a level of resilience, for example, or a departmental reorganization may split a single role in the plan across a number of individuals, meaning that this responsibility may have to be reassigned.

The major objective of ITSCM is to ensure that solutions have been developed and put in place to ensure that the required level of service (or better) can continue to be provided. Where these solutions involve the use of services supplied by external third-party suppliers, ITSCM will work with supplier management to ensure the necessary contracts are negotiated and agreed.

What Is Included in ITSCM?

Every IT service suffers from failures from time to time. ITSCM is not concerned with these service interruptions, which are handled through the incident management process. Neither does it get involved with managing risks as a result of business changes. Its focus is on the major events that have a catastrophic impact on the ability of the service provider to supply the vital services that enable the business to achieve its aims. The definition of catastrophic failure will vary between organizations. For example, the trading floor of a financial institution will feel a major impact within minutes, but other organizations may not be affected for hours or longer. Damage may be financial, but it may also be legal (failure to submit information in time to an official regulatory or government body). There may be damage to the "brand." Downtime on a global online book retailer's website, for example, would cause poor publicity, as well as missed sales opportunities. Undertaking a business impact analysis will help the business and the service provider agree on what the minimum requirements are for a particular organization. They will need to consider the various locations, the business processes carried out there, and the services used at each. From this, an appropriate ITSCM response can be designed to provide the required technical facilities to enable the critical work to continue at the agreed level.

The scope of the ITCM process includes agreeing on the policies and the services to be included in the plans, carrying out business impact analysis, and assessing and managing likely risks. Managing the risks entails identifying any steps that could be taken to reduce the likelihood of an occurrence or lessen its impact if avoidance is impossible, as long as the cost is justified.

Developing a strategy for service continuity, based on this business impact analysis and the risk management actions and aligned to the business continuity strategy, is a major part of the ITSCM process, shown in Figure 6.11. The strategy includes detailed recovery plans and involves regular testing and adjustments as necessary should requirements change. We will start by looking at the business impact analysis and the risk assessment processes that form part of the requirements and strategy phase of the process.

FIGURE 6.11 The ITSCM lifecycle

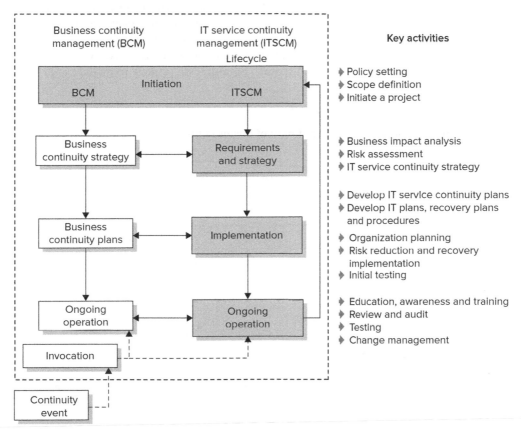

Based on Cabinet Office ITIL® material. Reproduced under license from the Cabinet Office.

Assessing Business Impact

The requirements and strategy phase of the ITSCM process—involving a detailed understanding of the requirement, through BIA, and an assessment of likely risks—is crucial. If these stages are rushed or incomplete, there is a real risk that the plans would not fit the business requirement, leading to severe, possibly terminal, business impact should the worst happen. The assessment identifies which are the key services, because it is these services that must continue, despite what has occurred.

BIA also considers various scenarios; the same event may not have an equivalent impact if it occurs at different times; the failure of financial reporting at year end would have a much greater impact than at another time, for example. The analysis should also consider whether the impact would escalate the longer the service was unavailable, because this would affect the choice of recovery option, favoring a faster recovery even at a greater cost.

ITSCM must understand how long recovery would take and what would be required to enable this recovery to take place. The BIA clarifies the relative business priority for each service. Where an impact would be severe from the start, implementing measures to reduce the chance of a service-affecting failure would be justified (failover, and so on). Where the impact takes some time to build up, a plan to restore the service within hours or days would be sufficient (see Figure 6.12). Each organization is likely to include a variety of recovery requirements.

FIGURE 6.12   Graphical representation of business impacts

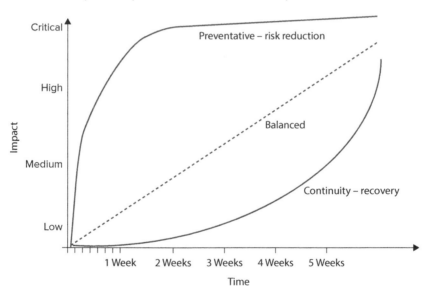

Based on Cabinet Office ITIL® material. Reproduced under license from the Cabinet Office.

Business impact analysis provides a mapping of the critical business processes against the IT components that provide the IT service that supports it. Only with this information can a decision be made as to what needs to be recovered and the necessary timescales. It is essential that senior business staff and those who actually carry out the activity are involved in the BIA; IT would otherwise decide this from an entirely technical viewpoint, being unaware that some apparently minor system may actually be required to deliver critical business processes. The business may also decide that the fast recovery options are too expensive and readjust their requirements.

Assessing Risk

Although the ITSCM plan provides a level of assurance that critical business processes could be recovered in a suitable timescale should a catastrophic event occur, it is preferable that the event does not occur at all. Many such events cannot be foreseen, or prevented, but a thorough risk assessment and management of the identified risks greatly reduces the likelihood. Risk assessment requires an understanding of likely threats and how vulnerable the organization is to those threats. Risk management then considers suitable cost-justifiable responses to these threats. The aim is to reduce the vulnerability to the risk, making it less likely to occur, or to minimize its impact, should it be unpreventable. As you learned earlier, risk management also takes place in the availability and information security management processes.

Risk assessment will compile a list of evaluated risks—some within an acceptable level of risk, some beyond it. The countermeasures should reduce the likelihood or the impact of a threat, reducing its score to within acceptable levels. Table 6.1 shows an example of the output from an assessment.

TABLE 6.1   Examples of risks and threats

Risk	Threat
Loss of internal IT systems/networks, PABXs, ACDs, and so on	Fire
	Power failure
	Arson and vandalism
	Flood
	Aircraft impact
	Weather damage, such as from a hurricane
	Environmental disaster
	Terrorist attack
	Sabotage
	Catastrophic failure
	Electrical damage, such as from lightning
	Accidental damage

TABLE 6.1   Examples of risks and threats *(continued)*

	Poor-quality software
Loss of external IT systems/networks, such as e-commerce servers, cryptographic systems	All of the above
	Excessive demand for services
	Denial-of-service attack, such as against an Internet firewall
	Technology failure, such as cryptographic system
Loss of data	Technology failure
	Human error
	Viruses, malicious software, such as attack applets
Loss of network services	Damage or denial of access to network service provider's premises
	Loss of service provider's IT systems/ networks
	Loss of service provider's data
	Failure of the service provider
Unavailability of key technical and support staff	Industrial action
	Denial of access to premises
	Resignation
	Sickness/injury
	Transport difficulties
Failure of service providers, such as outsourced IT	Commercial failure, such as insolvency
	Denial of access to premises
	Unavailability of service provider's staff
	Failure to meet contractual service levels

Business impact analysis and risk management enable the IT service provider and the business to devise an appropriate ITSCM plan combining risk reduction measures with recovery in the event of an unavoidable event. The plan will be cost-effective, because only the critical services will have a full, speedy recovery; other services will have a lower level of protection that fits their lower level of criticality.

Not all risks can be avoided. A disaster affecting a nearby location, such as a gas explosion, would inevitably impact the service being provided; if the interruption to the service is short-lived, it may be decided that invoking the ITSCM plan is not warranted.

Design Coordination

Service design involves many different aspects beyond designing a new application to provide new functionality (utility). Consideration must be given to how the service will operate, both now and in the future; what level of availability, security, continuity, and capacity will need to be provided; and the best approach to this (warranty). Other processes will interface with the service design processes. To ensure a successful outcome, the design activities must be coordinated.

The purpose of the *design coordination* process is to carry out the coordination of the many different activities of service design. The many processes and numerous interfaces involved are all potential sources of conflict. By providing a single point, complications and misunderstandings are avoided.

The objectives of this process include ensuring that all aspects of the design, including the architecture, processes, and metrics, are designed to provide the utility and warranty of the service to a level that meets the business requirement now and in the future. Where there are several competing projects, design coordination ensures the resolution of conflicting demands. It also ensures that the resources and capabilities needed for a successful implementation are in place and ensures that service design packages are compiled and transmitted to the appropriate transition staff when required. It ensures that everyone is clear about what needs to be handed over between the different lifecycle changes and the quality criteria they must meet.

Design coordination will check that the proposed design conforms to the agreed standards and that repeatable design practices are used so that there is a consistency of approach across services. It will try to identify any improvements to the design stage that could be used in future projects.

Design coordination covers all the various activities in design and ensures consistency across them. All activities regarding the design of any new services, changes to existing services, or the retirement of services will benefit from this process. It covers large projects, as well as those designs that are too small to merit a project being set up but whose activities would benefit from being coordinated. Some activities are too small to require coordination. The majority of design coordination will focus on major changes and larger projects, where the complexity of the tasks and the number of people involved present a risk that these tasks could become out of step with each other. Design coordination reduces that risk significantly.

Deciding which activities require design coordination and which do not is a matter for individual organizations to decide. Each organization must also consider how it wants to decide upon the level of coordination required.

 Real World Scenario

Fitting the Process to the Business Requirement

The internal service provider for a large retail organization was concerned about the quality of changes that had been implemented in the past, many of which required rework later because not all implications had been considered. It was agreed that all changes would be considered to have a design phase. Even smaller changes now had defined design activities, including implementation plans. The coordination process in this situation was usually straightforward, acting as a check to ensure that all the activities had been carried out. Where necessary, when changes were more complex, there would be a greater level of detailed coordination. The organization was happy that this level of involvement in all changes addressed the concerns.

Another organization took an opposite view, regarding such involvement in all changes as unnecessarily bureaucratic. It laid down criteria restricting the involvement of the service coordination process to major changes or projects. It was happy with the level of assurance this approach provided.

Both of these organizations were right; the level of coordination in each case fitted the business requirement and each organization's attitude toward risk. The first organization had poor experiences in the past, and implementing design coordination for all changes gave it the reassurance it required. Organizations such as government departments, global enterprises, and those with safety-critical systems are likely to want this level of assurance. The second organization was happy with a "lighter touch." Organizations that need to be dynamic and responsive to fast-changing requirements, such as those providing web services, are more likely to adopt this approach.

The design coordination process includes providing the required level of assistance to projects or changes that the organization has decided is appropriate. It ensures that all resources are managed effectively, avoiding scheduling issues and overcommitment of resources, by ensuring that resource planning is carried out in advance.

The process ensures that a standard approach is used wherever possible and that policies and guidelines are followed. It confirms that the service designs are documented and handed over with the service design package to transition. It carries out checks to evaluate whether the design is both fit for use and fit for purpose. It also ensures that the guidelines are updated when required. By monitoring the success of the service design activities, it identifies opportunities for continual service improvement and ensures they are implemented.

The process is concerned solely with the design phase. The role is one of coordination; the actual contents of the solution are the responsibility of the individual projects.

Summary

The processes discussed in this chapter are essential to an effective design; by effective, we mean not only a design that provides the required functionality but also one in which the requirements of the service in operation are fully considered. The design takes into account the immediate needs but also ensures the future requirements for changes, increased capacity, and so on, are fully considered. Through availability and IT service continuity management, the design ensures that the service will be available to an agreed level when required and will be protected from unnecessary risks. The business can be assured that the required level of information security has been built in and that IT management will be able to monitor and manage performance, because the metrics needed will have been included. The service coordination process ensures that all these processes work smoothly together to ensure an efficient handoff to the transition phase.

Exam Essentials

Understand the format of the service catalog as a database or structured document, forming one of the three service portfolio elements.   Be able to describe its contents and information about all live IT services, including those available for deployment. Understand the purpose of the service catalog as a single source of consistent information to authorized individuals on all current and forthcoming operational services and the importance of this information being kept accurate and current. There are two types of services included in the catalog: customer-facing services that are visible to the business and supporting services required by the service provider to deliver customer-facing services. Understand that the customer and the service provider will therefore have different views of each service. Understand also that different customer types such as wholesale or retail customers may have different views.

Understand the type of information held in the service catalog for individual services such as service details, status, interfaces, and dependencies and the way in which this information is used by other processes, such as service level management.   The scope of the service catalog includes only those services that have been or will be transitioned to the operational environment. Remember that these may be listed individually or in the form of service packages.

Understand what is meant by availability and how it is calculated. Remember that the user is concerned with end-to-end availability, and the failure of one component can make the whole service unavailable to that user. Measurement of availability takes into account only agreed service time so that agreed downtime and out-of-hours availability are not included in the calculation. Identifying vital business functions helps availability management target its activities to the best effect.

Be able to describe the availability concepts of reliability, resilience, maintainability, and serviceability. Reliability concerns how long a service, component, or CI can function without an interruption and the impact of this on overall availability. Understand what is meant by mean time between failure and how it is calculated. A resilient service design may suffer component failures without the service being affected. Understand the role of redundant equipment in providing resilience. Maintainability concerns how quickly a service, component, or CI can be restored to normal working status following a failure, as well as the impact of this on overall availability. Understand what is meant by mean time to restore service and how it is calculated. Serviceability is how well a third party is able to provide the response and fix times required in its contract following a failure, as well as the impact of this on overall availability.

Understand the purpose and importance of the information security policy. The level of security required is a business decision, and it is the responsibility of the information security manager to then ensure the required level of protection is provided. Understand the purpose of related policies such as password and Internet use policies and how they contribute to the overall protection of the organization's data. Understand the concepts of confidentiality (restricting access to data to authorized users), integrity (maintaining data free of any corruption or unauthorized change), and availability (able to be accessed when required) of data. Security rules must be clearly communicated so that all staff members are aware of them and senior management is enforcing them. SLAs, OLAs, and underpinning contracts play a central role in documenting and agreeing on responsibilities in this area. All security breaches must be documented and responded to appropriately and should be considered opportunities to improve security.

Understand the importance of suppliers to ensuring the quality of the overall service and the need to ensure that suppliers deliver value for money. Understand the link between underpinning contracts as part of service level management and the management of suppliers. Understand the lifecycle of supplier management, from the signing of the contract through the management of the delivery by the supplier against that contract to its renewal or termination. Be able to explain the importance of the supplier management policy and the role of the supplier and contract management information system. Understand the different categories of suppliers (strategic, tactical, operational, and commodity) and how suppliers are assessed in terms of value, importance, risk, and impact to determine which category is appropriate.

Understand the role of capacity management in providing the current and future capacity and performance that the business requires, when it requires it, and at a cost it can afford. Understand the use of demand management to affect this requirement. Be able to explain the subprocesses of business, service, and component capacity management and the role each plays in delivering what is required. Understand the involvement of the different functions in assessing and providing sufficient capacity. Understand the purpose and contents of the capacity plan and the requirement for it to be revised as requirements change. Understand the purpose and contents of the capacity management information system.

Understand how IT service continuity management (ITSCM) is responsible for providing an agreed level of service in the event of a major disruption to normal working conditions. Be able to differentiate between the responsibilities of business continuity management and ITSCM. Be able to explain the concept of business impact analysis and the requirement for the participation of the business in this exercise. The two stages of risk management are identification of risks and cost-justifiable risk mitigation. ITSCM is not entirely about recovering from a catastrophic event; it also addresses the need to prevent or reduce the impact of such an event. Understand the importance of keeping the plan up-to-date and the need to assess changes for possible impact on it. Remember that the plan needs to be rehearsed to ensure that it works as designed.

Understand the role of design coordination in providing a single point of coordination and control for all service design activities and processes. Understand the role of design coordination in managing resources and capabilities and its responsibility for compiling the service design package. It has a key role in ensuring quality and consistency across designs and ensuring the conformance of designs to governance requirements. Design coordination ensures the successful handoff of a service first from strategy to design and then to transition. The coordination process helps control cost, ensure adherence to warranty and utility requirements, and ensure activities are appropriately scheduled. A central coordinating role is able to learn from each design stage and implement improvements to all the service design activities.

Review Questions

You can find the answers in Appendix A.

1. Which of the following is the correct definition of the service catalog?

    A. A document that describes the IT service, service level targets, and responsibilities of the IT service provider and the customer

    B. The complete set of services managed by a service provider, used to manage the entire lifecycle of all services

    C. A database or document with information about all live IT services

    D. Justification for a particular item of expenditure, including information about costs, benefits, options, and risks

2. Which of the following is included in a service catalog?

    1. Customer-facing services

    2. Strategic services

    3. Supporting services

    4. Retired services

    A. 1 and 2

    B. 1, 2, 3, and 4

    C. 1 and 3

    D. 2 and 3

3. Which of the following statements about the service catalog is true?

    1. The service catalog forms part of the service portfolio.

    2. The service portfolio forms part of the service catalog.

    3. There is no relationship between the service catalog and the service portfolio.

    4. Customer-facing services appear in the service catalog, and supporting services appear in the service portfolio.

    A. 1 and 3

    B. 1 only

    C. 2 and 4

    D. 4 only

4. Availability is calculated using the formula AST-DT/AST × 100. What do the terms AST and DT refer to?

    A. AST = assumed service target, DT = delivery time

    B. AST = availability service target, DT = downtime

    C. AST = agreed service time, DT = downtime

    D. AST = agreed service time, DT = delivery time

5. Availability management considers VBFs. What does VBF stand for?

    A. Viable business factors

    B. Vital business functions

    C. Visibility, benefits, functionality

    D. Vital business facilities

6. Which of these statements is *not* correct?

    A. MTBF measures uptime—the time from the failure to service restoration.

    B. MTRS measures downtime.

    C. MTBSI stands for maximum time before service interruption.

    D. MTBSI measures the time from one failure until the next failure.

7. Which of the following are terms used in availability management?

    1. Reliability

    2. Resilience

    3. Resistance

    4. Attainability

    5. Serviceability

    6. Maintainability

    7. Detectability

    A. 1, 2, 6, 7

    B. 2, 3, 5, 6

    C. 1, 4, 6, 7

    D. 1, 2, 5, 6

8. Which of the following are responsibilities of information security management?

    1. Defining the protection required for systems and data

    2. Undertaking risk assessments

    3. Producing the Information security policy

    4. Implementing security measures to new systems during service transition

    A. 1 and 2 only

    B. All of the above

    C. 1, 2, and 3

    D. 2, 3, and 4

9. Information security management keeps information about security in what?

   A. SMIS

   B. IMSS

   C. KEDB

   D. ISDB

10. Which of the following are responsibilities of supplier management?

     1. Negotiating with internal suppliers

     2. Negotiating with external suppliers

     3. Monitoring delivery against the contract

     4. Ensuring value for money

   A. 1 and 2 only

   B. All of the above

   C. 1, 2, and 3

   D. 2, 3, and 4

11. Which of the following are categories of supplier described in ITIL?

     1. Strategic

     2. Operational

     3. Trusted

     4. Commodity

   A. 1 and 2 only

   B. All of the above

   C. 1, 2, and 4

   D. 2, 3, and 4

12. Which of the following are responsibilities of capacity management?

     1. Negotiating capacity requirements to be included in the SLA

     2. Monitoring capacity

     3. Forecasting capacity requirements

     4. Dealing with capacity issues

   A. 2, 3, and 4

   B. 1 and 2 only

   C. All of the above

   D. 1, 2, and 4

13. Capacity management considers three subprocesses. What are they?

   A. Service capacity, business capacity, component capacity

   B. System capacity, business capacity, component capacity

   C. Service capacity, business capacity, configuration capacity

   D. System capacity, business capacity, infrastructure capacity

14. Capacity management considers PBAs. What does PBA stand for?

   A. Proactive business assurance

   B. Patterns of business availability

   C. Patterns of business activity

   D. Proactive business assessment

15. Which of the following are responsibilities of IT service continuity management?

   1. Ensuring IT services can continue in the event of a disaster

   2. Carrying out risk assessments

   3. Ensuring the business has contingency plans in place in case of a disaster

   4. Ensuring all IT staff know their role in the event of a disaster

   A. 2, 3, and 4

   B. 1, 2, and 4

   C. 1 and 2 only

   D. All of the above

16. IT service continuity management carries out a BIA in conjunction with the business. What does BIA stand for?

   A. Business integrity appraisal

   B. Business information alternatives

   C. Benefit integration assessment

   D. Business impact analysis

17. Which of the following statements about design coordination responsibilities is incorrect?

   A. To ensure that the goals and objectives of the design stage are met

   B. To design the solution

   C. To provide a single coordination point

   D. To ensure the design meets the requirements

18. Outputs from design coordination include what?
    1. The service design package
    2. The CMS
    3. The governance requirements
    4. Suggestions for improvements to be made to the design stage
    A. 2, 3, and 4
    B. 1 and 2 only
    C. All of the above
    D. 1 and 4 only

19. Which of the following statements about the service catalogue is TRUE?
    A. The service catalog contains information on customer-facing services only
    B. The service catalog contains information on supporting services only
    C. The service catalog shows which IT service supports each business process
    D. The service catalog shows details of services under development.

20. Which of the following statements about IT Service Continuity Management (ITSCM) is TRUE?
    A. ITSCM defines the service that can be provided in the event of a major disruption. The business can then plan how it will use the service.
    B. ITSCM and Business Continuity Management (BCM) have no impact on each other.
    C. BCM defines the level of IT service that will be required in the event of a major disruption. ITSCM is responsible for delivering this level of service.
    D. It is the responsibility of ITSCM to deliver a single continuity plan, that will fit all situations.

Chapter

7

Service Design Roles

THE FOLLOWING ITIL FOUNDATION EXAM OBJECTIVES ARE COVERED IN THIS CHAPTER:

✓ **Unit 7: Roles**

   ▪ 7-1. Account for the role and the responsibilities of the

      ▪ Process owner

      ▪ Process manager

      ▪ Process practitioner

      ▪ Service owner

   ▪ 7-2. Recognize the responsible, accountable, consulted, informed (RACI) responsibility model and explain its role in determining organizational structure

✓ **Unit 9: Competence and training**

   ▪ 9-1. Competence and skills for service management

   ▪ 9-2. Competence and skills framework

   ▪ 9-3. Training

This chapter covers the people aspect of service design; specifically, we will be examining the various roles that are required to be carried out if this lifecycle stage is to deliver effectively. We will look at a method of showing these roles and the various levels of involvement in a process activity. Finally, we will look at how organizations can ensure that their staff can obtain the required skills to enable them to be effective.

Roles and Responsibilities in Service Management

There are many different ways to organize an IT department, and no two service providers are identical, so the exact configuration of roles within each organization will differ. Often two or more roles may be combined; in other organizations, a single role may be split. ITIL provides guidelines, not prescriptive rules, so each organization should consider what would best fit their own requirements.

We will first clarify what is meant by the term *role*. The official glossary defines it as follows:

> A set of responsibilities, activities and authorities assigned to a person or team. A role is defined in a process or function.

Within each of the processes we have covered, we have described a number of roles. The role may be carried out by an individual or a team, and one person may have multiple roles. The person responsible for the availability management of the infrastructure may often also be fulfilling the capacity management role. It may be that capacity management is divided between a number of people, with one considering network capacity, another responsible for storage, and so on.

It is important to remember that although roles may be shared, or combined, there can be only one process owner for each process and one service owner for each service.

Often a job title may be the same as a role description; service level manager is one such example. Job titles are for each organization to decide, and it may be the case that the job of service level manager includes the role of service level manager, along with one or more other roles, such as supplier manager, within that particular organization.

It is also often true that one task carried out by an individual may touch several processes. A technician may submit a request for change to overcome a capacity issue that has been identified by problem management. The action may have been identified as desirable as part of a service improvement plan (SIP), which has been logged on the CSI register. The technician's action therefore involves several processes: problem, change, capacity, service level management, and continual service improvement.

Every process has its own specific roles. Here we will be looking at the generic roles that appear in all lifecycle stages.

Service Owner

With every service interacting with so many processes, there is a danger that the service itself may no longer receive the required attention. To avoid this, ITIL recommends that each service should have a single service owner. This clarifies who is accountable for the service and ensures that there is a focus on the business processes that the service supports.

Whatever technology is used to deliver the service and regardless of whether aspects of the technology are provided in-house or are outsourced, the service owner remains accountable for delivering the service. This role is responsible to the customer for the service being developed, implemented, and maintained, but it is also accountable to the IT director or service management director for its delivery.

As we will examine, ITIL recommends that each process should have an identifiable owner. Each process may affect many services, and it is the service owner of each who will ensure the service is delivered effectively and efficiently, whatever process is being carried out. Service owners will often own more than one service. For each service, they will carry out the following responsibilities:

- Ensuring that the service is delivered and supported to the required standards, by working with all IT groups and process owners
- Ensuring that the customer's requirements are understood and that the tasks required to deliver them are implemented by working with the business relationship manager
- Communicating with the customer as required on all issues regarding the delivery of the service
- Using the service portfolio management process to define new service models and to evaluate the impact of any changes to existing services
- Ensuring that the service undergoes continual service improvement by identifying possible improvements and, with the customer's agreement, putting these forward as requests for change
- Ensuring that appropriate monitoring and reporting is taking place to enable an accurate view of the level of service being delivered
- Ensuring that the required levels of performance and availability are delivered
- Developing a thorough understanding of the components that make up the service and ensuring that the potential impact of their failure is realized
- Representing the service across the organization and attending service review meetings with the business

- Representing the service within IT and at change advisory board meetings and internal service reviews
- Being the escalation (notification) point for major incidents affecting the service
- Working with service level to negotiate service level agreements that meet the customer requirements and operational-level agreements that support the service provision at the agreed level
- Maintaining the service catalog entry
- Working with the CSI manager to identify improvements to be added to the CSI register and participating in the review and prioritization of these and their eventual implementation

As the owner of the service, this role is concerned with the impact of any process affecting the service. This means service owners should be considered stakeholders in these processes, with whatever level of involvement is appropriate.

For example, the service owner plays a major part in the major incident process and will attend or possibly run any crisis meetings. They will also be involved in investigating the root cause of problems affecting their service. The service owner will represent the service at CAB meetings and will be involved in discussions regarding if and when a release should go ahead. They will want to ensure that the service portfolio and catalog entries and configuration data held on their service is accurate.

As explained earlier, there will be a close relationship between the service level management process and the service owner who acts as the contact point for the service. The service owner will also liaise with the owners of the more technical processes, such as availability and capacity, to ensure that the data collected by these processes indicates that the performance and reliability of these services meets the agreed standard.

The service owner is responsible for ensuring that the IT service continuity management plan for their service is practical and that every element of the plan is in place. They will work with the ITSCM manager to make sure that all aspects are considered. They will often attend rehearsals of the plan to observe it in action to confirm that nothing has been forgotten.

The service owner understands the costs involved in delivering the service and will work with the supplier manager and other managers to ensure that costs are controlled and value for money is achieved. In organizations where the business is charged for IT services, they will ensure that the recovery of costs takes place as agreed.

Finally, the service owner ensures that the service follows the information security management policies.

Process Owner

As we have seen, the service owner is the focus for one particular service, across all process areas. The process owner, in contrast, is accountable for a single process, whatever the service it affects.

The process owner must ensure that the process works efficiently and effectively. Although the role may often be carried out by the same person who fulfills the process manager role, in larger organizations this is less likely. A global company may have a change management process owner and a number of process managers carrying out the process in different countries, for example. The process owner is accountable for ensuring the process is fit for its purpose and is being carried out correctly by the process managers and practitioners. The role therefore has both a design and an enforcement aspect.

The process owner is accountable for the following:

- Developing the process strategy, policies, and standards
- Designing the process and amending it as required to implement improvements that make it more effective or efficient
- Designing the metrics for the process and ensuring that these provide the necessary information to judge the effectiveness and efficiency of the process
- Ensuring that the process is documented, that this documentation is available to those that require it, and that it is updated as needed
- Where the process has changed, ensuring that the process documentation is updated and the changes communicated to the process practitioners (those who actually carry out the process steps)
- Auditing the process activities to ensure adherence to the correct process
- Ensuring that the required resources are available to carry out the process and that the staff members involved have been trained to carry it out
- Communicating to the process technicians the importance of adhering to the documented process and explaining the implications for IT and the business of nonadherence
- As part of continual service improvement, reviewing the process strategy and the effectiveness of the process itself to identify possible improvements
- Where improvements to effectiveness or efficiency are identified, having these included in the CSI register and working with the CSI manager to review, prioritize, and implement them as appropriate

The process owner role is critical to the success of the process. In organizations where no such single point of ownership exists, those carrying out the process may decide to drop or amend steps in the process, and there is no one with the overall authority to prevent this. In global organizations, this can mean the process may develop regional variations. In addition to the danger of losing focus on the purpose of the process, this may invalidate the reporting from the process, because each area may be inputting data differently.

In Chapter 1, we discussed a generic process model. Without a process owner, there is no one with the responsibility of ensuring consistency in applying the process, and there is no one to ensure that the process output still matches the process objectives. Process documentation may not be updated, because the responsibility for its upkeep would be unclear. Finally, there would be no one to assess the process and identify improvements.

Process Manager

The process owner is accountable for the success of the process but may often not be responsible for actually carrying it out. The responsibility for managing the day-to-day implementation of a process belongs to the process manager. In large or geographically spread-out organizations, there may be several process managers responsible for managing the implementation of the same process, each with a regional or infrastructure responsibility.

The process manager is accountable for the following:

- Liaising with the process owner to ensure that the process is implemented across all lifecycle stages as the process owner intended

- Ensuring the right numbers of staff are assigned to the various roles within the process and that they understand what is required of them

- Working with other process managers and service owners to ensure the services are delivered as required

- Monitoring the process metrics to confirm the process is working as designed

- As part of continual service improvement, reviewing the process performance to identify possible improvements

- Where improvements are identified, having them included in the CSI register and working with the CSI manager and process owner to review, prioritize, and implement them as appropriate

The role of process manager is important, because it is the process manager who ensures that the process is carried out correctly day-to-day. The process manager may be distant from where the process actually occurs (working in the head office, while the process takes place in branch offices, for example). The process manager, or managers, will ensure that the staff members understand what is required of them and have been provided with the right resources and training to carry out the tasks. As process managers are close to the process execution, they are in an ideal position to identify issues and possible improvements. The success of any improvement initiatives will depend heavily on the enthusiastic involvement of the process manager in ensuring that staff members adopt the improved process.

Process Practitioner

Dependent on the process, there may be one or more people carrying out the process activities. In a small organization or for a simple process, this may be a single person, who is also likely to be the process manager. For a large organization or for a complex process, there may be many people, each carrying out parts of the process. The people involved in carrying out the process activities are the process practitioners.

The process practitioner is usually responsible for the following:

- Completing process activities to the required standard

- Understanding the importance of the process, and their role within it, in delivering the service

- Working with all the process stakeholders to ensure the process inputs, outputs, and interfaces are working properly so that the process delivers the desired result
- Producing evidence that the process activities have been carried out correctly, in the form of records
- Identifying necessary improvements to the process or supporting tool

The process practitioner role is responsible for actually delivering the process activities. Under the guidance of the process manager (unless these roles are combined), the practitioner is responsible for carrying out the process as designed, consistently and efficiently. It may be tempting to believe that the practitioner has nothing to contribute other than carrying out the activities; this is far from the truth. As a practitioner, the staff member will experience first-hand any issues with the process, such as tools that do not support the process effectively, bottlenecks in the process flow, or ambiguities in the documentation. The process manager and process owner should therefore seek out the views of practitioners when attempting to identify possible improvements.

Each role has its own purpose. Even where the roles are carried out by the same person, that person should attempt to consider each aspect of the roles. The practitioner has the advantage of daily interaction with the process but may be too close to it to see it objectively; the process manager is judged on the outcome of the process so has a particular focus on the resources required to deliver these effectively and efficiently. They will monitor the process metrics closely to ensure that the outputs are being delivered on time and within budget. The manager will see only their own part of the process delivery, however. The process owner has the advantage of seeing the overall picture, comparing the delivery of the process in different locations and under different process managers. By understanding the strengths and weaknesses of each perspective, a complete picture of the process delivery can be achieved, and improvement initiatives can be gathered from each level.

Designing Roles Using the RACI Model

In the first part of this chapter, we looked at the roles ITIL describes in relation to processes. With many service management processes and multiple roles within each, it is important that these roles are clearly defined for each individual process. Where it is not clear who has the authority to make a decision, organizations can find that processes fail to deliver, because of contradictory decisions being made by different people or perhaps no decisions being made at all. Where processes are failing to deliver, this can often be traced to such confusion; everybody agrees something should be done but not who should do it. Delay or dissent can result, which affects the effectiveness of the process and ultimately the level of service delivered.

It is essential, therefore, that there should be an agreement as to the responsibilities and accountabilities for each process task. This is especially true where activities within a process are carried out by staff across business units. A process such as service asset and configuration management may involve staff from the technical teams within IT, who may define configuration item relationships and install or change those items; it may also involve non-IT teams such as finance or procurement.

It is a critical success factor for effective processes that responsibility and accountability are clearly defined. Best practice in this area involves mapping the tasks to roles and defining the level of involvement in the task for each role. The RACI model or matrix is commonly used across many industries to show the roles and responsibilities for activities and processes. It is a simple-to-understand, visual summary, and it clarifies the responsibilities and accountabilities to all stakeholders, removing confusion and allowing decisions to be made without delay.

The acronym RACI stands for the four levels of involvement in a process activity:

Responsible   Those who are defined as responsible are the people who "get the job done" by actually carrying out the task. There must always be at least one person responsible for each task.

Accountable   This single individual owns the task and ensures that the quality of the work carried out meets the required standard. The buck stops with them. To avoid any confusion, there can be only one person accountable for each task, and each task must have an accountable person.

Consulted   Where appropriate for the process, there may be people who are consulted for their opinion regarding a process activity. They provide information. This is not a mandatory role like Accountable and Responsible; there may or may not be a Consulted person for an activity.

Informed   These people are updated as to the progress of the activity. As with Consulted, this is not a mandatory role; it depends on the particular activity.

Where the RACI model is applied to the process as a whole, as opposed to its individual activities, the process owner would normally be defined as accountable for the end-to-end process.

Table 7.1 shows an example of a change management RACI matrix. Each row represents a specific activity, and each column shows the people involved and their level of involvement.

To build a RACI matrix for an activity, you must first identify the processes or activities and the roles. Through discussion with the people involved, agree on who is responsible for each activity or process and their level of involvement. There may be some activities where this is not clear, for example, when many roles have responsibility or where no one appears to be responsible. This situation can often be resolved by breaking the activity down into smaller activities. For example, a "new joiner" process may have the step "Grant access to the system" as an activity. Breaking this activity down into "Define access required," "Authorize access Request," and "Set up required access" should make it easier to define clear roles and responsibilities. When complete, the matrix should be discussed and agreed on.

The RACI matrix is useful when designing a new process to ensure that all aspects have been considered; it is also useful as a diagnostic tool when seeking to improve a failing process. Consideration should be given in this case to whether the accountability lies with the correct person or whether one person is responsible for too many activities, leading to confusion as to their priorities and possible delays. Once the roles have been documented, the process owner will verify that they are being correctly carried out.

TABLE 7.1   A simple RACI matrix

Activity	Director of service management	Service level manager	Problem manager	Security manager	Procurement manager
Activity 1	AR	C	I	I	C
Activity 2	A	R	C	C	C
Activity 3	I	A	R	I	C
Activity 4	I	A	R	I	
Activity 5	I	A	R	C	I

As discussed previously, individuals may carry out numerous activities across several processes. Someone working in the technical management function may have a role in availability, capacity, incident, problem, and change management. They will have a line manager within the technical management function but are also answerable to the various process owners for carrying out the process activities correctly.

There are two other advantages to using a RACI matrix other than the primary purpose of clarifying roles and levels of involvement within the process. First, the responsibilities defined for an individual or team can be helpful when thinking about what should be included in an operational-level agreement. Second, the workflow and handoff points between activities and individuals is clarified and shows where communication should flow. Continual service improvement will use this latter information to define what communication is required during CSI.

There may be difficulties encountered when using the RACI model. These could include the splitting of authority between process activities, which could make it difficult to understand who is accountable for the end-to-end process; remember that this overall accountability lies with the process owner. Using the RACI model will also show where delegation of responsibility or accountability has taken place without necessary authority also being delegated. Comparing the RACI matrixes across a number of processes may highlight that one person has responsibility for a number of closely related processes, such as incident and problem management or change and release and deployment management. These processes are meant to be separate, and combining the responsibility for them in this way may reduce checks and balances that support good governance.

RACI is a simple-to-use method to clarify roles and identify potential conflicts or issues; as such, it is invaluable when designing service management processes.

Competence and Training

Effective service management requires staff members who understand their job role, not only the tasks they need to perform but the importance of these tasks and their relationship to other processes. Developing staff competencies and skills is an important element in managing services successfully.

The best known and most popular service management training scheme is the ITIL Qualifications scheme. This scheme provides a modular approach to the ITIL framework. It comprises a series of qualifications focused on different aspects of ITIL best practices to various degrees of depth and detail. Each ITIL qualification has a specific credit value; these credits can be used by candidates who are interested in achieving the ITIL expert level. The expert level requires candidates to meet a specific set of key requirements, covering the full spectrum of ITIL best practices.

This section, covering the topics of competence and training, is not included in the foundation examination but is included in the syllabus, because an understanding of competence and skills is essential for service management.

Competence and Skills for Service Management

As discussed previously, the "people" aspect within the four p's of effective service management is crucial; good processes depend upon them. Service management products deliver little value if not operated by skilled staff. Third-party suppliers require competent staff within the service provider organization if they are to be effective.

Having the right number of people is not enough; they need to have undergone the training to enable them to be good at their jobs. (Remember that people are both a resource and a capability; education and training develops their capability.) Good staff training will ensure that individuals understand their roles. Training is not a one-off activity; as changes to processes, technology, and services occur, further training will be required. As we have discussed, staff will be involved across different lifecycle stages; someone based in an operational role may have involvement in design, transition, and CSI. Each role they carry out will require specific skills, attributes, and competences. All roles require the following:

- Everyone needs a reasonable awareness of the business in order to understand how IT in general, and the process in particular, helps the business achieve its objectives

- They need customer service skills. These are often thought to be necessary only for service desk staff; although they are essential for that role, they are also required by any role where the IT staff member may come into contact with the business. Desktop engineers, for example, interact with customers on a daily basis, and those involved in coordinating user acceptance testing or service reviews also have regular user contact, so customer service skills are a requirement for all.

- All staff members require the knowledge to carry out their roles; they also need to understand the policies and procedures involved.

Additional attributes may also be required, dependent on the role. These include management skills and the ability to run meetings, such as chairing, taking minutes, and so on. Being able to communicate effectively, in speech and in writing, is essential, and the ability to negotiate and persuade will help ensure others conform to what is required of them. Finally, all roles involve some interpretation of metrics, so analytical skills are also necessary.

Staff may also participate in CSI initiatives. The CSI core guidance describes the specific skills required for them.

Competence and Skills Framework

It can be helpful for service providers to adopt a standard framework for describing job titles, roles and responsibilities, and so on. The Skills Framework for the Information Age (SFIA) is an example of such a reference model. It defines the necessary skills for effective IT services, information systems, and technology. SFIA defines seven generic levels for tasks, with the associated professional skills required. It also defines core competencies. SFIA is used by many IT service providers. You can find more information on SFIA at www.sfia.org.uk.

Specific Training in the ITIL Framework

In addition to the core guidance provided in the ITIL volumes covering service strategy, service design, service transition, service operation and continual service improvement, and the complementary guidance, training is available to enable staff to understand this best practice service management framework and to develop the necessary skills and competencies to carry out its guidance.

The scheme, shown in Figure 7.1, is managed and controlled through the official accreditor, accredited examination institutes, and accredited training organizations to ensure that organizations can be confident in its quality. All training material used and individual trainers also have to meet quality standards. Students take examinations at the end of each course to achieve the relevant certificate, and the qualifications gained are evidence that the student has acquired the associated knowledge of ITIL best practices. The qualifications are recognized worldwide.

The scheme has four levels:

Foundation Level   This acts as an entry point to, and a prerequisite for, the rest of the scheme. This book is intended to prepare you to take the foundation exam.

Intermediate Level   Following the foundation level, organizations can develop particular knowledge and skills in their staff. Courses at this level are in two groups:

Lifecycle Courses   Five courses, each providing management level with knowledge particular to each lifecycle stage — service strategy, service design, service transition, service operation, and continual service improvement (three points per successful qualification)

FIGURE 7.1 The ITIL qualification scheme

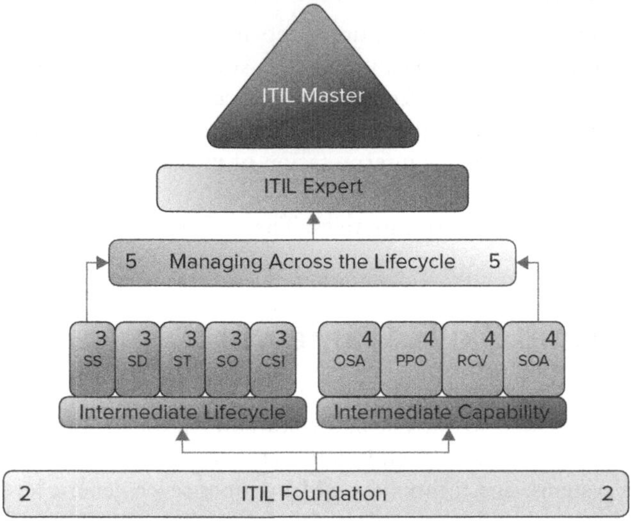

© The Official ITIL Accreditor 2012

Based on Cabinet Office ITIL® material. Reproduced under license from the Cabinet Office.

Capability Courses Four courses, each covering particular areas within service management at a practitioner (hands-on, how-to do; four points per successful qualification)

The four courses are:

1. Operational Support and Analysis: This course covers request fulfillment and the event, incident, problem, and access management processes. It also considers the four functions of the service desk and technical, IT operations, and application management.

2. Planning, Protection, and Optimization: This course covers capacity, availability, IT service continuity, information security and demand management.

3. Release, Control and Validation: This course covers change and service asset and configuration management, service validation and testing, release and deployment, request fulfillment, change evaluation, and knowledge management.

4. Service Offerings and Agreements: This course covers service portfolio and service catalog management, service level, demand, supplier, financial, and business relationship management.

Individuals may choose to do one or more of these courses to enhance their professional development. Each course is worth a number of credits, so students may collect these credits toward achieving ITIL Expert status, should they want.

ITIL Expert   This qualification level is awarded to individuals who successfully pass the managing across the lifecycle examination. Attendance for this course is dependent on achieving 17 points from within the lower levels of the qualification scheme.

ITIL Master   This qualification requires proof of implementation of best practices.

You can find more information on ITIL qualifications at `www.itil-officialsite.com`.

Summary

In this chapter we discussed the key roles involved in successful service management. We considered the importance of the process owner is ensuring that the process is (and remains) fit for purpose. The importance of the process manager and process practitioner in actually carrying out the process as defined by the process owner were also examined. Finally we looked at the role of the service owner in providing a single point of focus and accountability for a service. Defining these roles and allocating them to individuals is an important element of service management. Using the RACI matrix explained in this chapter enables an unambiguous definition of roles and responsibilities in each process, and ensures that accountability is clearly defined.

In this chapter we also considered the skills and competencies that are required and the ITIL qualification structure.

Exam Essentials

Understand the roles and responsibilities of the service owner.   The service owner is accountable for ensuring the delivery of the service. The service owner will liaise with process owners to ensure that the service is delivered to the highest standard possible.

Understand the roles and responsibilities of the process owner, the process manager, and the process practitioner.   The process owner is accountable for ensuring the successful delivery of a process across all services and takes a lead role in ensuring that the process outcomes match the objectives. There may be several process managers for each process, each responsible for managing the day-to-day implementation of the process by the process practitioners in their own geographical or infrastructure area. The process practitioner is responsible for carrying out the process tasks under the direction of the process manager. One person may carry out more than one of these roles, although there is a danger that process control may not be as strong when this is the case, because of individuals being too close to the process to be objective. All roles have a responsibility to identify possible improvements in the process, but it is the process owner's responsibility to evaluate them and implement the ones that have value.

Understand the purpose of the RACI model in defining roles and responsibilities within processes.   Be able to explain the difference between Responsible, Accountable, Consulted, and Informed. Understand that only one person can be accountable for each activity and that every activity must have, as a minimum, a responsible and an accountable person.

Review Questions

You can find the answers in Appendix A.

1. Who is responsible for producing evidence that the process activities have been carried out correctly, in the form of records?

    A. Process owner

    B. Process practitioner

    C. Process manager

    D. Service owner

2. What does RACI stand for?

    A. Responsible, Accountable, Consulted, Involved

    B. Recorded, Assessed, Consulted, Informed

    C. Review, Authorize, Consult, Inform

    D. Responsible, Accountable, Consulted, Informed

3. Which of the following is *not* one of the responsibilities of a service owner?

    A. Communicating with the customer as required on all issues regarding the delivery of the service

    B. Designing the metrics for the process and ensuring that these provide the necessary information to judge the effectiveness and efficiency of the process

    C. Representing the service across the organization and attending service review meetings with the business.

    D. Being the escalation (notification) point for major incidents affecting the service

4. Who is responsible for ensuring the right numbers of staff are assigned to the various roles within the process and that they understand what is required of them?

    A. Process manager

    B. Process owner

    C. Service owner

    D. Process practitioner

5. Which of the following is true?

    A. Accountability can be shared.

    B. There may be more than one person responsible.

    C. Someone must always be consulted for each process step.

    D. The process owner is the person informed for every process step.

6. What is the RACI model used for?

    A. Defining the different responsibilities of the service owner and the process owner, manager, and practitioner

    B. Defining the process requirements for a new service

    C. Risk assessment for each configuration item

    D. Defining the roles and responsibilities for a process

7. Which of these statements is *not* true?

    A. There may be several process practitioners for each process.

    B. There may be several process managers for each process.

    C. There may be several process owners for each process.

    D. Every process must have a process manager.

8. Which role should update process documentation following a change?

    A. The process manager

    B. The change manager

    C. The process owner

    D. The knowledge manager

9. Who does ITIL say is responsible for identifying improvements to a process?

    1. The service owner

    2. The process improvement manager

    3. The process manager

    4. The process owner

    A. 1 and 2 only

    B. 4 only

    C. All of the above

    D. 3 and 4 only

10. Which of the following activities should a service owner undertake?

    1. Representing a specific service across the organization

    2. Updating the known error database with details of errors that have been identified for the service

    3. Attending the CAB meeting to discuss changes to the service

    4. Attending service reviews with the business

    A. 1, 2, and 3 only

    B. 1, 3, and 4 only

    C. 1 and 2 only

    D. All of the above

Chapter

8

Understanding Service Transition and the Change Management Processes

---

THE FOLLOWING ITIL FOUNDATION EXAM TOPICS ARE COVERED IN THIS CHAPTER:

- ✓ 2-7. Account for the purpose, objectives and scope of service transition

- ✓ 2-8. Briefly explain what value service transition provides to the business

- ✓ Unit 3: Generic concepts and definitions:
  - ▪ 3-20. Change
  - ▪ 3-21. Change types (standard, emergency and normal)
  - ▪ 3-37. Change proposals

- ✓ 5-5. Explain the purpose, objectives, scope, basic concepts, process activities and interfaces for:
  - ▪ 5-51 Change management
    - ▪ Types of change request
    - ▪ Change models
    - ▪ Remediation planning
    - ▪ Change advisory board / emergency change advisory board
    - ▪ Lifecycle of a normal change

This chapter explores the service transition stage of the life cycle, and looks in detail at the change management process. In the next chapter, we will consider the other service transition processes. The service transition lifecycle stage is concerned with the delivery of a new or changed service into the live operational environment.

The service transition processes are used throughout the life cycle to provide control over the live operational environment. Change management is used both to deliver new services and to modify them later and so provides control over the infrastructure. The service transition process of service asset and configuration management provides a source of information which is used in transition, and the rest of the life cycle. Knowledge management is particularly important during transition, but also takes place throughout the life cycle.

Understanding Service Transition

During this lifecycle stage, you will explore the management and control of the infrastructure and service management processes.

The Purpose of Service Transition

Each stage of the lifecycle has a distinct purpose, and the purpose of *service transition* is to ensure that the services that have been agreed on and designed through the stages of strategy and design are now delivered effectively into operation.

Any new, modified, or retired service should be transitioned in accordance with the plans and documents that have been prepared to meet the expectations of the business. This is true if the service has been designed by the internal service provider or sourced from outside the organization. The efforts that have been made during the previous lifecycle stages—negotiating with customers to understand their needs and requirements and the agreements that have been put in place—all need to be considered when introducing a new service or a change to an existing service. It is in this stage that we are setting the expectation of the business, because this is the stage where we will test the new service for its ability to perform as required.

Think about this in terms of a project or implementation in which you have had some involvement. What were the things that went well during the handover to operational staff? What went badly and caused issues in support or customer experience? It is during transition that we address these issues and put in place measureable, repeatable activities that will enable a smooth handover into operations.

Transition is an important lifecycle stage, because it ensures that the business receives the services as agreed and that they can be used as intended. Ensuring the proper use of services is critical in achieving customer satisfaction; if your customer does not understand how the service is intended to work, they may find fault with something that it was never intended to perform.

This lifecycle stage is concerned with the experience for the customer and user and also for the support staff. All the stakeholders who will be receiving the new service or change to the existing services need to be considered as part of the transition planning. If a service is to be retired, the same careful and considered approach should be adopted so that the retirement of the service is seamless, particularly if there is a replacement service being implemented at the same time.

The Objectives of Service Transition

The objectives of this stage are to do the following:

- Plan and manage changes to services, the introduction of new services, or the retirement of services efficiently and effectively

- Manage risk associated with new, modified, or retired services being transitioned

- Successfully deploy releases into the live environment

- Set the expectations for the performance and use of the new or modified services

- Ensure that the changes to the services deliver the anticipated and required business value

- Provide relevant and good-quality knowledge and information about the services and service assets

So that we can achieve these objectives, a number of activities and processes have to take place as part of the service transition stage. It will be important to ensure that there are adequate plans made for the resourcing requirements for the transition, including providing the capacity that will be necessary for managing successful change. As part of the preparation for deployment, there needs to be a framework for risk assessment and evaluation of the required capabilities so that deployment can be managed efficiently and effectively.

During any transition, it will be necessary to ensure the integrity of the service assets. This is important throughout the whole lifecycle but becomes critical when introducing new services or changing existing services, because the management of changes to the service assets will introduce additional risks to the overall operation of the portfolio of services.

One of the key aspects of managing transition is ensuring that there is a well-organized manner of delivering the required outcomes, in an efficient and effective way. This requires you to have repeatable mechanisms for all of the activities that need to be carried out as part of this lifecycle stage. This includes the build, testing, and deployment of service releases, so as part of the transition, we have processes that allow for measureable management of these activities.

Finally, we have to ensure that the outcomes identified in the service design stage are delivered effectively into operation. This will include ensuring that the service can be managed, operated, and supported according to the constraints specified as part of service design. It is important to ensure, as part of this final activity, that users and support staff are adequately trained in the new or changed service or system. This will ensure that the new or changed service can be used at the time of deployment.

The Scope of Service Transition

The service transition stage provides guidance on the development and improvement of the capabilities required to deliver new services into the live environment. This covers the planning, build, test, evaluation, implementation, and deployment of new services or changes to existing services. It also provides information and guidance on the transition of services between service providers (internal and external) and the retirement of services that are no longer required. The guidance covers the relationship between strategy, design, and transition so that the requirements from service strategy, which are then developed in service design, may be successfully realized for operational use, while minimizing the risk and disruption of making changes.

The service transition lifecycle stage provides guidance on management and how transitions should work between all types of service providers, no matter what the situation. This includes introducing new technologies, working with suppliers and partners, and managing working practices.

So, the scope of service transition covers all aspects of introducing new services to the operational environment. It will have a close association with project management activity and may adopt a project management approach to the coordination of the activities.

The Value of Service Transition to the Business

Service transition offers value by providing guidance on how to adopt and implement standard and consistent approaches while delivering changes to services. Taking a consistent approach will enable projects to predict the risks, resources, spend, and timescales for delivery more accurately, which will result in the ability to manage higher volumes of change.

Because there will be a consistent approach to planning, the transition processes will be easier for stakeholders in the activities to follow, and there will be fewer issues with clashes of project resource requirements, such as two separate teams requiring access to the same testing environments. By working in this way, you will also be able to reduce the effort spent on managing test and pilot environments. This will also enable reuse of systems and service assets, because a planned approach will enable you to see where reuse can be achieved.

Other benefits include increased confidence on the part of the recipients of any changes, because there is clear planned communication, and expectations are correctly set for all stakeholders, including customers, users, suppliers, partners, and projects.

In addition, the overall management of the transition enables control of the assets and costs associated with transitions. So, the value to the business is realized in the successful transition of new or changed services within budget and according to the specifications set out in strategy and developed in design.

We are probably all familiar with the project that gets delivered into operation with minimal information, warning, or preparation. It used to be a common occurrence, and the consequent impact to the operational environment in terms of rework and additional effort required to begin supporting the project would often have significant additional cost implications.

The transition stage is there to ensure that this no longer happens. Taking the output from the service design stage, the service design package (SDP) transition is responsible for ensuring the seamless delivery of new or changed services into the live operational environment.

The next chapters will examine the processes in the service transition stage, which enable your services to be transitioned successfully, with the exception of change management which is detailed below.

Introduction to the Change Management Process

This section covers the *change management* process. This is one of the process areas we cover in detail; when you come to the exam, you can expect to have questions that ask you about the activities and concepts of the process as well as the purpose of it.

It is important to start with an understanding of the purpose, objectives, and scope of the process, because this sets the scene for how the process will be used in the service lifecycle. We will also cover the activities of the process and the concepts of the types of change (normal, standard, and emergency). In addition, we cover the role of the change advisory board (CAB) and how the change management process interfaces with the rest of the service lifecycle processes.

The Purpose of the Change Management Process

Let's begin by looking at the purpose of the change management process according to the ITIL framework. ITIL states that the purpose of this process is "to control the lifecycle of all changes, enabling beneficial changes to be made with minimum disruption to IT services." This simple statement cuts right to the heart of successful change management for an IT department.

If, in an organization that has not adopted best practices, you review your records for incidents following a change to your infrastructure, it is very likely that there will be an increase in incident volume specifically associated to the change that has been made. Uncontrolled change may trigger or be the cause of incidents in the infrastructure. According to the IT Service Management Forum (ITSMF), 80 percent of all incidents are caused by changes to the IT infrastructure.

It is for this reason that best practices in service management suggest that change management should be controlled. But there are other equally compelling reasons to address the issues caused by poor change control, not least of which is the reputation of the IT department in the eyes of their customers.

This is an extract from a conversation heard in an office on a Friday afternoon:

"IT is making a change over the weekend, aren't they?"

"Yes."

"Then I think I'll take Monday off to work from home; nothing will be working until Tuesday!"

This kind of attitude and expectation can be very damaging to the organization as a whole and demonstrates a lack of confidence in the IT department. Service management is about providing your customers with assurance that the IT services and systems that support the business will work as expected, when required. Unreliable changes that do not achieve their benefits cause adverse impact on the business as a whole, so the importance of controlling the change process is vital to business success.

Equally damaging is unplanned change, and often it is the IT department that carries this out. There is not usually malicious intent to bring down the service when making unplanned changes; it is much more likely to be carried out by a well-meaning individual with the intention of correcting an error that may have an impact on business performance. But if this is carried out without careful planning and assessment, there may be unintended and unexpected impacts on existing services.

Any failure in the management of change will potentially require additional work and rework following the implementation, and this has perhaps the most significant impact of uncontrolled change in your organization. It may incur additional costs, for which there may be no budget, and this can contribute to the view that IT departments are endless "money pits" into which the business pours funds for little perceived reward.

Objectives of the Change Management Process

The objectives of the process reflect some of the issues identified in the previous section on its purpose. A key objective is to keep abreast of the changes that happen in the business environment. This objective specifically states that while responding to the changing business needs, you should be reducing incidents, disruption to the services, and rework. In this way, the process can assist with maximizing the value of the IT services provided to the business.

It is an important objective to support your business, and as organizational needs evolve, the IT department or service provider should continue to ensure that the services align to business needs. This will require the management of changes to the services to meet the challenges of a changing business.

The next objective identified by the ITIL Service Transition publication begins to show the process in action. It states that the service provider should "ensure that changes are recorded and evaluated, and that authorized changes are prioritized, planned, tested, implemented, documented and reviewed in a controlled manner." This states the steps of the change management process as a clear objective and sets the expectation for how changes should be controlled. Note that the objective stresses authorized changes as part of the process flow and emphasizes the need for recording changes.

As part of the management of change in the IT environment, one of the objectives for successful change management is to control the items recorded in the configuration management system (CMS). This, of course, assumes that the IT service provider has a functioning CMS. We will be covering the CMS in Chapter 9, as part of the process of service asset and configuration management (SACM). The SACM process is an important one in the overall approach of the service lifecycle, because it helps identify the components that make up our services and how they all relate to one another. Once we have made the effort to capture this information to maximize its use, it needs to be maintained and kept accurate. The process of change management is key for enabling this and ensuring that we have relevant information maintained in the CMS.

The ITIL framework also suggests that an additional objective of the change management process is to optimize risk for the business. The reason for a change may often be to minimize risk, but it is also common to accept risk for a beneficial result. Often the reason for carrying out a change is that the risk of not doing it far outweighs the risk of doing it. We will be covering this important aspect when we cover the individual steps of the process later in this chapter.

The objectives set the expectations of what will be achieved by the process.

Scope of the Change Management Process

Change can be looked at in many different ways, so it is extremely important to understand the scope for this process so that it can be handled effectively. The ITIL framework defines a change as "the addition, modification or removal of anything that could have an effect on IT services."

This means the scope of this process covers everything from the architecture and infrastructure to the processes, documentation, metrics, and tools that support your services, as well as changes to IT services and configuration items.

With a scope as large as this, it is even more important to ensure the control of the environment with a manageable, repeatable process. ITIL suggests that the process should cover all stages of the service lifecycle, from strategy right through to operation and into continual service improvement. Changes to configuration items across the lifecycle should be managed in a controlled manner, including changes to contracts, agreements, or physical assets such as servers or networks and virtual assets in a virtualized environment. This should also include the management of changes to the five aspects of service design (which were covered in Chapter 4):

- Service solutions for new or changed services, which include the resources and capabilities needed for the service and the functional requirements for the solution

- Management systems and tools, particularly the service portfolio, allowing management and control of the services throughout their lifecycle

- Management and technology architectures required to deliver the services

- Processes that support the services by managing design, transition, operation, and improvement activities
- Measurement systems, methods, and metrics for the services

Defining the changes that are out of scope is equally important for the successful management of change. Typically these will include changes that have a significantly wider impact than just the services themselves, such as changes to departmental structures, business policies, or operations. These changes may have associated IT service changes, which would be managed through the change process, but the initial management would be through business and organizational change processes. But at the other end of the scale, the minor operational changes that need to be done as part of day-to-day management of the infrastructure may also be excluded from the change management process. Examples of these would be routine maintenance changes such as simple repairs to printers.

Management of change needs to take place at all levels of an organization—strategically, tactically, and operationally. Agreeing on the scope between the IT service provider, business, and any suppliers is essential for success, particularly where there are shared assets and a shared responsibility for the delivery of services to the organization. The ability to interface our IT change management process with those of the business and the suppliers to effect a seamless introduction of change will be a major factor in the successful management of changes in a complex environment.

The service portfolio, with its capture of the details relating to all services, including current, planned, and retired services, is a valuable tool for understanding the impact of changes in a supported environment.

Changes may be triggered from a variety of situations and still remain in scope for your process. Strategic changes may be introduced through a change proposal, whereas design driven changes may occur in response to design requirements as part of the development of a new service. Service operations or external suppliers may initiate changes that arise from improvement initiatives or in response to operational requirements for corrective actions. Change management is not responsible for the coordination of processes for the successful implementation of projects; this will be handled through the planning and transition support process.

So, defining the scope can be complex but is important for the successful management of the process and will require negotiation and discussion throughout the organization to ensure everyone has a clear understanding and expectation for the management of changes.

Types of Change

Many different types of change exist in operational environments. As we discussed in the previous section about the scope of change, it is a wide subject area. A change is captured as a formal request for alteration of a configuration item. There are a number of ways of handling this formal request; it could be a service call to the service desk, a completed request for change form, or even a project initiation document. A request for change is commonly referred to as an RFC.

One of the most common complaints when you try to introduce a new change management process is that it is too bureaucratic. There is often reluctance to update documentation if it is seen as unnecessary with no obvious benefit to the individual who has to complete it. When introducing a request for change form or procedural documentation, it is advisable to think about the culture of the organization and how processes are viewed. If processes are seen as unwieldy and ineffective, if you introduce a complicated or overly detailed form for requesting a simple change, then people are unlikely to use it. Many people do not like documentation, so the simpler the form and detail required, the more likely people are to support the process. So, introducing a formal document to capture change requests means that you have to be aware of the requirements of the business and be sensitive to its needs. The ITIL framework identifies different types of change, and each has a different handling procedure, so you can adapt the request for change (RFC) to meet the individual requirements of each change type.

There is sometimes confusion over the terminology that is used around the change management process. For clarification, the ITIL framework identifies the difference between a change, a request for change, and a *change record*.

Change   The addition, modification, or removal of anything that could have an effect on IT services.

Request for Change   Formal proposal for altering a configuration item, recorded either electronically or on paper. This is often misused to describe the change record or the change itself. It includes details of the change to be completed. RFCs are used only to request a change, not to manage and communicate the lifecycle of the change.

Change Record   A capture of the details of the lifecycle of a change. A change record is raised in response to a request for change—for every change, even those that are subsequently rejected. Change records should reference the configuration items affected by the change. They are stored in the configuration management system or service management tool.

Using the Change Model

The ITIL framework also talks about the advisability of using a change model. This is a set of predefined steps for use in a commonly occurring set of circumstances, allowing particular changes to be handled consistently in an agreed manner. This can be very useful for integration with support tools so that management of the change can be handled by automation. The change model should include the following:

- Steps for handling the change

- The order in which the steps should be carried out, including any dependencies

- Responsibilities throughout the process

- Timescales

- Escalation procedures

Change models can be used to manage specific types of change, such as standard changes, emergency changes, regular maintenance changes, and service requests from users. Now that we have clarified the terminology, we'll cover the different types of change that ITIL identifies: standard change, emergency change, and normal change.

Standard Change

A *standard change* is a change to a service or other configuration item, which has a preauthorized approach to its execution. These are changes with a well-known and clearly understood risk. Examples of this type of change are the provision of a user profile for a new starter or software download from a standard list or a desktop move for a single user. The approach follows a set of predefined and agreed steps providing a model that can be used and reused consistently. This model will determine the requirements for logging the change, handling the change, and implementing the change. It will be an established and tested procedure that has been proven in practice. The change authority that has the budget for the activity grants authorization of the standard change.

These key elements identify a standard change:

- There is a clearly defined trigger for the initiation of the change, such as an exception generated by an event management tool or a request via the service desk.

- The actions are understood, proven in practice, and documented.

- Authority is effectively given in advance.

- Financial authority either is in the control of the requestor or is granted in advance under an agreed budget.

- The risk is low or well known and understood.

 **Real World Scenario**

Example of a Standard Change

The following is an example of a standard change in a working environment. In the car manufacturing industry, cars are often sold by franchise garages or dealerships, rather than directly from the manufacturer. In one such organization, the manufacturer uses the standard change model for the IT requirements when introducing a new dealership. Let's explore whether this use of the standard change meets the specifications identified by the ITIL framework. The standard change in this case covers a number of activities, each of which is documented. The activities are all clearly understood (equipment and software are sent to the dealership, user profiles are set up, access profiles are applied to the firewalls, and so on) and so are the risks. There is a well-known and documented trigger for the change. Most importantly, because the decision is in the control of the business, the authority for the budget is agreed upon, and the authority for the implementation of the change is part of the business decision to engage the dealership. So, even though this change has a number of activities and involves considerable cost, it has been proven, the risks are well known and understood, and it is requested and classed as a standard change. It follows a defined model, which includes documentation specifying each step of the activities, including the lead times for ordering equipment, so that the requestors understand the timeframe for the whole activity. It meets the requirements for the key elements of a standard change.

Introduction of standard changes can greatly enhance the effectiveness of the change management process and increase the buy-in for the management of change within the organization, because it can be seen as improving responsiveness and efficiency and minimizing bureaucracy. Each standard change model should be approved and agreed upon prior to its use, and the records of the standard changes should be reviewed on a regular basis to ensure that there is no adverse impact from the implementation. The content of the individual change records for the standard changes will potentially vary, based on the requirement of the change itself, but it should contain sufficient detail to manage the change and provide a track record of the activity undertaken.

Emergency Change

Another change type, which has a different model, is the *emergency change*. This type of change is in response to or in order to prevent a business-critical error. There is the potential for the impact of a poorly handled emergency change to be greater than the incident it is attempting to solve because of tight timescales, reduced assessment, and testing of the change. The number of emergency changes should be kept to a minimum, because they are more likely than the other types to be disruptive and prone to failure. Ideally, changes should be planned, but emergencies do happen, and there needs to be a recognized approach to manage the implementation of the response. These procedures take into consideration the need for urgency but also the need to have a clear record of the actions that will be carried out in response to the emergency.

There needs to be a clear definition of the authority levels associated with emergency changes, and if that authority has been devolved (perhaps to a duty manager on a night shift or manager on call), this should be clearly documented as part of the procedures. If it is necessary, emergency changes may have to be assessed by a group of people or referred to an advisory board, which is known as the *emergency change advisory board (ECAB)*. The ECAB is the emergency authority for assessing emergency changes covering the same responsibilities as the change advisory board, which we will review in the normal change process. Any decisions to authorize an emergency change must be documented in the change record so that there is a clear audit trail for all activities.

Once authorized, there may be no time for full testing of the build and implementation while the change is carried out. This will increase the risk of failure, so as much testing as possible should be completed. It is also recognized that during this activity, there may be little time given to the update of the change record, so there is a recommendation that the documentation is updated after the implementation.

So, the key elements of the emergency change approach are as follows:

- Authorization and assessment may be completed by the ECAB rather than waiting for a CAB meeting.

- Testing may be reduced or, in extreme cases, be missed completely, if this is an acceptable risk to resolve the emergency.

- Documentation, once the change record has been raised, may be completed retrospectively.

Emergency changes should not be carried out to address poor planning. As can be seen, the approach increases the risk of failure and may cause additional issues in the operational environment. So, they should be tightly controlled and implemented only when absolutely necessary, according to a business-critical need.

Normal Change

The next type of change we are going to review is the normal change. This section will cover the normal change process flow and the roles and responsibilities of the change advisory board.

The typical process flow includes these steps:

1. Create and record the RFC.
2. Review the RFC.
3. Assess and evaluate the change.
4. Authorize the change.
5. Plan updates.
6. Coordinate change implementation.
7. Review and close the change.

We will cover each step of the process in turn (Figure 8.1).

FIGURE 8.1   The normal change process

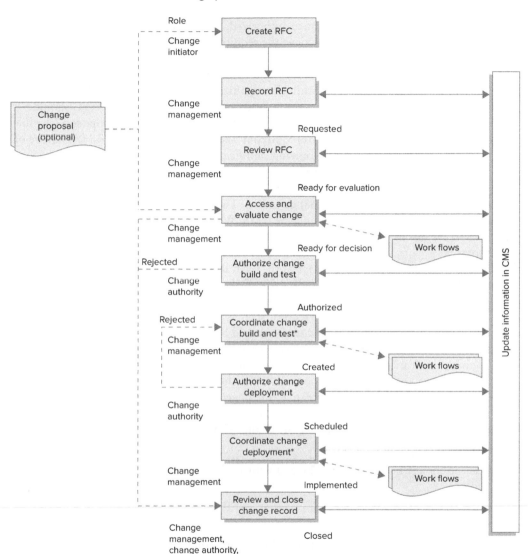

Based on Cabinet Office ITIL material. Reproduced under license from the Cabinet Office.

You can see in Figure 8.1 that there is a reference to a change proposal. A change proposal may be required if the change is potentially going to have significant and costly impact on the business. Authorizing the proposal for a change means that the wider implications can be reviewed against any other changes and proposed new services.

The proposal should include a high-level description of the change, a detailed business case including a risk assessment and profile, and an outline schedule for the design and implementation of the change. Once authorized, the proposal will be used as a basis for raising the changes required to achieve the requirement or perhaps chartering a new service.

The first step of the process is the creation of the *request for change (RFC)*. The change can be initiated by anyone within the organization (or supported by the service provider), and this request will trigger the creation of a change record. The RFC should specify the details of the change, including the risks, benefits, costs, and proposed schedule for implementation. The level of detail required in the request will depend on the nature of the request; for example, a change requiring significant technical engagement should cover the tasks in detail. But it may be that the relevant details cannot be provided at the point of request, so there needs to be clear guidance on the minimum content required.

Raising an RFC will trigger the change record. The details and updates captured in the change record will be managed through the CMS. We cover the description and use of the CMS in the discussion of the service asset and configuration management process in Chapter 9.

Change logging is an important part of the overall change process. Keeping an accurate change record provides an audit trail for the actions carried out in the lifecycle of the change. All RFCs should be logged with a unique identifier, and where the trigger for the change is captured in another record (such as an incident or problem), the original reference number of the initiating document should be captured as part of the change record. A good service management tool will have the functionality to link these records and be able to capture the relationship between the RFC and any associated configuration items, records, and other service components. It is the responsibility of change management to ensure that the change record is created and logged correctly.

Once the change has been raised and logged, the change should be reviewed against some basic criteria to establish whether the change should continue through the process:

- Is it completely impractical?

- Has the change been raised and logged with sufficient information and appropriate budget?

- Is it a repeat of an earlier RFC or one that is still being considered, or a previously rejected request?

If rejected, the initiator must be provided with a reason for the rejection and have right of appeal through normal management channels. This review is the responsibility of the change manager but can be carried out by others if there is agreement with the change management process owner. For example, for minor changes that require authorization, often the line manager of the initiator carries out the review, ensuring that no incomplete or impractical changes are raised.

Once the RFC has been accepted into the change process, the next step is that of evaluation and assessment. If the change has a significant impact, it may require a specific and separate formal evaluation activity; otherwise, the assessment can be managed as part of the normal change process. The framework provides a set of seven questions that should be asked during the assessment of a change. These are known as the seven Rs of assessment:

- Who *raised* the change?
- What is the *reason* for the change?
- What is the *return* required from the change?
- What are the *risks* involved in the change?
- What *resources* are required to deliver the change?
- Who is *responsible* for the build, test, and implementation of the change?
- What is the *relationship* between this change and other changes?

Assessment should include all potential factors that may impact the success of the change. This may require the RFC to be reviewed by a number of people, and it is the responsibility of the change manager to ensure that the assessment is completed. This is where the change advisory board is used. We cover the roles and responsibilities of the CAB later in this section.

Following the assessment, the *change schedule (CS)* can be updated. This is an important output from the change process and shows the details of all changes authorized for implementation and their proposed implementation dates. In fact, this is both an input and an output for the process, because the change schedule will need to be consulted when considering the scheduling for new changes. The schedule should be published so that all interested parties can understand when planned changes are to take place.

The *projected service outage (PSO)* document should also be updated at this point, with the impact to the business of the service outages clearly identified. This allows stakeholders to understand when any additional outages outside of the agreed service level agreement will take place and when the planned maintenance outages will take place.

Both the CS and the PSO provide important information for assessing new changes. It is the responsibility of change management to ensure that these documents are available and accurate for use by the CAB as part of the assessment activity.

Another important element for assessment is the *remediation plan*. A remediation plan should be in place for all changes so that if the change fails, the infrastructure can be returned to normal. Often concentration is placed on mitigation against the risk of failure, which is an important part of managing a change implementation, but if that mitigation is unsuccessful, then return to normal must be considered. This may be achieved by envoking service continuity plans, or back out or rollback plans, dependent on the nature of the change.

While we are engaged in the updates to our plans for the change and producing the documented outputs, the change record is updated with the plans for executing the change. In Figure 8.1, you can see that there are workflows associated with this step. This indicates the potential requirement for additional activity outside of the assessment itself, perhaps to obtain further information to enable an informed recommendation to be made, such as a feasibility study for a proposed activity.

Once a recommendation has been made for a change to be authorized, either by the change manager or by the CAB, it is time to engage the change authority for approval for the change to be built and tested. This includes prioritization of the change among other changes and releases.

Formal authorization is granted for each change by the change authority, which may be a role, person, or group of people. The levels of authorization will be determined by the significance of the change in terms of size, risk, cost, and potential business impact. Change authorization is often dependent on the culture of the organization. In a hierarchical organization, authorization may be part of that multilevel management structure, whereas another organization may take a more streamlined approach.

However the authority is structured, once a decision is made and communicated, there should be a right of appeal for the initiator if the change has been rejected at this stage.

Following authorization of the build and test of the change, the coordination of the build, test, and implementation of the change can take place. During this stage, the change will be assessed for release, either as part of a release package through the release and deployment process or as part of operational release into the production environment. You can see in Figure 8.1 that there are workflows associated with this step in the process so that engagement of technical resources can be managed and coordinated to deliver the required activity. Change management is responsible for ensuring that this step in the process takes place efficiently.

Once the build and test has been approved, then authorization for the deployment can take place.

You can also see workflows in the diagram associated with the coordination of the deployment step, indicating that activity outside the change management process may take place. The actual work of deployment is managed through the release and deployment process. Activities to plan, create, and deploy releases are part of the responsibility of the release and deployment process. Change management's responsibility during deployment is coordinating the activity being carried out if it is a simple change that is not part of a release.

Change management is responsible for ensuring that the changes are deployed as scheduled. The role of coordination will be shared with release and deployment management. Any release activity should be scheduled to minimize the impact to the business.

Finally, we come to the review and closure of the change. In this step, the change is evaluated to ensure that the actual performance has been achieved. If this has been realized, the change can be closed. But closure should take place only after a period of time has passed, so the true effects of the change can be assessed. All feedback should be captured and presented to the CAB or the change authority via the change process.

Where a change has not met the acceptance criteria for success, change management may identify a number of options. If it is possible, the change can undergo remediation and return to normal, or if this is not possible, then additional changes can be raised to correct any issues. These will be managed through the change process, and once the original change meets its acceptance criteria, it can be closed. It may also be agreed on that nothing will be done to achieve the original success criteria, if the business agrees that what has been delivered is sufficient to meet their needs.

Whatever the decision made, once closure has been agreed, this should be recorded as part of the change record, and the record should be closed. This is change management's responsibility.

Throughout the process, any activities associated with the role of the change manager may be carried out by a change practitioner, a change authority or the change management process owner, or a change management team, dependent on the size and structure of the organization.

The Role of the Change Advisory Board

The *change advisory board (CAB)* is a group of people brought together to review and assess changes to determine whether they should be authorized. In some organizations, the CAB will also act as the change authority for certain levels of change, but the main role is to provide advice and guidance. The makeup of the group is entirely dependent on the RFCs that are under discussion. The membership will, therefore, potentially change for each meeting. It is important to ensure that the group consists of all those who have an interest in the outcome of the change. This should include a customer representative who can assess the business impact of a change and also a technical representative who can assess the change for the requirements relating to the infrastructure. There will be a number of stakeholders involved in the execution of the change, including suppliers, and they should also be represented as part of the CAB. You may be familiar with a CAB in your own organization or, using your own experience, be able to identify the relevant roles who might attend a CAB in your own company. It is potentially quite a large group of people, and it may be quite challenging to arrange a meeting that all can attend face to face. Some organizations address this by holding "virtual" meetings, either through conference calls or electronically via email. Others adopt an approach that has a tightly controlled meeting schedule, and the relevant people are called in for the appropriate time slot to discuss the RFC that affects them.

To ensure the meeting is productive and efficient, it is the responsibility of the change manager to circulate the RFCs for discussion prior to the meeting. This means that each person can review the RFC and gather any relevant information that will aid in the discussion and decision making.

As the assessment is carried out, it is important that the CAB has visibility of all changes that are being considered or have already been approved. This will ensure that the RFC under review can be assessed for the impact and relationship to other changes.

The CAB Meeting

There should be a standard agenda for a CAB meeting, including the following:

- Change proposals
- RFCs to be assessed (prioritized in a structured approach)
- RFCs that have been assessed
- Change reviews

- Outstanding changes and progress updates on current changes

- Updates from and to the schedule of changes, and planned service outages identified

- Failed changes, backed-out changes, or unauthorized changes

- Proposed changes for future assessment at CAB

This agenda should remain flexible enough to allow for the review of all necessary change activity that has taken place since the last CAB meeting. There is no fixed interval for the frequency of CAB meetings; this is driven by the volume and nature of IT change taking place in the organization.

How the Change Management Process Interfaces with Other Service Management Processes

We begin by looking at the service transition processes that have an interface to change management, but it is important to remember that change management affects the entire service lifecycle, from strategy to continual service improvement.

There needs to be a close relationship between change management and transition planning and support so that transitions can be coordinated successfully.

Relationships between change management and release and deployment management should be carefully integrated with the project management and business change processes so that clear boundaries and dependencies can be established for transitions that involve project management. This may also include working with suppliers, so supplier management should engage with change management to ensure that all activity can be coordinated. If the change has a wide impact or scope within the organization, there may be other business processes that need to work with change management.

The process of change evaluation in the service transition phase is not covered specifically in the foundation course syllabus, but the concept of change evaluation is there to ensure that you have a review and evaluation of the actual performance of the change against the predicted performance as specified in the change proposal. Change management has to be able to integrate with change evaluation and should be able to indicate which changes are to be subjected to formal evaluation. Change management provides the trigger for change evaluation, and the timescales required for the evaluation should be part of the overall planning for the change, because the evaluation report will be an important input to the CAB or other change authority when making decisions on authorization.

When we consider the integration and cooperation between business processes, program and project management processes, and organizational change processes with change management, it is important to understand the requirements for supporting these activities even though they are outside the scope of change management. Change management representatives may be called on to attend meetings associated with these business programs so that all approaches can be consistently delivered.

Integration with other service management process is also vital for the success of change management. Many processes are going to interface with change because they will raise changes in response to either operational outages or improvement initiatives. Service asset and configuration management has very strong connections to change management, because the information it captures about the overall infrastructure provides valuable data that can be used for the assessment of change impact on the environment. Problem management raises changes and has a responsibility to attend the CAB for inclusion in the assessment activity for those changes. Processes such as information security and IT service continuity management need to be included in the change management assessment for the impact of changes on the security policies and continuity plans. Capacity and demand management are also critical in change assessment and may raise changes to address new requirements for capacity to meet altered demands. Service portfolio management provides input for the change assessment activity and may be responsible for raising strategic changes to address new requirements for the business. Service level management needs to be included in the change assessment to ensure that the agreed-on service targets will not be impacted. Availability management will also be a key process in the assessment of changes, because many of the business-critical targets will involve the availability of services.

This is only a selection of the processes that relate to change management, but it does show the breadth of engagement that change management has throughout the service lifecycle.

Summary

In this chapter, we covered the service lifecycle stage of service transition. We looked at the purpose, objective, and scope of the stage, as well as its value to the business.

We also considered the change management process as part of the service transition stage. We explored the purpose, objectives, scope, and basic concepts, process activities, and interfaces for change management.

The concepts covered included the following:

- Types of change request
- Change models
- Lifecycle of a normal change
- Change advisory board/emergency change advisory board
- Change proposals
- Outputs from the change management process
- Remediation planning

Exam Essentials

Be able to recall the purpose, objectives, and scope of service transition.   The purpose is to ensure that new, modified, or retired services meet the expectations of the business as agreed on in strategy and design. The objectives are to plan and successfully manage releases into production, ensuring good knowledge transfer and expectation setting for the delivery of the new or modified service. The scope covers the planning, build, testing, evaluation, implementation, and deployment of new or modified services into the live environment or the retirement of services.

Be able to identify the value service transition provides to the business.   This lifecycle stage provides value by delivering changes that are planned, built, tested, evaluated, implemented, and deployed according to expectation and specification, enabling controlled management of new or changed services into operation.

Understand the purpose, objectives, and scope of the change management process. The purpose of this process is to provide controlled change. The objectives are to manage changes in a controlled manner, managing risk and meeting the needs of the business, now and in the future. The scope of the process covers IT changes, not business or organizational changes, and is not used for minor IT operational changes.

Be able to identify a change model.   The change model is used to assist with management of the process, by providing a set of predefined steps for commonly identified situations.

Be able to identify a standard change.   A standard change follows a recognized change model, responds to a predefined trigger, has a predefined approach, has clearly understood or low risk, and is effectively preauthorized by the change authority.

Understand the process for an emergency change.   An emergency change follows an adjusted process flow from the normal process; assessment and authorization may include the ECAB, testing may be reduced, and the documentation may be completed retrospectively.

Be able to recall the steps and activities of the normal change process flow.   You will need to be familiar with the steps and activities of the normal process as previously detailed on the normal change process flow.

Understand the types of documentation for the change process and their uses.   All changes should be documented in an RFC, and this should be logged in a change record, which is captured as part of the CMS. A change proposal is needed only if the change has a major impact on the business in terms of risk, cost, or resources.

Be able to identify the elements that are used for assessment of changes.   The assessment of a change should include the benefits, costs, risks, resources, and relationships for the change.

Be able to recall the output documentation from the process. The change schedule (CS) and projected service outage (PSO) documents are outputs of the change process and are used to communicate change timescales and impact with stakeholders.

Understand the purpose of the remediation plan. The remediation plan allows mitigation against potential failure and return to normal if a change fails.

Understand how changes are authorized and by whom. Changes are authorized for action by the change authority, dependent on the size, risk, cost, and business impact of the change.

Understand the responsibilities of change management in respect of release and deployment of changes and how change management interfaces with other processes. Change management is responsible for the coordination of the deployment of the change and will work with release and deployment management. Change management interfaces with many other service management and business processes across the service lifecycle.

Be able to identify how a change is closed. Once a change has been deployed, it should be reviewed, and the change record can be closed, once it has met the acceptance criteria for success.

Understand the responsibilities of the change advisory board. The change advisory board (CAB) is responsible for assessing changes and making recommendation for authorization.

Review Questions

You can find the answers in Appendix A.

1. Which of these statements is the *best* description of the purpose of the service transition lifecycle stage?

   A. Ensure services agreed on and designed in strategy and design are delivered effectively into operation.

   B. Ensure services are designed to meet business expectations.

   C. Ensure services are operated according to service level agreements.

   D. Ensure services are measured and improved according to improvement guidelines.

2. Which of these is a recognized "business benefit" or "value statement" for the service transition lifecycle stage?

   1. Deliver changes to services with a consistent approach

   2. Manage the business strategic plans

   3. Control the assets of the infrastructure

   4. Improve business strategy through service transformation

   5. Provide increased confidence in the success of changes

   A. 1, 2, 3, and 4

   B. 2, 4, and 5

   C. 1, 3, and 5

   D. 1, 2, 3, 4, and 5

3. Which of these statements *best* reflects the purpose of change management?

   A. To deliver successful projects to operations

   B. To provide controlled change

   C. To provide success strategies for the business

   D. To deliver an accurate configuration management system

4. Which of these is part of the scope of IT change management?

   A. Business strategic changes

   B. Minor operational changes

   C. IT service changes

   D. Project changes

5. What is the benefit of using a change model?

   A. It allows a change to be accepted into release more easily.

   B. It allows the customer to bypass the normal change process.

   C. It allows project teams to use the change process for project changes.

   D. It allows predefined steps to be used when handling similar types of change.

6. Which of these statements represent acceptable criteria for defining a standard change?

    1. The risk associated to the change is low or clearly understood.

    2. The change follows a defined procedure or predefined steps.

    3. The change can be completed within 24 hours of being requested.

    4. The change can be traced to a predefined trigger.

    5. The change delivers its results to IT service providers only.

  A. 1, 3, and 5

  B. 1, 2, and 4

  C. 2, 3, and 4

  D. 1, 2, 3, 4, and 5

7. Which of these would be a reason to raise a change proposal for authorization?

  A. If the change has a major cost impact on the business

  B. If the change has been assessed as being technical

  C. If the change has been raised by a user

  D. If the change has been assessed by a supplier

8. Which of these is *not* a recognized output document from the change management process?

  A. Change schedule

  B. Project service outage

  C. Remediation plan

  D. Configuration schedule

9. Who is responsible for authorizing a request for change as part of the change management process?

  A. Change authority

  B. Customer

  C. User

  D. Supplier

10. Which of these is a valid reason for closing a change record?

  A. The release has been implemented.

  B. The change acceptance criteria have been met.

  C. The change has been authorized and implemented.

  D. The change has been released.

Chapter

9

Service Transition Processes

THE FOLLOWING ITIL FOUNDATION EXAM OBJECTIVES ARE COVERED IN THIS CHAPTER:

✓ **3-16. Service knowledge management system (SKMS)**

✓ **3-17. Configuration item (CI)**

✓ **3-18. Configuration management system**

✓ **3-19. Definitive media library (DML)**

✓ **3-35. Release policy**

✓ **5-6. State the purpose, objectives and scope for:**

  5-61 Release and deployment management

  ▪ Four phases of release and deployment

  5-62 Knowledge management

  ▪ Data-to-Information-to-Knowledge-to-Wisdom

  5-63 Service asset and configuration management

  5-64 Transition planning and support

We have covered the change management process in some detail, but these remaining processes do not require such an in-depth consideration for the Foundation syllabus. As a result, we will review only the purpose, objectives, and scope for each process, as well as some of the basic process steps and concepts.

In fact, the list of processes for service transition is longer than the list of processes we will be reviewing. The following processes are also included in this lifecycle stage:

- Service validation and testing
- Change evaluation

These last two processes are not covered in the syllabus, so you will not have any questions in your exam that relate to them. But so that you are aware of their content, here is a brief outline for each:

- Service validation and testing, is, as the title suggests, the process that ensures the service will perform as specified and be designed through service strategy and service design. It is when you engage with your customers and users to complete the required testing of the new or changed service.
- Change evaluation is the process that allows you to check the predicted performance against the actual performance achieved by the new or changed service.

Both of these processes are important for service transition as a whole but are outside of the syllabus scope for Foundation.

Transition Planning and Support

Let's begin by looking at the *transition planning and support* process, which is a key process for the service transition lifecycle stage. Setting up the transition and how it will be managed is crucial for the successful release of your new service into the operational environment. It is a very detailed area of the lifecycle and covers the interface between service transition, project management, and business engagement. It is here that you are looking at the resources and capabilities required to deliver your service design into the live environment, in the service operation lifecycle stage.

In the Foundation exam syllabus, this process is covered only by the requirement to understand the purpose, scope, and objectives of the process. More information about this process is available in the Lifecycle core publication of Service Transition, and further education on the process can be found in the ITIL qualification scheme.

The Purpose of Transition Planning and Support

The purpose of transition planning and support is as the title of the process suggests: to plan the transition activities. But of course, that is very simplistic, and there are more things to consider.

The need to plan transition activity should be clear, because there are so many disparate activities that need to be undertaken. Think about the different processes that exist in this lifecycle stage—everything from managing change through release and deployment, service validation and testing, and change evaluation all the way to managing service assets and configuration items. The key purpose of the transition planning and support process is to coordinate the required resources that will be employed during the transition.

When carrying out a transition, it may be necessary to engage with the technical and application management functions to obtain the necessary resources for managing the activity and ensuring that all aspects of the transition are carried out by staff with the relevant capabilities.

Technical and Application Management Functions

Technical Management Function   Custodian of expertise relating to management of the IT infrastructure. This function provides resources for managing the infrastructure in the service operation lifecycle stage and for other lifecycle stages, such as service transition and service design.

Application Management Function   Custodian of expertise relating to managing applications. This function provides resources for managing applications in the service operation lifecycle stage and for other lifecycle stages, such as service transition and service design.

There will be considerations regarding the impact of utilizing existing operational staff to help in the transition, and this needs to be managed appropriately to minimize service impact.

It is important to remember that during a transition, it is not only the IT staff members who will need to engage in the activities; you also need to have support and involvement from the business and user community. They will need to be included in the testing of the transition to ensure that the requirements specified in strategy and the solutions developed in design are delivered successfully to meet the requirements of the business.

So, in transition planning and support, there needs to be a careful assessment of the resources and capabilities across all of the stakeholders, as well as appropriate scheduling of the transition planned to ensure that these are available when they are needed.

The Objectives of Transition Planning and Support

The objectives of the transition planning and support process are to do the following:

- Plan and coordinate the resources for the transition. It is important to plan this so that the requirements identified in service strategy, which were captured in service design, are effectively realized in service operation.

- Coordinate all of the various sources for the transitional activity. This may include projects and service teams but also includes suppliers if third-party engagement is involved in the transition.

- Meet the predicted budget, timeframe, and quality estimates as the new or changed service is established in the supported environment. Meeting the estimated cost, quality, and time allocation is an important factor for demonstrating the efficiency and effectiveness of the transitional activity and contributes to customer satisfaction.

- Establish the new requirements as specified in the service design stage for the management systems and tools that will be part of the new service in operation. This will include the service management tools, as well as the management and technology architectures as defined in the service solution. There may also be new requirements for service management processes for the new or changed services, as well as measures and metrics to be established in order to deliver the required results and service quality.

- Ensure that repeatable processes are adopted by all engaged in the transition. Developing a framework of reusable processes and systems that can improve the efficiency of future transitions is an important part of this process. It will mean that the coordination and planning will continue to improve over time, delivering long-term benefits to the overall operation.

- Provide clear and comprehensive plans for the transition. These will be made available to the business and project teams for alignment with their change plans. It is extremely important to ensure that business and project teams are aware of the IT service changes and plans so that the overall approach can be managed and aligned to meet the needs and expectations of the business in a realistic timeframe.

- Identify and manage risks, in accordance with the risk management framework adopted by the organization. This will include controlling risks, as well as mitigating them to minimize disruption and failure of the transition. It is important to identify risks and make the relevant stakeholders and decision makers aware of them so that appropriate actions can be taken to safeguard against failure and disruption in the transition.

- Monitor and improve the process of transition planning and support and the service transition lifecycle stage.

The Scope of Transition Planning and Support

The scope of service transition planning and support covers the following:

- The maintenance of the policies and standards that are to be applied throughout the transition. This is important to ensure that the repeatable activity is managed appropriately and that you maximize the use of models for an efficient approach.

- Providing guidance for each new service or major change through the transition processes.

- Ensuring that the resources and management required for multiple transitions to take place at the same time are available. It is unlikely that there will be only one change, project, or new service introduction taking place at any one time. Transition planning should recognize and coordinate the efforts required for this to happen successfully.

- Prioritizing the resources required for transition may be required because conflicts over usage may occur. An example of this would be the use of the test environment by multiple projects or changes.

- Planning for future transition requirements in terms of budget and resources. Consideration should be given to business requirements that are currently being handled in the design stage so that any additional resources can be ordered or allocated in a timely manner.

- Reviewing process activities for performance improvement opportunities.

- Ensuring the coordination of the transition and planning process with business program and project processes and the activities taking place in the service design lifecycle stage.

Transition planning and support should not cover the detailed plans for build, test, and deployment for individual changes or releases, because the processes of change management and release and deployment management will cover this. Its scope and purpose is at a higher level, ensuring the coordination of multiple activities toward the deployment of changes into the live operational environment.

Service Asset and Configuration Management

One of the key ways that an IT department can show its efficiency is by demonstrating that it has control over the assets it manages. Remember, the services that IT provides are crucial to the support of the business, and you must try to deliver these in the most efficient and effective manner possible.

In this process, you look at the ways you can establish a logical model of the infrastructure to assist service management. Capturing accurate information about your components and service assets will enable you to be more efficient in the delivery of services.

The elements we will be reviewing in this section are the purpose, objectives, and scope of the process; the concepts of the configuration management system, configuration management database, and configuration items; and the configuration model and the definitive media library.

The Purpose of the SACM Process

The purpose of the *service asset and configuration management (SACM)* process is to ensure that you are able to control the assets that make up your services. To achieve that control, it will be necessary to understand what each of those assets are and how they are connected to each other.

Managing the assets that make up your services can be a complicated task in distributed environments. Components of your services may be in diverse locations, managed by a wide variety of teams; and the more complex your technology architecture, the more involved the management becomes.

Identifying the assets is only part of the requirement; you also need to ensure you have accurate records about them. This is a challenging task for any department. The information captured should include the relationships between the assets, to maximize the use of the data. Understanding the relationships between the items will aid in the management of the infrastructure and the identification of the impact of changes, by showing the connections between the infrastructure items. Corporate asset management simply provides a list of the items; service asset and configuration management shows the relationships between items and allows for a greater understanding of how all the elements of the infrastructure depend on each other.

If appropriate, you should capture not only the relationships between items but also their configuration. It is important to capture appropriate information so that the full benefit of the information can be realized. It will be necessary to understand what the data will be used for within the organization so that the level of detail can be agreed upon as part of the process.

So, part of the purpose of SACM is to ensure you have accurate meaningful and relevant information about your assets.

The Objectives of the SACM Process

The objectives of the SACM process are to do the following:

- Ensure the assets that are under the control of the IT department are properly managed. This means the assets need to be identified and, once identified, controlled throughout their lifecycles. Managing the assets that make up your services is an important part of the governance and control you should have to support your organization.

- Capture information about the services you provide. This requires you to identify, control, and record the services and configuration items you use to support your businesses. Once this information is captured, you need to report on and audit the data, allowing you to verify the configuration of the services and how they support the business. This should include versions, baselines, and constituent components of the services, attributes, and relationships about the services.

- Manage the integrity of the *configuration items (CIs)* that make up the services. We expand on configuration items later in this chapter, but essentially it is an item of infrastructure that is managed to deliver a service. This should include accounting for and protecting the configuration items by using the change management process to ensure that only properly authorized items are in use in the infrastructure. Change management should be used to control the lifecycle of CIs so that only authorized changes can be carried out.

- Establish an accurate and maintained configuration management system, enabling the sustained control and integrity of the components and services. Creating a viable configuration management system is a very important aspect of the SACM process.

- Maintain historical, planned, and current information about the state of configuration items and services as part of the control and management of the infrastructure. By capturing historic and planned status, it will be possible to use the information for trending and modeling, so its accuracy will be important.

- Support efficient and effective service management processes, by providing information that allows accurate decision making by service providers in the delivery of services. This information is a crucial part of other service management processes, and it is sometimes said that SACM underpins and supports the entire lifecycle.

The Scope of the SACM Process

The process of SACM is there to identify the elements of the infrastructure that are to be managed as service assets and then to apply controls to that management. Service assets that are to be managed throughout their lifecycle, in order to deliver services, are known as configuration items (CI). Other assets that cannot be managed in this way, even though they are part of the overall service delivery, are not configuration items. All configuration items are service assets, but not all service assets will be classified and managed as configuration items. An example of this is a server; this would be classed as both an asset and a configuration item. But the knowledge used by the support technician to manage the server would not be classed as a configuration item, even though it is obviously an important service asset. To extend this example, the information stored on the server, although it is a valuable asset, is also not classified as a configuration item.

In the case of virtual infrastructure, a virtual server may still be classified as a configuration item and service asset, and even though it is as intangible as "knowledge" or "information," it will still need the same management controls applied as its physical counterpart.

So, the scope of the process includes the management of all configuration items throughout their lifecycle.

Providing control over the entire lifecycle of a configuration item, and all configuration items that make up your services, requires a substantial amount of effort. The scope of this effort should be managed across the whole of the service lifecycle. It requires that all CIs be baselined (that is, identifying and agreeing upon the state of the infrastructure at a given point in time), maintained, and controlled through change management. Using the change management process will also help ensure that there is control over the management of releases into the production environment. No release should take place without the necessary authorization, which is part of the change process.

Capturing all this information is done by creating the *configuration management system (CMS)*. This system allows you to develop a logical model of the infrastructure, which provides details of the relationships among all of the CIs. Known as a configuration model, this is an important tool for service management processes.

Other items that make up the services, perhaps not traditionally captured as assets by the other parts of the organization such as work products (for example, organization models, process documentation, roles, and responsibilities in a RACI matrix), may be classified as CIs in the CMS.

The scope will also include any interfaces that may exist with internal and external configuration items, such as any shared assets that are part of the service provision.

In most organizations, there will be an existing business process for managing fixed assets. Some of these assets will be under the management of IT and will need to be included in the CMS as CIs. It will be important to ensure that there is cooperation between the two areas so that the management of these assets is maintained appropriately.

Configuration item information may be stored in smaller databases, known as configuration management databases (CMDBs). The configuration management system can be made up of a number of CMDBs, because the management and accuracy of a local database may be more effectively achieved. The CMS takes a federated approach to managing the data.

The Description and Definition of Configuration Items

We have spoken a lot about configuration items throughout the purpose, objectives, and scope of SACM, so it is important that we provide some full definitions according the process framework:

Service Asset   Any resource or capability that could contribute to the delivery of a service. Examples include a virtual server, a physical server, and the knowledge in the support team to fix the server.

Configuration Item   A service asset that needs to be managed in order to deliver an IT service. All CIs are service assets, but many service assets are not configuration items. Examples include a server and software license documentation. Every CI must be under the control of configuration management.

Configuration Record   A set of attributes and relationships about a CI. Configuration records are stored in a configuration management database that allows for localized management of the data source and is managed with a configuration management system. It is important to recognize the distinction that CIs are not stored in the CMDB; it is the information about the CIs that is stored there, in a configuration record.

These definitions are important both for taking the exam and as part of the process of SACM.

The concept of the configuration item is particularly important. As stated earlier, a configuration item is a service asset that needs to be managed in order to deliver an IT service. The type, size, and complexity of configuration items may vary widely, from a single module of software to a complete system or service, including all hardware, software, and documentation. Configuration items may be managed by grouping individual items together, as in a release.

One of the most crucial factors is to define the level of detail required to manage configuration items successfully. If there is too much detail, it will be difficult to accurately maintain and keep up-to-date the information about them; if there is too little information, then the CMS will not be useful enough. Configuration items should be identified, grouped together, and classified in a way that makes it possible to manage and trace them throughout the service lifecycle.

ITIL suggests a number of different categories for classifying CIs. These are only suggestions; each organization will have to agree on their own categories and the level of detail for each CI, whether an item is a CI in its own right or simply an attribute of another CI. For example, is a desktop PC a CI on its own, with attributes listed as memory, hard drive capacity, monitor, and so on, or are each of these elements identified as CIs that will be under management control?

The categories suggested by ITIL are as follows:

Service Lifecycle CIs   Examples include the business case, service management plans, and the service design package. These are documents that provide information on the plans and requirements for the services, including costs and benefits.

Service CIs   Examples include service capability assets such as management, processes, and people; service resource assets such as financial capital, infrastructure, people; and service model; service package; release package; and service acceptance criteria.

Organization CIs   Examples include documentation relating to organizational policies or standards.

Internal CIs   Examples include assets delivered by projects such as software or hardware.

External CIs   Examples include external customer requirements and agreements.

Interface CIs   Examples include documentation relating to end-to-end service provision across multiple service providers.

The Description of the Configuration Model

Service asset and configuration management provides a model of the services, assets, and infrastructure by capturing the details of each configuration item and their relationships to each other. You can see an example of this in Figure 9.1.

FIGURE 9.1   Diagram of a configuration model

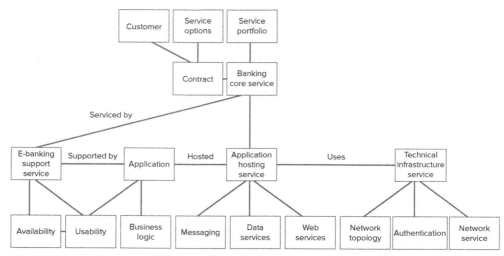

© Based on Cabinet Office ITIL material. Reproduced under license from the Cabinet Office.

Integrated into a service management system, the configuration model can provide important detail for the support of many service management processes. Imagine the benefits of having this level of connectivity of information about your infrastructure for use by the service desk. A user calls the service desk, and once the analyst has identified them in the system, information about the services, the infrastructure, and the service level agreements they use can be immediately accessible. The same detail can also be used for assessing changes, allowing complete understanding of the interdependencies when proposing to alter a CI. Information relating to cost will be available in the system, for use in financial management. Design for new or changed services will also make use of the configuration management system, enabling future enhancements to the infrastructure to be planned effectively and efficiently.

One of the key benefits of the system is that it is a consolidation of all the information sources into a single repository. That repository can consist of a number of smaller databases, linked so that the information can be connected to maximize the benefits of gathering the data.

The level of detail captured will depend on the value of information to the organization, the ability to manage the data, and whether it is feasible to maintain the level of change control required to ensure accuracy. This has to be an organizational choice, and it is part of the process to ensure that this is planned and executed in a controlled manner.

Using the Configuration Management System

The configuration management system is the system you use to manage the configuration model and deliver the information to those who need it. It is therefore extremely important to ensure that the tool is both fit for purpose and fit for use, just as you would with a system or service being provided directly to your customers and users.

The CMS holds all the information about the CIs that have been identified as part of the process of SACM. Figure 9.2 shows the relationship between the configuration records, actual CIs, and the larger, more complex service knowledge management system (SKMS), of which the CMS is a part.

FIGURE 9.2 Relationship between CMS and SKMS

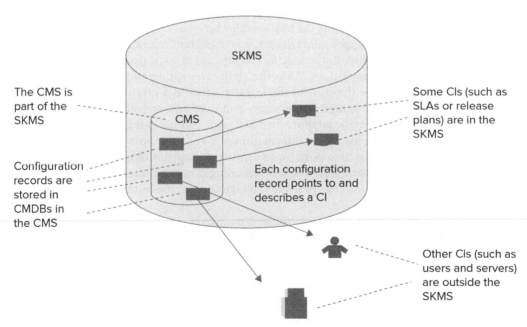

Based on Cabinet Office ITIL material. Reproduced under license from the Cabinet Office.

The SKMS (which we will cover in more detail in the "Knowledge Management" section) is an overarching system of tools and databases, used for managing all information relating to service management knowledge throughout the service lifecycle. Many CIs are available in the form of knowledge or information (for example, a service level agreement or a report template), and these items will be stored as part of the SKMS. SACM is not responsible for the management of the SKMS.

The CMS may include information from a number of *configuration management databases*, which allows for the localized management of the data source. Capturing information for a specific site, location, or section of the infrastructure may be easier to manage in smaller segments. However, each CMDB must be constructed with the intention of integration into the CMS, so the naming conventions, structure, and definitions of the data captured must support overall management through the CMS.

Populating the CMS can be achieved by integrating existing information sources and using discovery tools to automatically update or capture information about the infrastructure. These tools can be used to populate CMDBs and then used to verify the accuracy of the information as ongoing maintenance. Although some information may already be in existence in organizations in spreadsheets or databases, wherever possible this should be an automated activity.

All changes to CIs should be managed under the change management process, and any related records and information held in the CMS should be updated as part of this activity. As the CMS maintains the relationships between records such as incidents, problems, known errors, changes, and releases, it is important to ensure that all records are maintained accurately and link to the specific CIs affected in each case.

One of the many benefits of the CMS is the ability to capture and agree on baselines, identifying and agreeing on the state of the infrastructure at a given point in time. Baselines are reviewed and agreed for accuracy and used as a reference point for future activities. Baselines can provide support for the design and planning activities in the service lifecycle, providing historical information or a rollback point for major changes to the live environment. It is also possible to capture a snapshot of the infrastructure, which although unverified and not reviewed (meaning it may contain errors and inaccuracies) is a valuable tool for problem management or the initial assessment of success after a release.

Using a CMS means the data is captured by a multilayer mechanism, as defined by the structure of the SKMS. In this way, you have the ability to capture a variety of information sources, which are then integrated by the information integration layer. Ensuring these are manageable and provide a useful resource, you have a knowledge processing layer and a presentation layer providing access to the information in a usable state.

The integration of various information sources to support the delivery of services is a vital part of service management effectiveness and efficiency, including business information sources, such as HR information.

In Figure 9.3 you can see the different layers of the CMS, their relationship to the SKMS, and additional information sources.

FIGURE 9.3   Architecture of the CMS

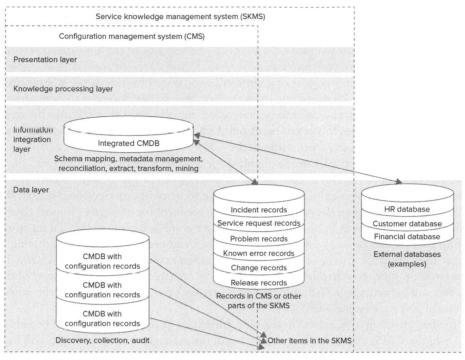

© Based on Cabinet Office ITIL material. Reproduced under license from the Cabinet Office.

Using the Definitive Media Library

As we have discussed, some information sources may exist outside of the SKMS or CMS, but there are also aspects of your services that are captured as records in the CMS or SKMS but are in fact physical libraries or stores.

Secure stores or libraries allow you to manage those elements of your infrastructure or CIs that you need to ensure retain their integrity, outside of their operational use. Consider the use of authorized software, purchased under license from a third party. You should ensure you keep a master copy of the software and its associated license documentation in a secure store for use in service continuity situations or to maintain a "clean" version for reinstallation should there be any issues of data integrity in the live environment. This will also apply to unlicensed software developed in-house by your organization.

Records of these CIs should be captured and managed in your CMS (perhaps as a specific CMDB), and in this way you can validate and control the use of the software versions in the live environment. SACM has a large part to play in license management and will be supported by release and deployment management to ensure that only authorized versions are used in the live environment.

Management of the secure library or store should be achieved by SACM controls through change management. The physical store may be actual disks or documents, but there may also be electronic stores if much of your software and its associated documentation is managed electronically. However the media is captured, the definitive media library (DML) is managed to ensure the integrity and security of the authorized versions of software in use in the live environment.

In reality, the DML may consist of a number of software libraries or file storage areas, which are managed and kept separate from the live, test, or development storage areas.

Hardware spares may also need to be controlled, but although this will also be managed by a secure physical store, this is not managed through the DML but as part of the overall management of the infrastructure through the CMS.

It will be important, as part of the planning for SACM, to define the structure, scope, and content of the DML. Consideration will need to be given to the security arrangements for the physical store but also for the security of any electronic media. Basic procedures for backing up electronic media and procedures for ensuring physical data storage is still viable will need to be created. There is no point in having physical data storage if you find that the master copy has lost integrity when you need to restore it. Archiving and changes to technology also need to be considered when managing the DML. What will be the retention policy; how frequently will versions be archived, and which versions of the software will be managed? Will only the latest version be archived, or should the previous versions of software be included?

Information about all CIs held in the secure libraries or physical stores will be held as records in the CMS, and the policies that control the management of the DML will form part of the SKMS.

Knowledge Management

Knowledge management is a process that impacts the wider service lifecycle, not just service transition. This process provides you with one of the key systems for service management, the service knowledge management system.

In this process, you will be considering the purpose, objectives, and scope of knowledge management, as well as the concepts of the Data-Information-Knowledge-Wisdom (DIKW) model and the SKMS.

The Purpose of Knowledge Management

The purpose of knowledge management is to ensure that ideas, perspectives, experience, and information are shared and that this is delivered at the right time and to the right place to enable informed decision making. You should try to reuse, not rediscover knowledge, so that you are more efficient.

Let's consider that statement in more detail. What are the right information, ideas, experience, and perspectives? These have to be considered in the context of the audience. What may be the right information for the IT department may be completely inappropriate for your customers, because it needs to be put into a context that the customer can understand. So, when you present information, you should be aware of the needs of the audience receiving it. Shared experience and ideas should be considered in this way so that relevant experiences and ideas are provided. It is very important to understand the perspectives that exist within your organization so that you can attempt to achieve a shared cultural perspective to improve the effectiveness of your cooperation across the organization.

The statement also talks about an informed decision. Here you need to think about the decision maker, so the appropriate person needs to be able to make a decision. Sometimes the decisions will be at a low level; at other times, it will be high-level strategic decision making. In either case, you need to ensure that the decisions can be made, so your information needs to be relevant.

Therefore, the purpose of knowledge management is to deliver relevant information, ideas, experiences, and perspectives to the correct audience so that they can make an informed decision.

If you capture these ideas, experiences, and information, you will be able to reuse them in order to continue to make decisions based on both new and historical information. The reuse of knowledge is a key concept in the process.

The Objectives of Knowledge Management

The objectives of knowledge management are to do the following:

- Improve the quality of decision making throughout the service lifecycle. The quality of decisions made must rest on the quality of the information provided to the decision maker. If the information provided is inaccurate or unreliable, then a considered decision cannot properly be achieved. So, this process should strive to ensure that the information provided is accurate, relevant, and secure for a decision to be made, throughout all of the lifecycle.

  Enable efficiency in the service provider and customer by encouraging the reuse of information. It is a key concept in the framework that you should use repeatable processes to deliver an efficient service, and the use of information should also be repeatable. Rediscovering the same knowledge is inefficient, so the drive from the process of knowledge management is to ensure you have captured your information in a repeatable and accessible format. If you manage to reduce the time taken to rediscover knowledge, then the efficiencies made will result in higher-quality services and greater customer satisfaction. This in turn can reduce the total cost of ownership for the services you deliver.

- Ensure that staff members have an understanding of the value of their services. Understanding the value of the services can be achieved only through the knowledge and experience shared between the business and IT communities within an organization.

Once you have established a clear and common understanding of the value of the services by communication with your user base, you can begin to make genuine improvements in the value of those services.

- Maintain a *service knowledge management system (SMKS)*. This objective is important for the success of knowledge management, because the delivery mechanisms you use for transferring knowledge will make information easily accessible. It will be important to ensure that the information shared is appropriately presented and controlled for the correct audience.

- Gather, store, analyze, share, use, and maintain knowledge, information, and data throughout the service provider organization. Without this objective, the process will not function at all; having a repeatable mechanism for capturing data so that you can carry out analysis, which allows you to provide the knowledge to support your services, is vital to knowledge management success.

The Scope of Knowledge Management

The scope of knowledge management crosses the whole of the service lifecycle. The detailed description of the process is located in the service transition lifecycle stage, so we will cover knowledge management from the perspective of transition. But knowledge management is essential throughout all stages of the lifecycle, and the ability to communicate, share, and deliver knowledge, information, and experience is important for service management success.

There is significant importance placed on the management of data and information across the service management processes. Each process will have an element of knowledge management or shared data. In the operational processes, you create records and data that need to be connected and managed. You should consider the relationship between knowledge management and service asset and configuration management. SACM manages the connection and relationship between individual CIs and service assets, some of which may be information sources or outputs. Knowledge management manages the achievement of the knowledge and its sharing and analysis. So, there is a very clear relationship between the two processes (the relationship between the configuration management system and the service knowledge management system was shown in Figure 9.3).

The management of knowledge is also vital for using the service management processes with your customers and users. So, the scope of the process extends into the relationship you have with your businesses, and you need to ensure that you share appropriate information with your customers and users, in an accessible format.

Using the Data-Information-Knowledge-Wisdom Structure

The application of knowledge management is usually displayed as the Data-Information-Knowledge-Wisdom (DIKW) structure, as shown in Figure 9.4.

FIGURE 9.4   Data-Information-Knowledge-Wisdom

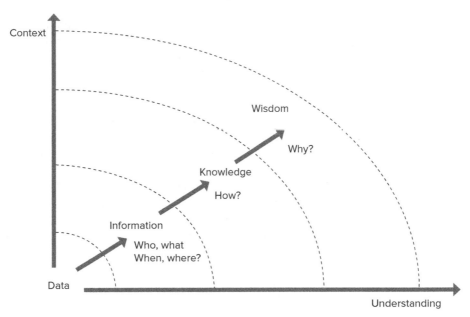

Based on Cabinet Office ITIL material. Reproduced under license from the Cabinet Office.

Data is the starting point for your generation of knowledge. Data is a set of discrete facts, for example, a capture of the volume of service desk calls recorded in the call-logging system (such as 100 service desk calls). Organizations usually have the capability to store significant amounts of data from a variety of systems when managing services. The ability to capture accurate data, which can then be analyzed and transformed into information, is key to the success of the process. Effort needs to be made to maintain the integrity of the data, including managing the volume of data captured and using the resources for storage and update.

You need to be careful that the reports you provide to your customers and users are more than just "data dumps" that have minimal value. You need to provide greater context and understanding to make your communication more meaningful.

You derive information from data by adding context. For example, the volume of service desk calls includes some for hardware faults and some for software (for example, of 100 service desk calls, 50 were related to router failures, and 50 were related to application errors). You begin to be specific and perform basic analysis, which allows for greater understanding of what the data is telling you.

It is important to ensure that your data can be captured, analyzed, and reused efficiently. Many reports produced by IT departments simply detail information, but this may not provide sufficient context or understanding for the audience. It is the next step in this structure that provides the additional context and understanding to add value to your communications.

Knowledge is formed when you apply experience, context, and understanding to the information analysis. This can be gained from your own perspectives or from those of others. Knowledge is based on current and past experience and is an accumulation of the analysis, experience, and context that you can apply. You are answering the question "How does this affect us?"

In the example given previously with 100 service desk calls, of which 50 are router failures, you now apply experience, further information, context, and understanding to identify how this affects you. Perhaps you have only 50 routers, in which case this is a serious and significant failure of equipment. Are they all the same model or all from the same vendor? The answers to such questions provide the context you can then apply to the information to ensure you can take the next step and make an informed decision. It may also be that this example is based in a large organization where 50 router failures are insignificant for the management of the infrastructure. The context of the information is key to understanding how the original data impacts your ability to manage service.

Taking the final step, you are now in a position to make an informed decision. This is where the knowledge provided can be applied to your environment to make improvements or react to the knowledge to deliver effective service.

To use the previous example of 100 service desk calls, 50 of which are router failures in an infrastructure that has only 50 routers, the decision you make may be to replace all the routers, change the vendor, or even invoke your service continuity plans.

So, the whole structure of DIKW is designed to ensure that you deliver useful, meaningful knowledge to enable informed decision making by the recipients.

Consider how this works for reports produced from your IT department. How often do you deliver information vs. knowledge, ensuring that sufficient context and understanding are part of the delivery?

Using the Service Knowledge Management System

The *service knowledge management system* is a focused system that allows you to manage the data and information that is generated by the service management processes and the service measures. The system is designed to ensure that you gain sufficient knowledge from the data sources through a series of processing layers. This enables connection of the various data sources, integration of the information, and a processing layer to allow you to query, report, and analyze. The final layer is the presentation layer, ensuring that your knowledge is presented in an acceptable format to allow decisions to be made.

This structure includes integrating your existing data capture in the CMDBs and CMS that are part of the SKMS. It also includes sources such as the service portfolio, definitive media library, information in SLAs, OLAs and contracts, budgets, cost models, and service improvement plans. Finally, it integrates the various information systems from availability, capacity, and supplier management.

Figure 9.5 shows a simple diagram of this structure.

FIGURE 9.5 Structure of the SKMS

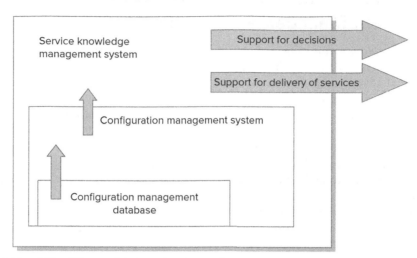

Based on Cabinet Office ITIL material. Reproduced under license from the Cabinet Office.

Other information sources will come from the integration of operation data from incident and problem management. This will include known error information and knowledge bases in use in operations.

Some of the information managed through the SKMS will include service reports and documentation supporting your services. These may be CIs, and the records about them will be managed through the CMS, whereas the actual information will be managed through the SKMS. Both of these will be under the control of change management to ensure that no unauthorized alterations are made and the integrity and accuracy of your information sources are maintained.

Release and Deployment Management

The role of release and deployment management in this lifecycle stage is to ensure the successful introduction of changes into the live environment, minimizing the unpredicted impact to the business.

To deliver releases into the live environment successfully, you need to have control over the release management activities, and in this process we cover the purpose, objectives, and scope of the process, as well as the concepts of the release policy and the four phases of release and deployment.

The Purpose of the Release and Deployment Management Process

Release and deployment management is an important part of managing your live environment. The process ensures that the build, test, and deployment of the release is delivered with minimal adverse impact to the business.

One of the key purposes of the process is to ensure that this activity is planned, scheduled, and controlled in accordance with the needs of the organization.

This is one of the most visible processes of transition, because it is where the interaction of the IT department and the business community meets to engage with the new or changed services. During release and deployment, you will carry out pilots and testing of new services in order to understand whether the service design can be realized effectively in operation.

Release and deployment management needs to deliver the new functionality required by the business, and it is important to ensure that the new or changed services do not negatively impact the existing services.

The Objectives of the Release and Deployment Management Process

The objectives of release and deployment management are to do the following:

- Define and agree on deployment plans with the stakeholders of the release. This is an important aspect of the process, because the agreement of a schedule and management of the activity with the customers and stakeholders who will receive the release is important in setting expectations for the desired outcome.

- Create and test release packages. Release packages may consist of a number of related configuration items, and it is the responsibility of release and deployment to verify the components are compatible and can be released together.

- Maintain the integrity of a software release package throughout the release. All release packages should be stored as part of a definitive media library, and the records should be kept in the configuration management system relating to the release. This includes managing the constituent components of the release package and keeping accurate records about each CI. Hardware releases will be managed in the same way but without the requirement to check them into the DML.

- Follow the agreed release plans according to the schedule, including deploying the software release from the DML. Keeping to the plans and schedule will ensure that the engagement agreed with the stakeholders can take place efficiently, in the timeframes allocated.

- Manage the release package effectively, ensuring it can be tracked, installed, tested, and verified. This includes the potential for uninstalling or backing out the release. Delivering the release in a controlled manner is crucial to its success.

- Ensure that the new or changed service meets the utility and warranty requirements. It is important to ensure that the supporting systems and technology for the release are contributing appropriately to achieve the requirements.

- Manage and record any unplanned outcomes, risks, and issues from the release. Capture of any deviations from the expected performance is an important part of the lessons learned for the release, and suitable changes should be made to ensure the final outcome meets the requirements specified in the original plans.

- Ensure there is suitable knowledge transfer to the stakeholders of the release to enable proper use of the new or changed service. This should be completed according to the plans and schedule, including the timely delivery of any training requirements for the recipients of the release, both users and the IT operations staff.

- Ensure that sufficient training is provided for the support teams in operations to enable full capability for maintenance and support according to the utility and warranty requirements. This element of a release may be easy to overlook, particularly because some of the operations teams may be engaged in the deployment of the release, but it is crucial to the success of the deployment that operations are able to support the release effectively and efficiently from the start.

The Scope of the Release and Deployment Management Process

The scope of release and deployment management covers the processes, systems, and functions required to deliver a release into the live environment. This includes the packaging, build, test, and deployment of the release, enabling the release to be executed according to the design package, and the specified utility and warranty requirements. The scope includes the handover to the service operation teams.

All aspects and CIs associated with the release should be managed, including, for example, physical and virtual assets such as servers and networks, applications and software, training for IT staff and users, and services including the supporting agreements and contracts with suppliers.

There are exclusions to the scope of release and deployment, because some aspects are managed as part of other processes. For example, although ensuring that testing takes place is part of the responsibility of release and deployment, the activity of testing and managing the test environment and plans will be carried out by the process of service validation and testing.

Release and deployment is not responsible for authorizing activity toward the release deployment. This will be referred to the change management process and the change authority. Interacting with project management and project authorization may also take place, but any IT change activity should be coordinated through change management.

Creating the Release Policy

To ensure effective management of releases, there should be a defined release policy for each service or group of services. The policy is important for the overall control of release and deployment within service management. Specifying the requirements that should be managed for any release for the service or services, this document should be under change control and managed as a service asset. Not all changes will require release and deployment management for their implementation; for example, minor operational changes will be managed through change management and operational activity. Release and deployment is used for significant or complex changes, and the policy should set out the requirements that need to be considered for successful implementation.

As part of the policy, there should be a definition of the types of release, which will be under the control of release and deployment management. This should be included to set expectations for customers and stakeholders regarding the nature of the release and how it will be managed. A suggestion for release types is a major release; these are releases that will have a significant impact on the business environment, because of either complexity or size, and will often include new functionality. Other suggested types are the minor release, providing minimal impact or only minor upgrades or enhancements, and the emergency release, carried out in response to a business-critical requirement or for a small enhancement. The release policy will define when an emergency release may be carried out and in what circumstances.

The policy should cover some or all of the following elements:

- A unique identification structure or naming convention to ensure releases can be easily identified and tracked. This should include a description for the associated release.

- Definitions of the roles and responsibilities required for the management of the release throughout all its stages.

- Use of the definitive media library for all software asset releases.

- The expected frequency for specific types of release.

- The approach for grouping changes into a release and how any additional updates are to be included if enhancements are required.

- Any automation that can be applied to the build, installation, and deployment to deliver a repeatable mechanism to improve efficiency.

- How the configuration baseline will be taken prior to the release and what means will be used to verify its accuracy in terms of components before agreement and recording.

- The entry and exit criteria for each stage of the release, including the authority required, as well as definitions of the acceptance criteria for entry into controlled test and development environments and other supported environments such as disaster recovery or training.

- The criteria for the final handover into operations, including the criteria for the completion and exit of the early life support stage.

Managing the Four Phases of Release and Deployment

There are four phases to release and deployment:

Release and Deployment Planning   This phase starts with the authorization from change management to plan a release and ends with change authorization to create the release. It is here that the plans for creating and deploying the release are produced. This is an important aspect of the process, because a properly planned release will improve the efficiency of the deployment.

Release Build and Test   During this phase, the release package is built, tested, and checked into the DML if it is software and documentation only or contains these elements. The trigger for this phase is the authorization from change management for the release build to take place and ends with the authorization to include the baselined package in the DML. This phase will take place only once during any release. Service asset and configuration management has control over the DML, so the processes of change, SACM, and release and deployment will work closely together.

Deployment   This phase starts with change management authorization for deploying the release package from the DML and/or hardware store if applicable. The package is deployed to the live environment, and this phase ends with handover to the service operation teams and/or early life support. Depending on the selected deployment mechanisms, there may be a number of stages in the deployment activity. In *early life support*, the development and deployment teams are still working alongside the operational teams as the release goes live. This provides support for the release in the initial stages, when the majority of the issues will be identified. This step in release and deployment management is crucial for the support of the release as it goes live and provides speedy resolution of issues and faults. This will improve customer and user satisfaction with the new service and will also assist in the transfer of knowledge to the support teams and the users.

Review and Close   This is where experience and feedback are captured, performance targets are reviewed, achievements are assessed, and lessons are learned. Improvements identified, either to the process or to the release, should be formally captured, and actions should be taken to address any issues.

In Figure 9.6, you can see the various points where the change process provides authorization and triggers for the phases of the release. This would be managed as part of the original change record and would not require separate requests for change. Some organizations may take a different view, particularly in the case of major releases, and require further documented authorization through raising individual requests for change. But either approach is acceptable, because it is important to ensure that your change and release and deployment processes are flexible enough to meet your organization's requirements. The important factor is that authorization is provided through change management to trigger each phase of the release.

FIGURE 9.6   The phases of release and deployment

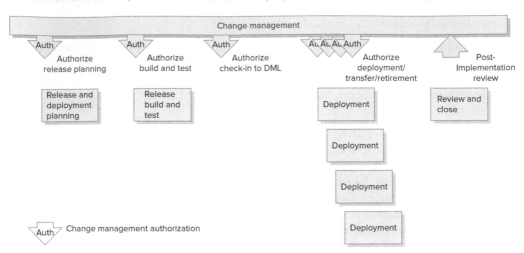

Based on Cabinet Office ITIL material. Reproduced under license from the Cabinet Office.

Summary

In this chapter, we covered the processes in the service transition lifecycle stage.

You learned about the purpose, scope, and objectives of the processes, as well as some of the key concepts associated with them. The processes covered were as follows:

- Transition planning and support
- Knowledge management
- Service asset and configuration management
- Release and deployment management

You also learned about the following concepts:

- Data-Information-Knowledge-Wisdom
- Service knowledge management system
- Configuration items and the configuration management system
- Definitive media library
- The four phases of release and deployment
- The release policy

These processes are all associated with the service transition lifecycle stage, but some have a "whole lifecycle" application. The key processes for the application across the whole lifecycle are as follows:

- Knowledge management
- Service asset and configuration management
- Change management

It is important to remember that all the activities and processes in service transition are working toward delivering a new or changed service into the operational environment in a controlled manner, with minimal disruption and adverse impact to the business.

Exam Essentials

Understand the purpose, objectives, and scope of the transition planning and support process.   This process ensures that all transitions are managed efficiently.

Understand the purpose, objectives, and scope of the service asset and configuration management process.   This process ensures that you capture accurate and reliable information about the assets that make up your services. It applies to all service assets and configuration items.

Recall that configuration items are identified and recorded as part of the configuration management system, and identify the purpose of the system.   The configuration management system is used to integrate information about the infrastructure and provide a comprehensive view of the CIs and relationships that make up your services.

Understand the configuration model, a configuration baseline, and a snapshot.   The configuration model provides a model of the services, assets, and infrastructure by capturing the details of each configuration item and their relationships to each other. A configuration baseline is a capture of the state of the infrastructure at a specific point that is reviewed and agreed upon and used for trending, comparison, and planning. A snapshot is a capture of the infrastructure at a point in time but may contain errors and inaccuracies because it is not reviewed and agreed upon.

Understand the nature and purpose of the definitive media library.   The definitive media library is a specific secure area set aside for managing software media. It may consist of physical and electronic stores for master copies of licensed or authorized software in use in the live environment, as well as the associated documentation.

Understand the purpose, objectives, and scope of knowledge management.   This process ensures knowledge is available in the right place at the right time to enable informed decisions, reducing the need for knowledge rediscovery.

Be able to recall the DIKW model.   Data-Information-Knowledge-Wisdom is a model used to transition from data to information to knowledge to wisdom, ensuring that you add context and understanding to the communications you provide to the organization you support.

Understand the use of the service knowledge management system. The service knowledge management system is the overarching system for managing knowledge relating to service management. It integrates all the existing data sources from your service management processes and enables the DIKW structure for knowledge management across the whole service lifecycle.

Understand the purpose, objectives, and scope of the release and deployment management process and the release policy. This process ensures that releases are planned, scheduled, and controlled so the new or change services are built, tested, and deployed successfully into the operational environment. The release policy describes the manner in which releases will be carried out, provides definitions for release types, and specifies the activities that should be managed under the control of the process.

Know the four phases of the release and deployment management process. The four phases are release and deployment planning, release build and test, deployment, and review and close. All four should be triggered by authorization from the change management process.

Review Questions

You can find the answers in Appendix A.

1. Which of these is the *best* description of the purpose of transition planning and support process?

    A. To provide overall planning and coordination of resources for service transition

    B. To provide coordination for all change management activities

    C. To provide planning for all designs in the service lifecycle

    D. To provide planning for operational activities during release management

2. Which of these statements about transition planning and support is/are correct?

    1. Transition planning and support identifies and manages risks, in accordance with the risk management framework adopted by the organization.

    2. Transition planning and support ensures that repeatable processes are adopted by all engaged in the transition.

        A. 1 only

        B. 2 only

        C. Both

        D. Neither

3. Which of these statements is *not* part of the purpose of the SACM process?

    A. To control the assets that make up your services

    B. To manage the changes to your service assets

    C. To identify service assets

    D. To capture accurate information about service assets

4. SACM is a process that supports which of the following stages of the service lifecycle?

    1. Service strategy

    2. Service design

    3. Service transition

    4. Service operation

    5. Continual service improvement

        A. 1, 3, and 5

        B. 2, 3, and 4

        C. 2, 3, 4, and 5

        D. 1, 2, 3, 4, and 5

5. Which of these statements *best* describes a configuration record?

   A. Any resource or capability that could contribute to the delivery of a service

   B. A service asset that needs to be managed in order to deliver an IT service

   C. A set of attributes and relationships about a CI and stored in a configuration management database

   D. Categorization of the CIs that make up the services

6. The configuration management system (CMS) is composed of four separate layers. Which of these is the correct identification of those layers?

   A. Presentation, knowledge processing, information integration, data

   B. Presentation, information integration, configuration item, data

   C. Presentation, knowledge processing, configuration item, configuration database

   D. Presentation, configuration item, configuration database, knowledge model

7. Which of these statements is *not* an objective of knowledge management?

   A. To improve the quality of decision making throughout the service lifecycle

   B. To capture and maintain information about the assets that make up your services

   C. To enable efficiency in the service provider and customer, by encouraging the reuse of information

   D. To maintain a service knowledge management system

8. Which of these statements is *not* a recommended part of a release policy?

   A. A unique identification structure or naming convention to ensure releases can be easily identified and tracked

   B. Definitions of the roles and responsibilities required for the management of the release throughout all its stages

   C. Definition of the configuration management database naming convention

   D. Use of the definitive media library for all software asset releases

9. Which of these is *not* one of the phases of the release and deployment process?

   A. Release and deployment planning

   B. Deployment

   C. Review and close

   D. Verification and audit

10. Early life support is an important concept in the release and deployment management process. In which phase of the release and deployment process does early life support happen?

    A. Release build and test

    B. Review and close

    C. Deployment

    D. Release deployment and planning

Chapter

10

Delivering the Service: The Service Operation Lifecycle Stage

---

THE FOLLOWING ITIL FOUNDATION EXAM OBJECTIVES ARE DISCUSSED IN THIS CHAPTER:

- ✓ **2-9. Account for the purpose, objectives and scope of service operation**

- ✓ **2-10. Briefly explain what value service operation provides to the business**

- ✓ **Unit 3: Generic concepts and definitions**

   3-33. The role of communication in service operation

- ✓ **6-1. Explain the role, objectives and organizational structures for:**

   The service desk function

- ✓ **6-2. State the role and objectives of:**

   The technical management function

   The application management function

   The IT operations management function

This chapter covers the how the IT service provider organizes to deliver the services to the required standard. The service operation stage is when the service is actually being delivered, and often is a much longer stage than the previous stages of strategy, design and transition. We will cover the purpose, objectives, and scope for each process, along with the value it provides to the business. We will discuss the generic concepts and definitions involved in this lifecycle stage and consider the importance of good communication in achieving successful service operations. Finally, we shall look at the service operation functions identified in ITIL. These are the service desk, technical management, application management and operations management functions.

Understanding the Purpose, Objectives, and Scope of Service Operation

The output from service strategy, design, and transition becomes visible in service operation. It is in the operational stage that the service, which was originally considered in strategy, put together in design, and rolled out in transition, actually delivers the benefit that the business requires. It is also a much longer stage of the lifecycle than the first three stages; the service should continue to meet the business requirement for months or even years.

The majority of IT staff is involved (to a greater or lesser extent) in the service operation stage. They may contribute to other lifecycle stages; their main focus is the delivery of the operational services. In this chapter, we examine the four functions involved in the service lifecycle.

The Purpose of Service Operation

The purpose of the service operation stage of the service lifecycle is to deliver the service at the level that was agreed through the service level management process. This includes all the activities required to deliver the service as well as managing the technology used to deliver the service (such as applying updates, backing up data, and so on).

Service operation must deliver the service effectively but also has to ensure that the cost of that delivery is within the operational costs that formed part of the original business case. Should a service be operated at a higher cost than was originally envisaged, the benefits that were planned, such as cost savings, may never be realized.

Many of the processes that we have discussed when examining the other lifecycle stages take place during the service operation stage. Service level management, for example, is a process that is undertaken as part of service design; once operational, however, the monitoring and reporting of the service performance takes place during the operation phase. The same is true of capacity and availability management; ongoing monitoring and adjustments of these aspects take place during service operation. It is essential, therefore, that *all* of the processes that are operated during the operation phase work effectively and efficiently. Continual service improvement (CSI) also depends on service operation producing the required information to allow improvement opportunities to be identified, baselines to be taken, and the success of any improvements measured.

Service operation staff members must view the service as a whole and be given the tools they need to evaluate whether the delivery meets the standard required. It is a common error to have staff members concentrate on individual aspects of a service or to ignore those parts of the service provided by third parties, losing sight of the end-to-end service as it appears to the customer. Technology can be used to spot deviations from expected service or response levels very quickly, allowing remedial action to be put in place immediately.

The Objectives of Service Operation

It is the job of the service operation phase to deliver the service as agreed on in the SLA; this ensures that the business receives the level of service it expects. Some service outages are inevitable; service operation will work to reduce both the number and impact of outages. The service operation process of problem management aims to reduce repeat incidents that disrupt business activities, while incident management aims to resolve those incidents that do occur as quickly as possible.

Service operation is also responsible for controlling access to IT services. The access management process ensures that only authorized users can have access to the services provided.

The Scope of Service Operation

The scope of service operation described in the ITIL framework includes the "processes, functions, organization, and tools" that are used to deliver and support the agreed services. This lifecycle stage is responsible for performing the critical day-to-day activities and processes that ensure the service meets the business requirement and enables the business to achieve its objectives. It also collects the performance data that will be required by continual service improvement to identify and track improvement opportunities. The ITIL Service Operation publication provides guidance on the successful management of the following:

The Services Themselves   This includes all the activities required to deliver the services consistently within the agreed service levels. These activities may be carried out by the service provider, an external supplier, or the user or customer of that service.

The Service Management Processes   These include the service operation processes of event, incident, problem and access management, and request fulfillment. (We will be looking at the service operation processes in Chapters 11 and 12.) In addition to these processes, service operation has responsibility for carrying out activities associated with processes that originated in other lifecycle stages. Figure 10.1 shows these processes. Capacity management, for example, is a design process; however, the day-to-day monitoring and tuning of capacity takes place in service operation.)

FIGURE 10.1   Service operation involvement in other lifecycle processes

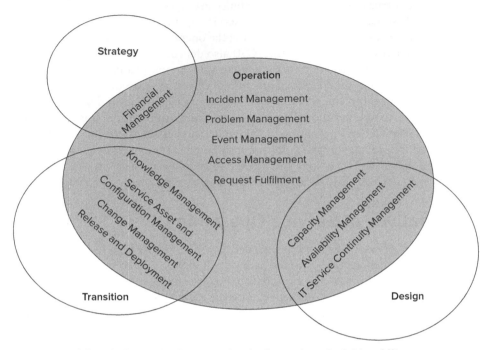

Strategy

Operation

Financial Management

Incident Management

Problem Management

Event Management

Access Management

Request Fulfilment

Knowledge Management

Service Asset and Configuration Management

Change Management

Release and Deployment

Capacity Management

Availability Management

IT Service Continuity Management

Transition

Design

Based on Cabinet Office ITIL® material. Reproduced under license from the Cabinet Office.

The Technology   Delivering IT services depends on the use of appropriate technology (network, desktops, servers, databases, data, monitoring tools, and so on). Service operation is responsible for managing the technology that delivers the services.

The People   Despite automation, service operation depends on the actions of the support staff members to ensure the service runs as it should. Their management of the technology and processes is the key to successful service delivery. In this chapter, we will be examining the people who deliver the service.

The Value Service Operation Delivers to the Business

The ITIL framework offers guidance on the best practices that can be used in the various lifecycle stages, and following this advice can deliver real benefits. In the area of service operation, the benefits to be achieved from following best practices include the following:

- Financial savings from reduced downtime as a result of the implementation of the service operation processes of problem and incident management. Problem management will reduce the frequency of failures so that less time (and therefore money) is wasted by the business not being able to work. It will ensure that skilled IT staff members concentrate their efforts on identifying and removing the root cause of the incident, thus preventing recurrence. Meanwhile, efficient incident management ensures that the service is restored as soon as possible, often by service desk staff members using defined workarounds. This both speeds up the service restoration and reduces costs, because the more expensive IT staff members are not called on to resolve simple incidents.

- Service operation includes the production of management information regarding the efficiency and effectiveness of the service delivery. This is used by other processes to target, justify, and implement continual service improvement initiatives.

- By carrying out the access management activities, service operation ensures that services are protected from unauthorized access, in accordance with the organization's security policy.

- The request management process enables the business to obtain standard services quickly and with minimum bureaucracy.

- By using technology to automate routine tasks, based on the information provided by the event management process, service operation reduces the number of staff members required to operate the service. This means as the number of users grows and the complexity of the services increases, the number of people needed to support the users remains broadly the same. This reduces costs and frees up technical staff members to concentrate on identifying improvements and new opportunities. Automation also delivers a more reliable and consistent service.

Organizing for Service Operations

ITIL describes four main functions that are responsible for carrying out all the lifecycle processes. These are the technical management, application management, operations management functions, and the service desk. The IT operations management function is further divided into IT operations control and facilities management. We will cover each of these in turn and then look at where the responsibilities of each function overlap. It is important to remember that ITIL is not prescriptive and does not specify an organizational structure or names of teams. The responsibilities of the functions described here should be carried out, but each organization will have its own structure.

Technical Management

Whatever the name given to the team or teams in any particular organization (infrastructure support, technical support, network management, and so on), the function referred to in the ITIL framework as *technical management* is required to manage and develop the IT infrastructure. This function covers the groups or teams that together have the technical expertise and knowledge to ensure that the infrastructure works effectively in support of the services required by the business.

Role

The technical management function has a number of responsibilities:

- It is responsible for managing the IT infrastructure. This would include ensuring that the staff members performing this function have the necessary technical knowledge to design, test, manage, and improve IT services.

- Although we discuss this function under service operation, the function provides appropriately skilled staff members to support the entire lifecycle. Technical management staff members would be involved in drawing up the technical strategy and ensuring that the infrastructure can support the overall service strategy. Technical management staff members would also carry out the technical design of new or changed services and would be involved in planning and implementing their transition to the operational environment.

- Once the service is live, technical management provides technical support, resolving incidents, investigating problems, responding to alerts, and specifying any changes or updates required to have the service operate efficiently. Technical management staff members will identify service improvements and work with the CSI manager to design, test, and implement these improvements.

It is the responsibility of the manager or managers of this function to ensure the correct number of staff members, with the correct skills to carry out the required tasks. Specifying the numbers and skill levels required is discussed as part of strategy and detailed as part of service design (as discussed in Chapter 3 and Chapter 4). Transition tests that the staff members are able to support the service as designed, and CSI identifies any improvements or training requirements. The technical manager must decide whether to employ new staff members with the correct skills, to train existing staff members, or to use short-term contract resources to meet a particular requirement. Larger organizations may have a team of subject-matter experts that can be called upon when required by subsidiary departments, without the need for those skills to be developed across the organization.

Most of the everyday operational support activities will be undertaken by the operations support staff members, but it is the responsibility of technical management, as the experts in the technology, to guide and support the operations staff members.

Objectives

The objectives of technical management include the following:

- Providing the appropriate technical infrastructure to support the business processes. This should take account of the availability and capacity requirements, providing a stable resilient infrastructure at an affordable cost.

- Planning and designing the technical aspects of any new or changed service.

- Implementing these technical aspects and supporting them in the live environment, using the technical expertise that the function possesses to ensure that any issues that arise are swiftly resolved.

Applications Management

The second service operation function described in the ITIL framework is that of *application management*. This function shares many features with the technical management function, although in this case it is the application software that is supported and managed throughout its lifecycle, rather than the infrastructure. Application management and applications development are not the same, and it is important to understand the differences between them:

- Application *management* is involved in every stage of the service lifecycle, from ascertaining the requirements through design and transition and then operation and improvement.

- Application *development* is mostly involved in single, finite activities, such as designing and building a new service. We discuss this in more detail later in this chapter.

As with technical management, the application management function may not be called this in many organizations. Whichever group of staff members is responsible for managing and supporting operational software applications is the application management function. As with technical management, this function may be split across a number of teams.

Application management may carry out some tasks as part of application development projects, such as design or testing. This is not the same as the work of application development itself.

Role

The application management function is involved in all applications. Even when the function has recommended purchase of the application from an external supplier, there is still a requirement for management activities to take place. These activities are very similar to those of the technical management function:

- It is responsible for managing the IT applications. This would include ensuring that the staff members performing this function have the necessary technical knowledge to design, test, manage, and improve IT services.

- It is the custodian of technical knowledge and expertise related to managing applications.

- Although we discuss this function under service operation, the function provides appropriately skilled staff members to support the entire lifecycle. Application management staff members would be involved in drawing up the application strategy. They would carry out the design of new or changed applications and would be involved in planning and implementing their transition to the operational environment. Once the service is live, application management provides support, resolving incidents, investigating problems, and specifying changes or updates required to have the service operate efficiently. Application management staff members will identify service improvements and work with the CSI manager to design, test, and implement them.

Application management staffing and training responsibilities are the same as those identified for technical management, and the function similarly interacts with the other stages of the lifecycle.

Application management also performs other specific roles:

- Application support ensures that the operations management staff members are given the correct training to enable the applications to be run efficiently.

- As part of service design, application management may carry out a training needs analysis covering the service operation staff members and provide the required training, but this role is a continuous one, providing day-to-day support to the operations staff members.

Objectives

The objectives of application management are to do the following:

- Identify functional and manageability requirements for application software

- Help in the design of applications

- Assist in their deployment

- Support the applications in the live environment

- Identify and implement improvements

To be successful, application management must ensure that applications are well-designed, taking account of both the utility and warranty aspects of service design. They must be able to deliver the right functionality at a reasonable cost, if the business benefit is to be realized. The provision of the correct numbers of appropriately skilled staff members is essential so that these skills may be applied to resolve any application failures.

Application Development vs. Application Management

As discussed earlier, application management and application development have separate aims and responsibilities. These two groups may work closely together or may be quite separate, with different reporting structures and a different interface with the business. Application development, as we said earlier, is normally a finite activity to develop an application, moving on to the next requirement when finished. Application management, on the other hand, remains involved throughout the lifecycle of the application.

- Development focuses on the utility aspects, and most of its work is carried out on applications developed in-house. Management activities consider both warranty and utility and are carried out whether the application is internally developed or purchased.

- Development is concerned with functionality and does not consider how it is to be operated or managed, whereas application management is concerned with how this functionality is to be delivered consistently.

- Development is often carried out as part of a project, with defined deliverables, costs, and handoff dates. This differs from application management, whose activities are ongoing throughout the service lifecycle and whose costs may not be separately identified.

- Developers may not have an understanding of what is required to manage and operate an application because they do not support the applications they have developed, instead moving on to the next development project. Similarly, application management staff members may have little involvement in development, meaning that they have a reduced understanding of how applications are developed.

- Development staff members work to software development lifecycles. Application management staff members are often involved only in the operation and improvement stages of the service lifecycle.

Figure 10.2 shows the differing roles of the application management and application development teams; the application development team is primarily concerned with the functionality of the application, whereas the application management team considers how the application infrastructure will support the application and how it will be built, deployed, and monitored in operation.

FIGURE 10.2   Role of teams in the application management lifecycle

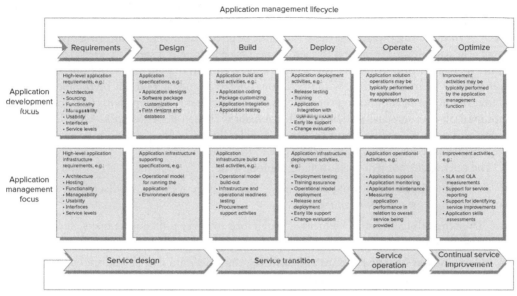

Based on Cabinet Office ITIL® material. Reproduced under license from the Cabinet Office.

There is a growing tendency to end the division between the two teams, because it is confusing for the business to understand. Ideally, this will mean a broadening of the development role to include considering how applications will operate, and it will mean more involvement in development for staff members who will be managing the application.

Operations Management

The role of *operations management* is to carry out all the day-to-day activities that are required to deliver the services provided. The applications and technical management functions are the subject-matter experts in their respective fields and define what operational activities are to take place; operations management's role is to make sure these are done.

The service design stage defined the required service levels, and the transition phase carried out tests to ensure that these were achievable; operations management is responsible for ensuring that these service levels are met consistently. Although the primary focus is on stability and availability, operations management will seek to continually improve by implementing changes that will help protect the live service or by reducing costs and opportunities for human error by implementing automation of routine tasks.

The quality of the service delivered to the business is dependent on operations management. This role is divided into two parts, covered next.

IT Operations Control

This part of operations management oversees the IT infrastructure. In larger organizations, this may be carried out as part of an operations bridge or Network Operations Center (NOC). In these organizations, there are dedicated staff members monitoring operational events on consoles and reacting to them as necessary, often in a separate area from the rest of IT. In smaller organizations, the line between technical management and operations control may be more blurred, with operations control being carried out by the technical management team, monitoring the systems from their desks, perhaps with one or two wall-mounted plasma screens. Whichever arrangement is chosen depends upon what suits the organization, but it is important that there are clearly defined expectations to ensure that the operations control tasks are carried out to the level required.

The operations control tasks include the following:

- The centralized monitoring and management of system events, as discussed, sometimes referred to as *console management*.

- The scheduling and management of batch jobs to carry out routine tasks, such as database updates.

- Carrying out backups of data and ensuring that this data can be restored if and when required. This may include the backup of entire systems or the restoration of individual files that a user may have corrupted.

- Although most printing is now carried out directly by the users, there may be certain requirements for centralized printing; pay slips will need to be printed in a secure environment to ensure confidentiality, and large print volumes may make centralized printing more efficient. The printing and distribution of these or other electronic output is an operations control task.

- Operations control will also undertake maintenance activities, under the guidance of the technical or application management functions; this could include archiving data, applying system packs, updating virus signatures, and so on.

Facilities Management

The other part of operations management is *facilities management*. Staff members involved in this will be responsible for the physical IT environment. This would include the following:

- Ensuring the necessary power is supplied (including any requirements for its quality, such as the prevention of any power spikes).

- Operating and maintaining any uninterruptible power supply (UPS) and generators. Facilities management is responsible for ensuring that these are available and for testing to ensure that they will work as designed, in the event of a power failure. This role may cover just a server room in a smaller organization or one or more data centers for larger ones.

- Ensuring the power provided at any disaster recovery sites has the required protection from failure and ensuring the maintenance of satisfactory air conditioning/cooling for rooms housing IT equipment, whether this is a server room or a complete data center.

Many organizations have undertaken data center or server consolidation projects in recent years to take advantage of technical advances. The facilities management function would be responsible for managing any such projects. In the case where the data center management is carried out by a third party, it would be the responsibility of facilities management to ensure that the external service provider was carrying out the required tasks to the agreed standard and managing any exceptions utilizing the supplier management process.

To be effective, operations management needs to understand the technology and how it supports the services provided, although this level of knowledge will be less than that provided by the technical and application management functions. There is a risk that operations staff members do not interact with the business as part of their work and so may fail to appreciate the business impact of failures or to understand the business importance of services, thinking of them in purely technical terms. It is essential that they have adequate understanding of the business aspect; the information showing how technology supports the business is available in the CMS, but specific training may be required to ensure that they have the necessary appreciation of the impact technology has on the business.

The importance of stability of services has been already mentioned; one way of maintaining that stability is to ensure that routine tasks are carried out consistently, no matter which staff members are on shift. This requires that properly documented procedures and technical manuals are available to operations staff members.

The performance of the operations management function should be measured against clear objectives, based on the performance of the service, not merely of the technology. Delivering the service to the required level, within the agreed cost, is essential, so operations management should be able to demonstrate the effectiveness of what they do but also prove that they are operating at maximum efficiency. Operations management should always strive to optimize the use of existing technology and exploit new technical advances to provide the required level of service at the best cost.

Objectives

The objectives of IT operations management include continuing to provide stable services to enable the business to obtain the business benefits from the service, while also investigating possible improvements to enable the service to be provided more cost-effectively.

Service operation's other objective is to overcome any failures that do occur as quickly as possible in order to minimize the impact to the business.

Overlapping Responsibilities Between Functions

The responsibilities for managing many aspects of the operational environment are often shared, with the technical management and application management teams providing specialist support for each area, while operations management carries out the monitoring and maintenance activities and dealing with the simpler faults. Figure 10.3 shows this overlap; under the headings of technical management and application management there are examples of areas of responsibility such as networks and specialist applications, with the figure showing how the responsibility for these is shared with service operations. The figure also shows those activities that are entirely service operations' responsibility, such as backups. The service desk is shown for completeness, but its responsibilities and those of the other functions do not overlap.

FIGURE 10.3   Service operations functions

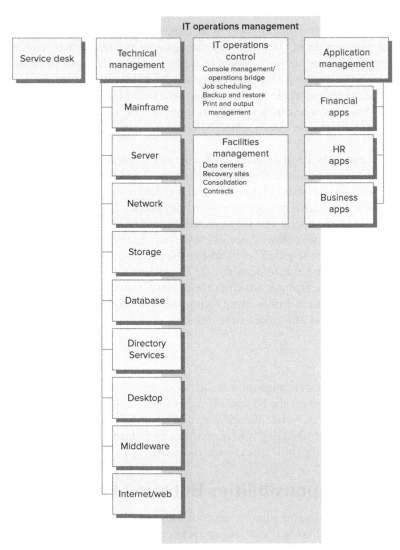

Based on Cabinet Office ITIL® material. Reproduced under license from the Cabinet Office.

The Service Desk Function

The final service operation function described by the ITIL framework is that of the service desk. A *service desk* is a functional unit consisting of a dedicated number of staff members responsible for dealing with a variety of service activities, usually made via telephone calls, web interface, or automatically reported infrastructure events. We will cover this function in more detail, because it plays a critical role in customer satisfaction. Although the service desk staff members do not have the same level of in-depth technical knowledge as the staff members in the other functions, their role is just as important.

The service desk function is the most visible of the four functions; every hour of every day they come into contact with business users at all levels. A poor service desk can result in a poor overall impression of the IT department, while an efficient, customer-focused team can ensure customer satisfaction even when the service is operating below the agreed service level.

An essential feature of a service desk is that it provides a single point of contact (SPOC) for users needing assistance. It provides a single day-to-day interface with IT, whatever the user requirement. It provides a variety of services:

- Handles incidents, resolving as many as possible, where the resolution is straightforward and within the service desk authority level

- Owns incidents that are escalated to other support groups for resolution

- Reports problems to the problem management staff members

- Handles service requests (including ensuring that requests for software to be installed have the required license)

- Provides information to users

- Communicates with the business about major incidents, upcoming changes, and so on

- Manages requests for change on the user's behalf if required

- Manages the performance of third-party maintenance providers, ensuring that they provide the agreed service

- Monitors incidents and service requests against the targets in the SLA and provides reporting from the service desk tool to show the level of service achieved

- Updates the CMS as required

- Gathers availability figures, based on incident data

Staffing

The service desk will use a service management tool and other technical resources to enable it to carry out its tasks and will follow defined processes (especially incident management and request fulfillment). Although these tools and processes are important, the people aspect of the service desk is critical. The interactions with the customers and users require good communication skills, in addition to technical knowledge. Knowing the answer is only part of the job; explaining it in terms that users understand is essential.

Recruiting and retaining good service desk staff members is the key to customer satisfaction. This function often acts as an entry level to the other functions, providing staff members with an understanding of all the services, the technology that supports them, and the business impact of failure. This provides an excellent basis for future technical specialization.

Service desk staff members require a mix of technical knowledge and interpersonal skills. The technical knowledge may not be in depth, but it covers all the services provided by the IT service provider. The service desk analyst can be said to know a little about a lot of services, rather than a lot about a few.

The ability to correctly prioritize incidents based on business impact and urgency (see the discussion of incident management in Chapter 11) requires that the service desk analyst has a good level of awareness about the business processes. Added to this knowledge is the requirement to be patient, helpful, assertive when dealing with support teams or third parties who are failing to meet targets, well-organized, and calm under pressure.

Service desks are organized differently dependent upon the particular requirements of the organization. We cover various service desk structures later in the chapter. The skill level required may also vary; the service desk may be tasked with resolving a high proportion (75 percent to 80 percent) of incidents, or it may be limited to logging and escalating them for resolution by another team. Service desks are often outsourced to specialist providers; the decision whether to do this will be based on the overall IT strategy. If the decision is made to outsource, the third-party supplier's performance must be monitored and managed closely to ensure that this essential service is being provided to the highest standard.

Role

The provision of a single point of contact is accepted in many industries as being central to good customer service. Without a service desk, users would have to try to identify which IT support team they should approach. This could be confusing for the business, leading to a delay in having their issue resolved. Technical staff members would waste time dealing with issues outside their specialist area or issues that could be dealt with by more junior staff members.

Providing a good service desk leads to a number of benefits:

- Increased focus of customer service
- Increased customer satisfaction
- Easier provision of support through the single point of contact
- Faster resolution of incidents and fulfillment of requests at the service desk, without the need for further escalation
- Reduced business impact of failures because of faster resolution
- More effective use of specialist IT staff members

- Accurate data regarding the numbers and nature of incidents, taken from the service desk tool

Objective

As we have said already, the main objective of the service desk is to provide a single point of contact. The next most important objective is to restore service in the event of a failure. This may not mean a complete resolution of the incident, but the provision of a work-around, to enable the user to continue working. Fulfilling a request, resetting a password, or answering a "How do I ... ?" query all help the user get back to work as soon as possible.

Other responsibilities of the service desk include the following:

- Logging all incidents and requests, with the appropriate level of detail
- Categorizing incidents and requests for future analysis
- Agreeing on the correct priority with the user based on impact and urgency (utilizing SLAs wherever possible for consistency)
- Investigating, diagnosing, and resolving incidents whenever possible
- Deciding upon the correct support team to whom to escalate the incident should the service desk be unable to resolve it
- Communicating progress to the users
- Confirming closure of resolved incidents with the user
- Carrying out surveys to ascertain the level of customer satisfaction

We will cover some of these activities in more depth when we look at the incident and request processes.

Service Desk Organizational Structures

The best structure for the service desk is dependent upon the size and structure of the organization. A global organization will have different needs from one with all its employees based in the same location. Here we look at the most common structures; the best option may be a combination of them.

Local Service Desk

This option provides a service desk co-located with the users it serves; an organization with three offices would have three local service desks. There are advantages with this approach, in that the service desk is local, so it understands the local business priorities. Where the offices are spread across different countries, local service desks provide support in the language of the local users, work in the same time zone, have the same public holidays, and so on. This structure can also be useful when different locations have specialized support needs. The basic principle of a single point of contact is retained, because, from the user perspective, they have only one number to call and are unaware of any other desks that may exist.

This is an expensive option, because each new office location would require a new service desk too. At quiet times, there would be several service desk staff members spread across the various desks waiting for calls. There are potential issues with incidents and requests being logged in different languages, possibly in different systems; this makes incident analysis and problem identification difficult. Sharing knowledge is also more difficult: an incident that could be resolved by one service desk might be escalated by another, because the resolution has not been shared between the desks.

To overcome these issues, IT management must ensure that information is shared effectively. Procedures need to be put in place to ensure that issues affecting more than one location are managed effectively, without duplication of effort, or each service desk assuming that another desk is responsible. Figure 10.4 shows the local structure.

FIGURE 10.4 Local service desk structure

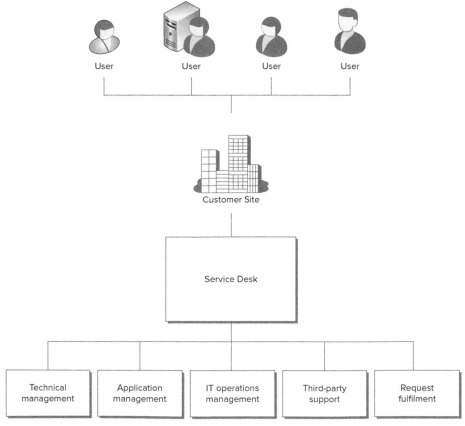

Centralized Service Desk

A more common structure for service desks is that of a centralized service desk. In this model, all users contact the same service desk. This has the benefit of providing economies of scale, because there is no duplication of provision. Specialist technology, such as intelligent call distribution or an integrated service management tool, may be justified for a centralized service desk, but not when implementing this technology across many sites. There are no issues with confusion regarding ownership of major incidents, and knowledge-sharing becomes much more straightforward. Offering a service at times of low demand is more cost effective when only one service desk needs to be staffed.

Staff members on a centralized desk will gain more experience of particular incidents, which a local service desk may encounter only occasionally, leading to an increased ability to resolve these issues immediately. Where the centralized desk is supporting users in many countries, the language issue may be resolved by either of the following:

- Employing staff members with language skills and using technology to allocate calls requiring support in a particular language to staff members who have that language ability. Staff members would then log the call in the main language.

- Standardizing on one language; callers would need to report incidents in that language, and support would be provided in it. This option depends on the type of organization and whether its users may reasonably be expected to be able to converse in the language. Local superusers may be required to support users without the necessary language ability and to log calls on their behalf.

To provide support to a global organization, a 24/7 service may be required. Where the resolution requires a physical intervention (unjamming a printer, for example), the service desk would require local staff members to provide that support, answerable to the service desk.

Consideration should also be given to maintaining service continuity, because an event that affects a centralized service desk would impact support across the entire organization. A plan to provide the service from another location, possibly using different staff members, in the event of a disaster must be developed and tested, in conjunction with IT service continuity management. There should also be plans in place to ensure the service desk's resilience in the event of disruption to the network or a power failure.

Figure 10.5 shows the centralized structure.

Virtual Service Desk

The third organizational option described by ITIL is that of a virtual service desk. This option consists of two or more service desk locations that operate as one desk. Calls and emails are distributed across the staff members as if they were in one centralized location. This ensures that the workload is balanced across all the desks. To the user, the virtual service desk appears as a single entity; the users may be completely unaware that this is not the case in reality. The virtual service desk retains the single point of contact principle.

The considerations we discussed earlier regarding knowledge sharing and clear ownership apply even more in this scenario, as does the need for all calls to be logged immediately.

FIGURE 10.5   Centralized service desk structure

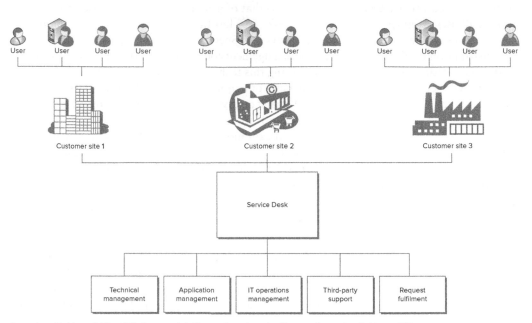

Based on Cabinet Office ITIL® material. Reproduced under license from the Cabinet Office.

Users will become very frustrated if they call the service desk and explain an issue in detail, only to find when they call for a second time that the service desk analyst can find no record of their first call.

The ability to route calls to analysts with particular language knowledge or to adopt one language for all users can be considered, as with a centralized desk. Calls must be logged on one common system, using one language, because the next analyst to handle the incident may be in another location.

The virtual service desk structure allows for a variety of ways of working. Many call centers use home-based staff members, who log on to the service desk telephone system and are allocated calls. Extra staff members from other teams can supplement the core service desk staff members at busy times, without the users being aware. Many of us have had the experience of calling a local company, only to have the call answered offshore outside of normal hours or during bust times.

Offshoring support (providing support from another geographical location where staff members' costs may be lower) can be cost-effective but requires careful management to ensure consistency of service. Managers need to be culturally sensitive, because users may become irritated by staff members behaving in a way in which they find unfamiliar.

Offshore Support Difficulties

A large insurance company in the United Kingdom decided to offshore its service desk. Overseas staff members were recruited carefully, with tests to validate their language and technical skills. After some months, an analysis of telephone traffic showed that many customers were hanging up as soon as they realized that their call was being answered offshore. Focus groups of users were interviewed to try to understand why this was happening.

The answer was not the level of technical support but a combination of the lack of local knowledge and cultural issues. The offshore staff members had been coached in customer service and were putting the recommendations into effect, explaining to the user what they were doing, thanking the user after every piece of information was provided, and so on. The users were not used to this level of service and expressed a wish that "the service desk staff members just got on with the task and stopped talking about it!"

One benefit of a virtual structure is that it has built-in resilience; should one location go offline because of a major disruption affecting that location, the service would continue with little or no impact.

Figure 10.6 shows the virtual service desk structure.

Follow the Sun

The fourth structure described within ITIL is known as *follow the sun*. This is a form of virtual service desk, but with this structure, the allocation of calls across the various desks is based on time of day, rather than workload.

"Follow the sun" enables a global organization to provide support around the clock, without needing to employ staff members at night to work on the service desk. A number of service desks will each work standard office hours. The calls will be allocated to whichever desk or desks are open at that time. Typically, this might mean a European service desk will handle calls until the end of the European working day, when calls will then be allocated to a desk or desks in North America. When the working day in North America finishes, calls are directed at another desk or desks in the Asia-Pacific region, before being directed back to the European desk at the start of the next European working day.

This option is an attractive one for many global organizations, providing 24-hour coverage without the need for shift or on-call payments. The requirements for effective call logging, a centralized database, and a common language for data entry referred to earlier for the virtual structure apply equally here. Procedures for handoff between desks are also required to ensure that the desk that is taking over knows the status of any major incidents, and so on.

FIGURE 10.6 Virtual service desk structure

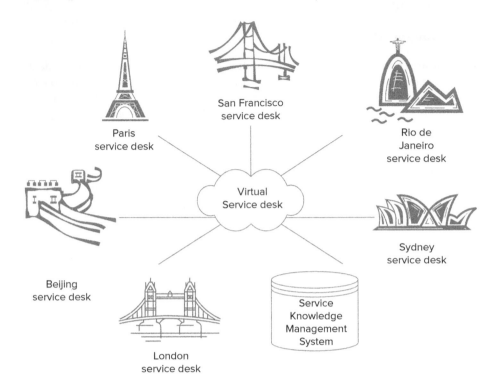

Paris service desk

San Francisco service desk

Rio de Janeiro service desk

Virtual Service desk

Sydney service desk

Beijing service desk

London service desk

Service Knowledge Management System

Based on Cabinet Office ITIL® material. Reproduced under license from the Cabinet Office.

To the user, the single point of contact still applies; they have one number to call, no matter who answers it or where the service desk analyst may be located.

Specialized Service Desk Groups

Another possible variant on the previous structures is to provide specialist support for particular services. In this structure, a user may call the usual service desk number and then choose an option depending on the issue they have. Typically, the message would say, "Press 1 if the call is regarding system X, press 2 if it is regarding system Y, or hold for a service desk analyst if your call is in regard to anything else."

Although this approach can be useful, especially where in-depth knowledge is required to resolve a call, it is not popular with users when it expands to numerous options to choose from, followed by another message saying "Thank you. You now have a further *n* options."

There is a danger that the user does not always know what support they need and may choose the wrong option, leading to delay and frustration. For example, a printer that will not print may be because of a hardware fault, a network issue, an application malfunction, or a user error. The user will not know which option to choose.

This specialist support option works best for a small number of complex services that require a level of both business and technical knowledge beyond what can reasonably be expected of a service desk analyst. Another possible reason to use this option is when the service contains confidential data. In this situation, the organization may wish to limit access to a small number of specialist support staff.

Summary

This chapter covered the purpose, objectives, and scope of service operation and covered how people are grouped into functions to deliver the service. The importance of the service operation stage was covered; it is in this stage that the services deliver business value and the return on the investment of the earlier lifecycle stages is realized (or not!).

We covered which processes from other lifecycle stages require service operation action. We looked at the overlapping responsibilities of the operations management function with the technical management and application management functions. We covered the role and importance of the service desk in providing a single point of contact for IT for the business, together with the various service desk structures that may be suitable for different situations. We also considered the skills and attributes required for service desk staff members.

In the following chapters, we will be covering the major service operation processes of incident and problem management in some depth, and looking in less detail at the other processes of this lifecycle stage: access management, request management, and event management.

Exam Essentials

Understand the purpose of the service operation: to deliver the services that have been designed and transitioned as efficiently as possible.   During this stage, faults that were not detected during transition will be identified and resolved, and the delivery of the service will be optimized.

Service operations is required to deliver the services in line with the SLAs that have been agreed with the business.   The transition stage should have validated the SLA targets through testing and piloting the service; it is for service operations to continue to meet the SLA targets during the operational stage of the service lifecycle.

By delivering the services efficiently and within service targets, service operations ensure that the business benefits from the service as planned.   Be able to name and describe the four service operation functions: technical management, application management, IT operations management, and the service desk.

Understand the role of the technical and application management functions in providing resources to the other lifecycle stages and in specifying the operational tasks that service operation staff members should carry out. Understand the overlap between these functions and operations management.

Explain the difference between application development and application support. Understand the two areas of operations management: operations control and facilities management. Be able to think of examples of the responsibilities of each of these areas, such as monitoring environmental conditions (IT facilities management) and console management (operations control).

Know the role and importance of the service desk function. Be able to list the skills and attributes that service desk staff members should possess, such as business awareness, technical awareness, customer focus, and so on. Be able to describe the different service desk structures of local, central, virtual, and follow the sun, as well as when each might be used. Understand the advantages and disadvantages of each option.

Review Questions

You can find the answers in Appendix A.

1. Service operation includes which of the following activities?
   A. Testing the service
   B. Rolling out the service
   C. Deciding whether to retire the service
   D. Optimizing the service

2. Many processes from other lifecycle stages also take place during the operation stage. Which of the following processes does not fall into this category?
   A. IT service continuity management
   B. Availability management
   C. Service level management
   D. Design coordination

3. Which of the following is the correct list of functions described in ITIL?
   A. Technical management function, facilities management function, service desk function
   B. Infrastructure management function, desktop support function, application management function, service desk function
   C. Technical management function, operations management function, application management function, service desk function
   D. Infrastructure management function, service desk function, application development function

4. Which of these activities is facilities management *not* responsible for?
   A. Maintaining air conditioning to the required level in the server rooms
   B. Defining the infrastructure requirements to support the services
   C. Ensuring the power supply at any disaster recovery sites meets the requirement
   D. Testing the UPS and generators

5. Match the activities to the following functions.
   1. Activity: Console management
   2. Activity: Identifying functional and manageability requirements for application software
   3. Activity: Providing a single point of contact

4. Activity: Designing and managing the infrastructure
   a. Function: Service desk
   b. Function: Technical management
   c. Function: Application management
   d. Function: Operations management

A. 1d, 2a, 3c, 4b

B. 1d, 2c, 3a, 4b

C. 1a, 2b, 3c, 4d

D. 1b, 2c, 3d, 4a

6. The service desk is *not* responsible for which of the following?

   A. Providing a first point of contact

   B. Resolving straightforward incidents

   C. Preventing incidents from recurring

   D. Providing updates to users

7. The service desk carries out two processes. What are they?

   1. Incident management

   2. Design coordination

   3. Request fulfillment

   4. Change management

      A. 2 and 4

      B. 1 and 3

      C. All of the above

      D. 3 and 4

8. Which of the following should service desk staff members possess?

   1. Specialist technical knowledge

   2. Customer service skills

   3. Technical ability

   4. Business knowledge

      A. 1 and 2

      B. 2 and 3

      C. All of the above

      D. 2, 3, and 4

9. Operations management is split into two aspects. What are they called?

    A. Facilities management, operations development

    B. Facilities ownership, operations control

    C. Console management, facilities management

    D. Facilities management, operations control

10. Which of the following is *not* a service desk structure described in ITIL?

    A. Virtual

    B. Matrix

    C. Follow the sun

    D. Local

Chapter

11

The Major Service Operation Processes

THE FOLLOWING ITIL FOUNDATION EXAM OBJECTIVES ARE DISCUSSED IN THIS CHAPTER:

✓ **Unit 3: Generic concepts and definitions**

- 3-26. Incident
- 3-27. Impact, urgency and priority
- 3-29. Problem
- 3-30. Workaround
- 3-31. Known error
- 3-32. Known error database (KEDB)

✓ **5-7. Explain the purpose, objectives, scope, basic concepts, process activities and interfaces for:**

- 5-71 Incident management
- 5-72 Problem management

Incidents and Problems: Two Key Service Management Concepts

The two processes of incident and problem management are among the most important of all the ITIL processes. They are often the first to be implemented by an organization that has decided to adopt the ITIL framework. The differentiation between incident management and problem management is an important distinction, and an organization that has adopted both of these processes has made a major advance toward improving their services and their service management.

Both these processes are carried out by every IT service provider, whether they are called by these names or not. All service providers fix faults as quickly as possible when they occur (incident management) and try to ascertain why the fault occurred so that it can be prevented from happening again (problem management). Many organizations do not differentiate between the two processes, however, and problem management in particular may not be carried out in a consistent fashion. A failure to appreciate the difference between problems and incidents may result in delayed service restoration following an incident and in allowing incidents to recur, causing business disruption each time.

ITIL provides guidance for the best approach to these two key processes. Effective incident management will improve availability, ensuring that users are able to get back to work quickly following a failure. Problem management will improve the overall quality and availability of services (and as such works in conjunction with continual service improvement); it also makes best use of skilled IT staff, who are freed from resolving repeat incidents and are able to spend time preventing them instead.

Incident Management

In ITIL terminology, an *incident* is defined as an unplanned interruption to an IT service, a reduction in the quality of an IT service, or a failure of a CI that has not yet impacted an IT service (for example, failure of one disk from a mirror set).

This is an important definition; because the incident is an interruption to service, restoring the service or improving the quality of the service to agreed levels resolves the incident. Note that incident resolution does not necessarily include understanding why the fault occurred or preventing its recurrence; these are matters for problem management. By understanding this distinction, you can see that resolving an incident does not need the skill that resolving a problem requires. If the service can be restored by a simple reboot, then the user can be instructed to do this by the service desk staff, without involving the more skilled (and therefore more expensive) second-line technicians.

From the user and business perspectives, the focus is on being able to get back to work, and there is little interest in the cause of the failure. Repeat occurrences will impact their work and increase the number of calls to the service desk so an investigation of the cause, and the permanent resolution of the underlying problem, will be required, but this can take place without impacting the users.

The incident management process is responsible for progressing all incidents from when they are first reported until they are closed. Some organizations may have dedicated incident management staff, but the most common approach is to make the service desk responsible for the process.

 Sometimes the resolution of an incident is possible only by understanding the cause and fixing the underlying fault. A hardware or network failure due to a failed hardware component where there is no resilience will need to have the component replaced or repaired before service can be restored. In the majority of incidents, however, service can be restored to the individual user without a permanent problem resolution.

The Purpose of Incident Management

The purpose of *incident management* is to restore normal service operation as quickly as possible and minimize the adverse impact on business operations, thus ensuring that agreed levels of service quality are maintained. *Normal service operation* is defined as an operational state where services and CIs are performing within their agreed service and operational levels.

As explained, by focusing on service restoration, incident management enables the business to return to work quickly, thus ensuring that the impact on business processes and deadlines is reduced.

The Objectives of Incident Management

The objectives of the incident management process are to ensure that all incidents are efficiently responded to, analyzed, logged, managed, resolved, and reported upon. By carrying out these tasks in an efficient and effective manner and by ensuring that affected customers are updated as required, the IT service provider aims to improve customer satisfaction, even though a fault has occurred. At all times during the incident management process, the needs of the business must be considered; business priorities must influence IT priorities.

The Scope of Incident Management

Incident management encompasses all incidents: all events have a real or potential impact on the quality of the service. Incidents will mostly be logged as the result of a user contacting the service desk, but event management tools may report an incident following an alert (see the discussion of event management in Chapter 12); often there will be a link between the event system and incident management tool so that events meeting certain criteria can automatically generate an incident log. Third-party suppliers may notify the service desk of a failure, or technical staff may notice that an error condition has arisen and log an incident.

 As discussed in Chapter 12, not all events are incidents; many are informational or a confirmation that a component is functioning correctly.

Requests may be logged and managed at the service desk, but it is important to differentiate between these requests and incidents; in the case of requests, no service has been impacted. Incident and problem management seek to reduce the number of incidents over time, whereas the IT service provider may want to handle increasing numbers of requests through the service desk and the request fulfillment process as a quick, efficient, and customer-focused method of dealing with them.

Efficient incident management delivers several benefits to the business; it reduces the cost of incident resolution by resolving incidents quickly, using less-skilled staff. Where incidents need to be escalated, the resolution is faster (because the relevant information required will have been gathered and an initial diagnosis will have been made). Faster incident resolution means a faster return to work for the affected users. Effective incident management improves the overall efficiency of the organization because nonproductive users are a cost to the company.

Incident prioritization is based on business priorities, which ensures that resources are allocated to maximize the business benefit. The data gathered by the service desk about the numbers and types of incidents can be analyzed to identify training requirements or potential areas for improvement.

As highlighted in the discussion of the service desk in Chapter 10, incident management is one of the most visible processes, as well as one that all users understand the need for. So, it is one of the easier areas to improve, because an improved incident resolution service has easily understood benefits for the business.

Basic Concepts for Incident Management

ITIL describes a number of basic concepts to keep in mind when implementing the incident management process. They are covered in the following sections.

Timescales

Time is of the essence in incident management because every incident represents some loss or deterioration of service. Every aspect of the process needs to be optimized to produce the fastest end result. Service-level agreements, operational-level agreements, and underpinning contracts will define how long a support group or third-party has to complete each step, with measurable targets.

Service management tool sets should be configured to capture how long it takes to log and escalate an incident, how many incidents are resolved within the first few minutes without requiring escalation, and how long support teams take to respond to and to fix incidents. These times should be monitored, and steps should be taken to identify bottlenecks or underperforming teams so that improvement actions can be taken.

Incident Models

Using *incident models*, which are incident templates prepopulated with the necessary steps to resolve common incidents, is one method of speeding up resolution. They enable faster, more consistent logging and resolution. The steps may instruct the service desk how to resolve the incident or may predefine the information to be gathered as well as the correct escalation group.

Major Incidents

All incidents should get resolved as quickly as possible, but some incidents are so serious, with such an impact on the business, that they require extra attention. The first step is to agree on exactly what is defined as a *major incident*. Some organizations will define all priority one incidents as major; others may restrict priority one incidents to those whose impact will be felt by the external customers. In this definition, an incident with a major impact within the organization would not normally be classed as major. An incident that (for example) prevents customers from ordering goods from the organization's website and that is therefore affecting both revenue and reputation would be included. The definition must align with the priority scheme to avoid confusion.

The purpose of defining an incident as a major incident is so that it can receive special focus. Specific actions to be undertaken are defined in advance so that when the major incident occurs, everyone knows what they are expected to do. Typical actions might include the following:

- Notification of key contacts within the service provider organization and the business as soon as the major incident is declared
- Regular updates posted through agreed channels—intranet, key users, and so on
- Recorded greeting put on the service desk number to inform callers that the incident has occurred and is being dealt with to reduce the number of calls being handled by the desk
- Appointment of a major incident manager (this may be the service desk manager) and the appointment of a separate team to focus on resolving the incident

> Where the service desk manager is managing the incident, another manager may be appointed to head up the team; they would then report progress to the incident manager. This is necessary to avoid a situation where the two roles, that of managing the situation and keeping stakeholders informed and that of pursuing a solution, are in conflict.

As with any incident, some major incidents can be resolved without understanding the cause (perhaps by restarting a server); some require the underlying cause to be understood. In the second case, problem management would become involved. It is essential, however, that the focus of incident management remains on restoring service as quickly as possible.

As we discussed in Chapter 10, a major responsibility of the service desk is communicating with the users; this is particularly true in the case of major incidents. Regular updates should be provided. The service desk staff members are also accountable for ensuring that the incident record is kept up-to-date throughout the incident, although it may be the technicians in other teams who actually enter the information. An accurate record is essential during the incident so that there is no confusion; it will also be used after the incident is resolved, as part of the major incident review. Regular updates showing the steps taken and whether they were successful will allow improvements to be identified for future events.

Incident Status

Incident management tracks incidents through their lifecycle, moving from when the incident is identified through diagnosis and resolution and finally closure. Incident management must ensure that incidents are resolved as quickly as possible and so will remind resolving groups of the associated target times, making sure no incident is forgotten or ignored.

Most service management tool sets will allow a number of statuses to be defined for each incident to facilitate progress tracking. Typical statuses include the following:

Open The incident has been identified and logged. It may be being worked on by a service desk analyst, or the service desk may be considering which second-line team it should be escalated to. Incidents resolved by the first-line team may move directly from Open to Closed, because the service desk analyst obtains the user confirmation that the incident has been satisfactorily resolved.

Assigned This may mean the incident has been sent to a support team but not allocated to a particular individual.

Allocated or In Progress This is usually defined as when a support technician has been allocated the call.

On Hold   This status is sometimes used when the user is not available or has not the time to test the resolution. It is used to "stop the target clock," because the service provider cannot do anything further to resolve the incident without the user.

On Hold status should be used with caution; support staff may be tempted to use it when they are too busy to work on the incident or when they are awaiting the actions of a third-party supplier. This is not its purpose, and using it in this way distorts reporting against OLAs and UCs, because the failure to provide the support and meet the target is hidden by the fact the clock is stopped.

Resolved   This status indicates that the technician has completed their work, but it has not been confirmed by the customer that this was successful. It is common to use the service management's automated email facility to automatically email the user when an incident is resolved, asking for a response within x days if the user is still not happy. If no reply is received, the incident is automatically closed.

- If the user is unhappy, the call is put back into In Progress, and further work is carried out to resolve it.

- The service desk should attempt to contact users to obtain permission to close calls before the automated closure, especially for high-impact incidents, where the user may not be aware of the resolution.

Closed   This status confirms that the incident is over to the user's satisfaction. The incident management process has no further involvement, although problem management may now investigate the underlying cause.

Expanded Incident Lifecycle

The expanded incident lifecycle is used by the service design availability management process and within CSI. The expanded lifecycle breaks down each step of the process so that they can be examined to understand the reasons for the failed targets. For example, the diagnosis of the incident may ascertain very quickly that the resolution requires the restoration of data, which takes three hours; this information would be used to pinpoint where improvements should be made. Delays in any step of the lifecycle can be analyzed, and improvements can be implemented to speed up resolution; implementing a knowledge base or storing spare parts on-site are two typical measures that are taken to shorten the diagnosis and repair steps.

Managing Incidents

We are going to look at the lifecycle of an incident and each of the process steps that take place. Refer to the flow chart pictured in Figure 11.1.

FIGURE 11.1 Incident management process flow

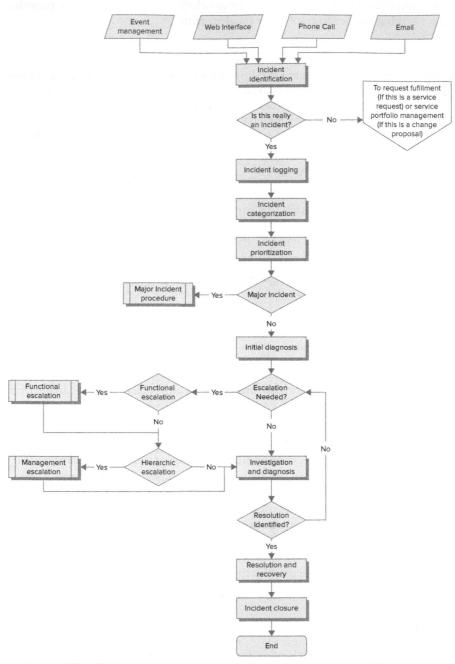

Based on Cabinet Office ITIL® material. Reproduced under license from the Cabinet Office.

Step 1: Incident Identification

Incident management is a reactive process; we cannot start to resolve an incident until we know it has occurred. As we said earlier, it is essential that incidents are resolved in the shortest possible time, because each represents business disruption. Whenever possible, therefore, we should be trying to realize that an incident has occurred before the user notices or, failing that, before they have reported it to the service desk. Chapter 12, on event management, shows how monitoring tools can be used to identify failures. The event management process should link directly to incident management so that any incidents spotted are worked on immediately and resolved quickly.

 Where an automated response to an incident is used, such as restarting a server following a failure, an incident should still be logged for future analysis.

Where event management is not in place, incidents will be identified by users contacting the service desk.

Step 2: Incident Logging

 All incidents must be logged, no matter how they are identified.

The *incident record* contains all the information concerning a particular incident; details of when it was logged, assigned, resolved, and closed may be required for service-level management reporting. Details of symptoms and the affected equipment may be used by problem management. Steps taken to resolve the incident may be used to populate a knowledge base. It is essential therefore that all relevant information is added to the record as it progresses through its lifecycle.

A good integrated service management tool makes good recordkeeping much easier, because it can automatically populate the record with user details (from Active Directory or a similar tool) and equipment and warranty details (based on the CI number). Automatic date and time stamping of each update and identification of who made the update will both improve the completeness of the information in the record.

Service management tool sets differ, but a typical list of required information in an incident record would include the following:

- Unique reference number, generated automatically
- Incident category (covered in the next section)
- Incident impact, urgency, and priority
- Date/time of every update, from logging to closure
- Name of who logged and updated the incident

- Method of notification (telephone, automatic, email, in person, and so on)
- Full user contact details
- Symptoms, questions asked by the service desk, and the answers given by the user
- Steps taken to try to resolve the incident (successful or otherwise)
- Incident status (covered earlier)
- Related CI/problem/known error
- Assignee group and individual
- Closure category

Step 3: Incident Categorization

Incidents are categorized during the logging stage. This can be helpful in guiding the service desk agent to the correct known error entry or the appropriate support team for escalation. A simple category structure should be used, however; too complex a scheme leads to incidents all being logged as "other" or "miscellaneous" because the agent does not want to spend the time considering which category is correct. This makes later analysis very difficult. A multilevel scheme, as shown in Figure 11.2, achieves granularity without facing the service desk agent with a long list to choose from. Incidents should be recategorized during investigation and on resolution, if the original choice was incorrect. (The service desk agent will have chosen the most appropriate category based on the information available at the time, but further investigation may have shown that, for example, a printer fault was actually a cabling fault.)

FIGURE 11.2 Multilevel incident categorization

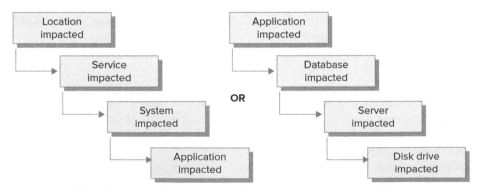

Based on Cabinet Office ITIL® material. Reproduced under license from the Cabinet Office.

 The process step that checks whether the call is actually a request is there to identify and filter out any requests which have been misreported as incidents

Step 4: Incident Prioritization

Incidents need to be prioritized to ensure that the most critical incidents are dealt with first. It is often said that all users believe that their own incident is the highest priority, so it is important to agree during service-level negotiations what criteria should be used to decide priority.

The ITIL framework recommends that two factors should be considered: business impact and urgency (how quickly the business needs a resolution). Business impact can be assessed by considering a number of factors: the number of people affected, the criticality of the service, the financial loss being incurred, damage to reputation, and so on. Dependent on the type of organization, other factors such as health and safety (for a hospital or a railway company or similar) and potential breach of regulations (financial institutions, and so on) may be considered.

During the life of an incident, it may be necessary to adjust the priority of an incident if the assessment of the impact changes or a resolution becomes more urgent.

 **Real World Scenario**

The Numbers Game

A global engineering company outsourced its hardware maintenance. The contract stated that prioritization, and therefore target resolution times, would be based on the number of CIs affected. One day a printer failed and was duly reported. It was allocated the lowest priority, with a target of five days because it was a single printer. What was not appreciated, however, was that this was not an office laser printer but a factory printer that printed barcodes to show which spare parts were packed in each box. With no way of indicating what was in the boxes, they could not be packed, so after 24 hours the production line was closed down, and all the staff members working on it were all sent home! It took another 24 hours before senior management realized what was happening and the financial loss that was being incurred.

In this situation, the outsourcer had followed the contract, but those involved in negotiating it had neglected to consider prioritization criteria beyond a very simplistic approach.

Deciding the priority must be simple, because the incident has to be logged quickly. Employing service desk staff with good business knowledge and ensuring they are trained to be aware of business impact will help a realistic assessment of business impact to be made. Table 11.1 shows a simple but very effective way to determine priority.

Table 11.2 shows how the determination of priority made using the matrix in Table 11.1 can in turn be employed to set a target resolution time for the incident.

TABLE 11.1   Impact and urgency: a matrix for determining an incident's priority

Impact	Urgency		
	High	Medium	Low
High	1	2	3
Medium	2	3	4
Low	3	4	5

TABLE 11.2   Target resolution

Priority code	Description	Target resolution time
1	Critical	1 hour
2	High	8 hours
3	Medium	24 hours
4	Low	48 hours
5	Planning	Planned

Assigning the Correct Priority

Sometimes a user insists on a high priority, even if the impact and urgency do not justify it; this puts the service desk agent in a difficult position. The incident should be logged at the higher priority to avoid arguing with the customer, who may already be agitated. The incident can be reviewed later, perhaps during a service review, and the point can tactfully be made that escalating an incident to a higher priority than justified could mean another incident, with a genuinely high priority, may not be actioned.

One tactic used by some organizations is to agree, within the SLA, that all high-priority incidents require a form to be completed by the user justifying the high priority for analysis during the major incident review. A significant number of users, when told of this requirement, decide that perhaps a lower priority is satisfactory after all!

Many organizations struggle with applying the prioritization rules when the user reporting the fault is very senior. Some organizations will have a formal procedure in place to give these VIPs faster service; some will apply the business impact and urgency evaluation to their incident as with any other caller (although the business impact is likely to be higher with these users). There needs to be clear guidance to the service desk agent whether to (for example) prioritize a VIP's printer fault over a fault affecting online sales.

Some organizations address this issue by formally recognizing the needs of VIPs for fast service and defining a special service level (gold service) for them within the SLA, documented in the service catalog.

Step 5: Initial Diagnosis

The initial diagnosis step refers to the actions taken at the service desk to diagnose the fault and, where possible, to resolve it at this stage. The service desk agent will use the known error database provided by problem management, incident models (covered earlier), any other diagnostic tools to assist in the diagnosis, and possible resolution. Where the service desk is unable to resolve the incident, the initial diagnosis will identify the appropriate support team for escalation.

One technique used by the service desk agent is "incident matching." By checking for previous incidents with the same classification, the service desk agent may be able to identify a repeat incident and the appropriate resolution steps. This speeds up the resolution and increases the first-contact fix rate.

FIGURE 11.3 Incident matching

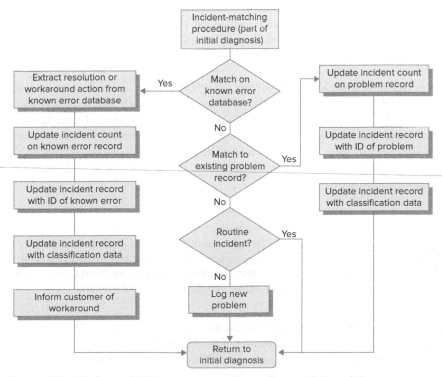

Based on Cabinet Office ITIL® material. Reproduced under license from the Cabinet Office.

As we have stated previously, time is of the essence in incident management, so the length of time an agent has to resolve the incident will be limited. If the incident can be resolved at first line, it is far more efficient for the user and the IT provider that this is done; holding onto the call for too long, however, delays the eventual resolution. Consideration needs to be given to what the time limit should be; five to ten minutes is common.

Part of this stage is the gathering of information to assist the second-line technician in resolving the incident quickly. Again, sufficient time is required for this step; "saving" time by passing the incident to a second-line technician quickly but with sparse details is not helpful. The second-line technician will need to contact the customer to obtain the information, adding delay and frustration. Support teams should provide guidance to the service desk about the type and level of information they should be gathering.

Step 6: Incident Escalation

The ITIL framework describes two forms of escalation that may take place during *incident management*: *functional escalation* and *hierarchic escalation*. We will look at each of these in turn.

Functional escalation takes place when the service desk is unable to resolve the incident; this may be realized immediately because of the type of incident such as a server failure or because the service desk agent may have spent the maximum time allowed under the organization's guidelines attempting to resolve the incident without success. It then needs to be passed to another group with a greater level of knowledge. The second-line support group that receives this escalated incident will also have a time limit for resolution, after which the incident gets escalated again to the next support level. Sometimes, as with the service desk, it is obvious that the incident will require a high level of technical knowledge, and in such a case the incident would be immediately escalated, without any attempt by second-line support staff to resolve it.

The service desk must know the correct group to escalate an incident to, to avoid unnecessary delays, so the service desk staff needs to have sufficient technical knowledge to be able to identify which incident goes to which team. Operational-level agreements will specify the responsibilities of each group. There may be occasions where cooperation between support groups is required or where the incident needs to be referred to third parties such as hardware maintenance companies. The OLAs and UCs should specify what should happen in this situation.

 Incident ownership remains with the service desk. Incidents may be escalated to support groups or third parties, but the service desk retains ownership of the incident, tracking progress, keeping users informed, and obtaining the user's agreement to its eventual closure.

The second type of escalation is hierarchic escalation, which takes place for high-priority or major incidents. This escalation consists of informing the appropriate level of management about the incident so that they are aware of it. This ensures that the management is able to make any decisions that are required regarding prioritization of work, involving suppliers, and so on. In the case of a major incident, the IT director may be expected to brief the business directors about the progress of the incident; even if this is not the case, business managers may go directly to senior IT managers when a serious incident has occurred, so it is essential that the IT managers have been thoroughly briefed themselves.

It is also sometimes necessary to use hierarchic escalation when the incident is not progressing as quickly as it should or if there is disagreement among the support groups regarding to whom it should be assigned.

A good service management tool will be able to automatically escalate incidents, based on the SLA targets, updating the record with details. For example, a tool could be set to notify a team leader when 90 percent of the SLA target time had passed and to inform the team leader's line manager when the incident breached the target.

Step 7: Investigation and Diagnosis

The major activity that takes place for every incident is investigation and diagnosis. The incident will have undergone the initial diagnosis step covered earlier; this identifies whether the service desk can resolve the incident because the incident has been seen before. The investigation and diagnosis stage here is different; it involves trying to ascertain what has happened and how the incident can be resolved.

The incident record should be updated to record what actions have been taken, and an accurate description of the symptoms, and the various actions taken, is required to prevent duplication of effort; it will also be useful when the incident is reviewed, perhaps as part of problem management. Typical investigation and diagnosis actions would include gathering a full description of the issue and its impact and urgency, creating a timeline of events, identifying possible causes such as recent changes, interrogating knowledge sources such as the known error database, and so on.

Step 8: Resolution and Recovery

Potential incident resolutions should be tested to ensure that they actually resolve the issue completely with no unintended consequences. This testing may involve the user. Other resolution actions might include the service desk agent or technician remotely taking over the user's equipment to implement a resolution or to show the user what they need to do in the future. Once the incident is resolved, it returns to the service desk for closure.

Step 9: Incident Closure

When the incident has been resolved and the service restored, the service desk will contact the user to verify that the incident may be closed (covered earlier). This is an important step, because the fault may appear resolved to the IT department, but the user may still be having difficulties, especially if there were actually two incidents, with the symptoms of one being hidden by the other. The second incident would become apparent only after the first was resolved. The service desk may contact the user directly, or an email could be sent with a time limit when the incident will be closed, as described earlier.

The category assigned to the incident when it was logged should be reviewed. The initial incident categorization is based on the available evidence at the time; following the resolution, it may be altered to reflect the confirmed cause (covered earlier). If the underlying cause of the incident is still unknown, despite the fact it has been resolved, a problem record may be raised to investigate the underlying cause and to prevent a recurrence. Finally, a user satisfaction survey may be carried out.

Interfaces Between Incident Management and the Lifecycle Stages

Incident management is a key process that is carried out by all service providers. There are several links between the process and other processes both within service operation and within the service design stage.

Service Design

Several of the service design processes interface directly with the incident management process. These processes are among those we discussed in Chapter 10, where many of the process activities take place in the service operation lifecycle stage. Service-level management interfaces with incident management because SLAs will contain incident targets; the other service design processes may result in incidents if the processes fail to prevent a security breach, a lack of capacity, or unplanned downtime.

Service level management   As we have seen, there are numerous links between incident and service-level management. Incidents have target response and resolution times; these targets are set in the SLAs. Incident management in return provides the management information from the service management tool set to enable SLM to report on the success achieved in meeting these targets. Incident reporting enables SLM to identify failing services and to implement service improvement plans for them (in conjunction with continual service improvement).

Information security management, capacity management, and availability management   Incident management collects data on the number of security-related incidents and capacity issues. It provides the data on downtime that availability uses to calculate availability reports, and analysis of incident records helps availability management understand the weak points in the infrastructure that need attention. An efficient incident lifecycle also improves overall availability.

Service Transition

The service transition processes of SACM and change management interface with incident management; SACM provides useful information to the incident process, and changes may be the cause of incidents or the means by which incidents are resolved.

Service asset and configuration management   Incident management uses SACM data to understand the impact of an incident, because it shows the dependencies on each CI. It provides useful information regarding who supports particular categories of CI. By logging each incident against a CI and checking that the user of the CI is as recorded in the CMS, incident management helps keep the CMS accurate.

Change management   Changes are often implemented to overcome incidents. Incidents may often be caused by changes. An important input into incident investigation is the change schedule; asking the question "What changed just before this incident occurred?" can often highlight the cause of incidents. In the case of a major incident caused by a change, the decision may be made to back out the change. Information identifying how many incidents were caused by changes should be fed back to change management to improve future changes.

Service Operation

There is a strong interface between incident management and problem management, as we will be covering in the rest of this chapter. Access management issues may also cause incidents.

Problem management   As you will learn when we discuss problem management in the rest of this chapter, incident management and problem management have many links. Incident management provides the data on repeat incidents that problem management uses to identify underlying problems. The permanent resolution of these problems helps incident management by reducing the number of incidents that occur. The incident impact and urgency information helps problem management prioritize between problems.

Problem management provides known error information, which enables incident management to restore service.

Access management   Incident management raises incidents following security breaches or unauthorized access attempts. This information can be used by access management to investigate access breaches. Failure to ensure users are granted the necessary access they require to do their job may result in incidents being reported when the user is greeted with an error message when attempting to carry out a task.

Problem Management

According to ITIL official terminology, a *problem* is defined as an underlying cause of one or more incidents. *Problem management* is the process that investigates the cause of incidents and, wherever possible, implements a permanent solution to prevent recurrence. Until such time as a permanent resolution is applied, it will also attempt to provide a workaround to enable the service to be restored and the incident to be resolved.

It is important to understand the differences between incidents and problems and to realize that an incident *never* becomes a problem.

A Mechanical Incident, Problem, and Workaround

One morning, as you leave your house to go to work, you find that your car will not start. You have an *incident*.

You have little mechanical knowledge, but you do know how to apply a *workaround*—to use jumper cables. You do this, the car starts, and your incident is over.

Every morning for a week, the same thing happens, and each time you apply the workaround to overcome the incident and restore service. The underlying *problem* could have several possible causes: a faulty battery, a mechanical fault preventing the engine from charging the battery, a light in the trunk left permanently on, and so on. The problem investigation has to be carried out by someone with a greater mechanical knowledge than you.

On the weekend, you take the car to a mechanic, who diagnoses the root cause and applies a permanent resolution (replaces the battery, fixes the wiring, or whatever is required). Your car will now start each morning!

Many organizations make the mistake of thinking that problem management is not essential. Typically they will state something like "this year we will concentrate on incident management; maybe next year we shall try some problem management." This is unwise. Until and unless problem management is undertaken, incidents will recur, inconveniencing the business and occupying support staff time. Problem management will reduce incidents, freeing up more time to undertake more problem management. It is a virtuous circle; the more time spent on it, the more time is freed up by it.

The Purpose, Objectives, and Scope of Problem Management

The purpose of the problem management process is to document, investigate, and remove causes of incidents. It also provides another very useful benefit; by providing workarounds, it reduces the impact of incidents that occur. It proactively identifies errors in the infrastructure that could cause incidents and provides a permanent resolution, thus preventing the incidents.

Problem management aims to identify the root cause of incidents, to document known errors, and to take action to remedy them. Problem management has three simple objectives:

- Prevent problems and resulting incidents from happening
- Eliminate recurring incidents
- Minimize the impact of incidents that cannot be prevented

The scope of problem management includes diagnosis of the root cause of incidents and taking the necessary action in conjunction with other processes (such as change management and release and deployment management) to permanently remove them.

Problem management is also responsible for compiling information about problems and any associated workarounds or resolutions. By identifying faults, providing workarounds, and then permanently removing them, problem management reduces the number and the impact of incidents. It has a strong relationship with knowledge management, because it is responsible for maintaining a known error database and could also be said to be part of continual service improvement.

There are important similarities and differences between the two principal service operation processes. The same service management tool will usually be used to track both incidents and problems, and a good tool will facilitate the linking of incident occurrences to specific problem records. Similar categories and prioritization classifications may be used. However, problem management may be a process of which the business is unaware. Once a workaround has been applied and an incident resolved, the user may think no more about it. Meanwhile, the IT service provider uses problem management to prevent recurrence. An effective workaround can take some of the pressure off support staff, allowing them to take the time to investigate the underlying cause, without being chased for a resolution, as the service has been restored.

As we have said, an incident is an unplanned interruption to an IT service or reduction in the quality of an IT service. Sometimes an incident cannot be resolved until the cause is known and remedied; a server fails and will not restart, for example, because of a hardware fault.

Unlike incident management, which is entirely reactive (you cannot resolve an incident until it has occurred), problem management has both reactive and proactive features.

- Problem management will react to incidents and attempt to identify a workaround and a permanent resolution.

- It will also proactively try to identify potential incidents and take action to prevent them from ever happening. This might include analysis of incident trends, such as intermittent but increasingly frequent complaints about poor response times, to identify a potential capacity issue. By working with capacity management, proactive measures can be taken to provide sufficient capacity and avoid any major breaks in service. Event management reports may also be analyzed to the same end, in this case, preventing an incident before the user is aware of any issue.

- Problem management may assist in a major incident review, trying to identify how to prevent a recurrence.

Reactive and proactive problem management activities normally take place as part of service operation, but problem management is also closely related to continual service improvement. Where improvement opportunities are identified as a result of problem management, they should be entered into the CSI register.

Problem Management Concepts

As stated earlier, problem management is not an interesting optional activity; it is fundamental to providing a consistent service, in line with SLA commitments. By providing workarounds to enable resolution of incidents with the first-line staff, better use is made of the more skilled and therefore more expensive second- and third-line staff, who are freed up to use their skills in problem investigation.

Reactive and Proactive Activities

The process steps for managing problems that are raised in reaction to incidents and those that are proactively identified are broadly similar. The main difference is the trigger for the process. Reactive activities take place as a result of an incident report and help prevent the incident from recurring or provide a workaround if avoidance is impossible; these activities complement the incident management process.

Proactive problem management analyzes incident records to identify underlying causes of incidents. It may be that analysis of previous incidents reveals a trend or pattern that was not apparent when each incident occurred. For example, users may complain of poor response periodically; it is only when all these complaints are analyzed that it becomes apparent that the poor response is always reported against the same module or from the same location. This would trigger a problem record to be raised to identify the common cause linking all these incidents. We will look at this in a bit more detail in the following sections.

Proactive problem management process depends on the reporting capability of the service management tool; it must be able to produce reports that show the trend and allow drilling down into the data to find the connections that explain it. This may require incident reports sorted by category, date, time, location, application, or associated configuration item. Proactive steps are triggered by attempts to identify improvements and as such complement CSI.

Problem Models

It may be useful to use problem models to handle problems that have not and will not be resolved, perhaps because the cost or risk is too great or because the technology is due for replacement. These problem models are similar to the incident models described earlier, identifying the steps to take. They are used in addition to entries in the known error database.

When Is a Problem Raised?

Sometimes it is helpful to raise a problem record while the incident is still open. Each organization will decide its own criteria for when a problem should be raised. For example, a problem may be raised when the support teams are sure that the incident has been caused by a new problem, because the incident appears to be part of a trend or because there is no match with existing known errors. The incident may have been resolved by the service desk or support teams without knowing the cause and so there is a risk that the fault may recur. This is particularly true in the case of a major incident; the underlying cause needs to be identified as soon as possible to prevent future disruption to the business. (The problem diagnosis activity may take place in parallel with the incident resolution and may continue after the successful resolution, until the underlying cause is identified and removed.) It is also possible that suppliers may inform their customers of problems that they have identified.

Managing Problems: The Problem Management Process

Now we are going to examine the problem management process step by step. Refer to Figure 11.4 as we discuss each activity.

FIGURE 11.4   The problem management process

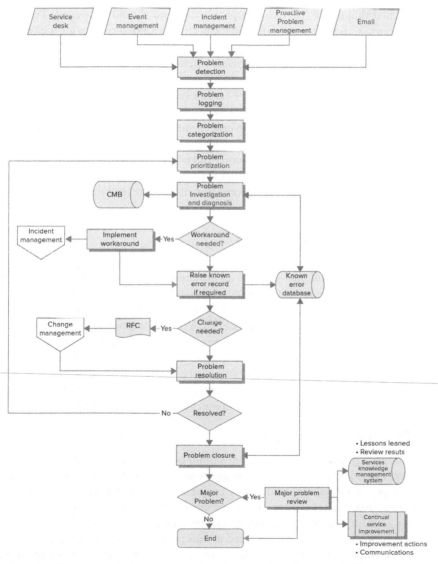

Based on Cabinet Office ITIL® material. Reproduced under license from the Cabinet Office.

Step 1: Detecting Problems

The first step in the process is to identify that a problem exists. As we discussed previously, problems may be raised either reactively in reaction to incidents or proactively. In addition to the triggers identified earlier, a problem may also be identified as a result of alerts received as part of event management. The event monitoring tools may identify a fault before it becomes apparent to users and may automatically raise an incident in response.

Step 2: Logging Problems

Having identified that a problem exists, a problem record should be logged. The problem record must contain all the relevant information, time-stamped to provide a complete picture. Wherever possible, the service management tool should be used to link problem records with the associated incident records. Incident details need to be copied into the problem record. Some tool sets enable the creation of a problem record from an incident, with automatic linking between the two. This can be very useful and saves a lot of time cutting and pasting details from one record to another. Be careful, however. Remember that the incident has not "become" a problem; the incident must continue to be managed to resolution whether the problem is resolved or not.

Typical details entered in a problem record and copied from the incident would include details of who reported it and when, details of the service and equipment used, and a description of the incident and actions taken. The incident record number and the priority and category would also be required.

Step 3: Categorizing Problems

Problems should be categorized in the same way as incidents, and using the same categorization scheme will make linking incidents and related problems together much easier.

An essential prerequisite for identifying trends in incidents is the accurate and consistent categorization of incidents. If every service desk analyst logs the same fault differently, it will be impossible to discern a trend. The example of poor response could be logged as a user complaint, a network issue, an application issue, or even "miscellaneous" or "other." The problem manager should emphasize the importance of accurate categorization to the service desk. The use of incident models can be very helpful here because they standardize the way common incidents are recorded. Enforcing categorization on incident resolution, as mentioned earlier, will also help ensure incident categories are accurate.

Step 4: Prioritizing Problems

As with incidents, the priority of a problem should be based on the impact to the business of the incidents that it is causing and the urgency with which it needs to be resolved. The problem manager should also consider how frequently the incidents are occurring. It is possible that a "frozen screen" that can be resolved with a reboot is not a high-priority incident; if it is occurring 100 times a day, the combined impact to the business may be severe, so the problem needs to be allocated a high priority. The impact to the business must always be considered, so factors such as the cost of resolving the incident, and the time this is likely to take, will be relevant when assessing priority.

Step 5: Investigating and Diagnosing Problems

The next stage in the process is to investigate and diagnose the problem. There may not be the resources to investigate every problem, so the priority level assigned to each will govern which ones get the necessary attention. It is important to allocate resources to problem investigation, because until the problem is resolved, the incident will recur, and resources will be spent on incident resolution.

The ITIL framework suggests a number of different problem-solving techniques, which are helpful in approaching the diagnosis logically. The CMS can be very helpful in providing CI information to help identify the underlying cause. It will also help in identifying the point of failure, where several incidents are reported; the CMS may identify that all the affected CIs are linked to the same CI. The KEDB may also provide information about previous, similar problems and their causes. Where a test environment exists, this can be used to re-create the fault and to try possible solutions.

Step 6: Identifying a Workaround

Although the aim of problem management is to find and remove the underlying cause of incidents, this may take some time; meanwhile, the incident or incidents continue, and the service is affected. When a user suffers an incident, the first priority is to restore the service so that they can continue working. A priority of the process, therefore, is to provide a workaround to be used until the problem is resolved. The workaround does not fix the underlying problem, but it allows the user to continue working by providing an alternative means of achieving the same result. The workaround can be provided to the service desk to enable them to resolve the incidents, while work on a permanent solution continues. The problem record remains open, because the fault still exists and is continuing to cause incidents. The details of the workaround are documented within the problem record, and a reassessment of its priority may be carried out.

It is possible that IT or business management may decide to continue to use the workaround and suspend work on a permanent solution if one is not justified. A problem affecting a service that is due to be replaced, for example, may not be worth the effort and risk involved in implementing a permanent solution. In the previous example regarding the car that fails to start, the owner may decide not to repair the fault if the car is to be replaced within weeks. Until it is replaced, the owner uses the workaround of jumper cables, rather than pay the mechanic to fix the fault.

Step 7: Raising a Known Error Record

When problem management has identified and documented the root cause and workaround, this information is made available to support staff as a *known error*. Information about all known errors, including which problem record it relates to, is kept in the *known error database (KEDB)*. When repeat incidents occur, the support staff can refer to the KEDB for the workaround.

There may be times when a workaround is available although the root cause is not yet known (for example, a reboot restores the service, although we do not know what causes the error). On other occasions, we may know the cause but not have a workaround because a change has to be implemented to fix the fault.

Sometimes a known error is raised before a workaround is available and sometimes even before the root cause has been fully identified. This may be just for information purposes; a workaround may be available that has not been fully proven. Rather than have a rigid rule about when a known error should be raised, a more pragmatic approach is advisable; a known error should be raised as soon as it becomes useful to do so.

Problem Resolution

When problem management has identified a solution to the problem, it should be implemented to resolve the underlying fault and thus prevent any further incidents from disrupting the service. Implementing the resolution may involve a degree of risk, however, so the change management process will ensure the risk and impact assessment of the RFC is satisfactory before allowing the change. Ultimately, the decision whether to go ahead with the resolution despite the risk is a business decision; the business damage being done by the problem may mean the business is prepared to accept the risk in order to have the fix implemented. For more discussion about the acceptance of risk by the business, see Chapter 8.

- Often a change to resolve a problem will be an emergency change because of the impact of the problem on the business and the urgency with which it needs to be fixed.

- In the circumstance mentioned earlier, where a permanent resolution is not justified, the KEDB should be used to document the workaround. The entry should state that the problem is not to be resolved to prevent any unnecessary work being done on it.

- There may be workarounds that mitigate rather than remove the impact of the fault; these should be documented and used until a better resolution is found. Having a workaround like this available, although not entirely satisfactory, may allow the priority to be reassessed.

Problem Closure

When a permanent solution to the problem has been identified, tested, and implemented through the change management process, the problem record can be updated and closed. Any open incidents caused by the problem can be closed too. The KEDB should be updated to show that the problem is resolved, so any future incidents will not have been caused by it; however, the information contained within the problem record may prove useful in addressing a future, similar problem.

Major Problem Review

Each organization should define what constitutes a major problem; this may be all priority one problems, anything above a particular priority level that continues or some other criteria. Once a major problem has been resolved, a review should be held to identify any lessons that can be learned from what occurred. This review should happen close enough to the time of the event that those involved can still remember what happened. The importance of good recordkeeping is apparent at a review; a well-documented problem, with a full history of steps taken, will provide useful information. A problem record with little detail will mean important items will be forgotten, or those present may have differing recollections.

It is important to remember, for this and other reviews, that lessons can be learned from what went well, not just from what went badly. Concentrating on what went wrong may lead to a list of recommendations about what *not* to do next time but gives little guidance about what should be done instead. Even when a problem causes a lot of disruption, there may still be positive lessons to be learned. For example, the business may comment that it was really helpful to have regular updates from the service desk regarding the status of the incident that resulted from the problem, because this allowed them to plan how to make best use of staff time.

The output from the review should cover what went well, whether anything was done that was against the agreed process, any suggestions for improvements for the future, and any ideas about how the problem could be prevented in the future. Follow-up actions should be assigned to the relevant teams, process owners, or third-party supplier, and internal improvements can be entered into the CSI register. It is important that action is taken on any improvements identified, whether technical changes to monitoring or logging tools, changes to process activities, or addressing training needs which have been identified.

The review may highlight underlying causes that can be handled as part of proactive problem management. The service-level manager (possibly accompanied by the problem manager) should report to the next service review what improvements have been identified and implemented to help prevent future major incidents. This provides assurance to the business that the IT service provider is not complacent and is making a genuine effort to improve the service.

Interfaces

As we discussed in the section about incident management, the major relationship that problem and incident management have is with each other. Problem management does interface with other processes, however. The following sections show these interfaces, grouped by the lifecycle stage.

Service Strategy

Problem management interfaces with the service strategy financial management process. The cost of overcoming problems has to be considered before actions can be taken.

Financial management for IT services   Problem management uses this process to assess the financial impact of possible solutions or workarounds. This information can be used to decide whether a permanent resolution is financially justified. Having the information from financial management to be able to assess the cost of downtime and having the cost of providing support for services with unresolved problems will also help you prioritize problems. Problem management can use information from financial management to prove the cost-effectiveness of resolving underlying causes, rather than spending time resolving multiple occurrences of the incident.

Service Design

The service design processes are intended to deliver services without problems. Not all problems can be foreseen, however, and the service design processes of availability management, capacity management, and IT service continuity management all take proactive steps to identify possible issues and deal with these problems before they result in incidents. This is very similar to problem management. How the service-level management process interfaces with problems is different; SLM is dependent on problem management to identify the root cause of incidents and resolve them in order to prevent downtime that could cause a service level target to be breached.

Availability management   Availability management has very similar aims to problem management: to prevent downtime. The proactive activities undertaken by availability management are directly related to proactive problem management; availability attempts to proactively identify risks that could result in a loss of service and to take preventative action. Problem management can supply information to availability management about the success of any measures taken.

Capacity management   Some performance problems can be caused by capacity issues. Capacity management will be involved in resolving these issues and also taking proactive measures to prevent capacity issues. Again, problem management can supply information about the success of any measures taken.

IT service continuity management   When a significant problem is causing or will cause major disruption to the business, it may be necessary to invoke the ITSCM plan until the issue is resolved. ITSCM also attempts to proactively identify risks that could result in a major loss of service and to take preventative action.

Service level management   SLM agrees with the business about the level of service to be provided. Incidents and problems will impact the service and may cause the service targets to be breached. The service-level manager has to report to the business about any failures and what is being done to avoid them in future. Problem management actions can be reported at the service review and may form part of the service improvement plan. SLM can assist in the prioritization of problems by providing information about the business impact and the effect on services of proposed resolutions. It should be noted, however, that SLAs should not contain target problem resolution times; by definition, a problem is the unknown cause of incidents, so it is not possible to know how long a problem may take to fix. It may be necessary to wait for a recurrence in order to gather sufficient evidence to diagnose the problem.

Service Transition

Problem management interfaces with several of the service transition processes. As discussed in relation to incident management, changes may be the cause or solution to problems also. SACM provides invaluable information to enable common factors to be identified across multiple incidents. Release and deployment is involved in contributing to problem management's known error database, which is also related to knowledge management.

Change Management   When a change is required to resolve a problem or implement a workaround, it is submitted to change management in the form of an RFC. Problem management will depend on information from change management to know whether such a change was implemented successfully. Problem management also has an interface to change management when changes introduce problems or cause incidents.

Service Asset and Configuration Management   The CMS provides essential information to problem management: identifying faulty CIs. The CMS is particularly useful when it is used to identify which CI is common to several incidents and which may be the source of the fault (for example, when several users, using different applications, complain about a performance issue, the CMS may show that all the users are using the same network equipment). The CMS is also helpful in identifying the impact of a problem, because it shows the dependencies for each CI.

Release and Deployment Management   When a change to resolve a fault is approved by change management, it is the change and deployment management process that will implement it in the live environment. As part of deploying a new release, it is responsible for ensuring any known errors from development are entered into the KEDB. Problem management also has an interface to change management when releases introduce problems or cause incidents.

Knowledge Management   The KEDB is an essential input into knowledge transfer; the SKMS may hold both problem records and the KEDB.

Continual Service Improvement

Problem management and continual service improvement have similar objectives; problem management activities can also be seen as CSO activities.

The Seven-Step Improvement Process   The aims of CSI and problem management are very closely allied. Both seek to drive out errors and improve service quality. As stated earlier, actions identified to resolve or prevent problems may be entered into the CSI register. The seven-step improvement process can be used by CSI or problem management to identify and resolve underlying problems.

Summary

In this chapter, we explored two of the major processes in the service operation lifecycle stage, covering the purpose, objectives, scope, basic concepts, process activities, and interfaces for incident management and problem management.

We examined how each of these processes supports the other and how each interfaces with other processes from other stages of the service lifecycle. You gained an understanding about the importance of these processes to the business and to the IT service provider.

We examined the following key ITIL concepts:

- Incident
- Impact
- Urgency

- Priority
- Problem
- Workaround
- Known error
- Known error database (KEDB)

Exam Essentials

Understand the purpose and objectives of incident management in reducing downtime by resolving incidents quickly. Be able to describe the scope and basic concepts such as major incidents, incident models, and the importance of timely resolution. Identify sources of incident reports other than users reporting them to the service desk; suppliers, support staff, or event management alerts are all possible sources. Understand that incident management is a reactive process. Be able to list and explain the interfaces that incident management has with other processes, especially problem management and service-level management.

Understand that the aim of incident management is to restore service, not to identify the cause. This focus on service restoration means that less-skilled staff are required to resolve incidents than problems. Be able to describe the differences between an incident, a problem, and a service request.

Explain how priority is calculated, using business impact and urgency. Understand what these terms mean.

Be able to explain the concept of incident and problem models and their use. Be able to describe the lifecycle of an incident and the use of the different statuses assigned to each stage. Be able to list the key information that would be recorded in an incident record. Be able to describe the difference between the two types of escalation (hierarchic and functional) and when each is used.

Understand the purpose, objectives, scope, basic concepts, process activities, and interfaces of problem management. Understand that a problem is the unknown, underlying cause of one or more incidents and that the aim of problem management is to find the cause of incidents and remove it to prevent recurrence. Be able to describe the relationship between problem management and other processes.

Understand the concepts of a workaround and a known error. Be able to explain why some problems might not resolved, when it is not cost-effective to implement the fix, and when a workaround exists. Be able to explain how the known error database is used.

Review Questions

You can find the answers in Appendix A.

1. Which is the best description of an incident?
   A. An event that has significance and impacts the service
   B. An unplanned interruption to an IT service or reduction in the quality of an IT service
   C. A fault that causes failures in the IT infrastructure
   D. A user error

2. When should an incident be closed?
   A. When the technical staff members are confident that it will not recur
   B. When desktop support staff members say that the incident is over
   C. When the user confirms that the service has been restored
   D. When the target resolution time is reached

3. Which of the following is *not* a satisfactory resolution to an incident?
   A. A user complains of poor response; a reboot speeds up the response.
   B. A user complains of poor response; second-line support runs diagnostics to be able to monitor it the next time it occurs.
   C. The service desk uses the KEDB to provide a workaround to restore the service.
   D. The service desk takes control of the user's machine remotely and shows the user how to run the report they were having difficulty with.

4. Incident management aims to restore normal service operation as quickly as possible. How is *normal service operation* defined?
   A. It is the level of service that the user requires.
   B. It is the level of service that the technical management staff members say is reasonable.
   C. It is the level of service defined in the SLA.
   D. It is the level of service that IT believes is optimal.

5. A service management tool has the ability to store templates for common incidents that define the steps to be taken to resolve the fault. What are these called?
   A. Major incidents
   B. Minor incidents
   C. Incident models
   D. Incident categories

6. Which incidents should be logged?

    A. Major incidents

    B. All incidents that resulted from a user contacting the service desk

    C. Minor incidents

    D. All incidents

7. What factors should be taken into consideration when assessing the priority of an incident?

    A. Impact and cost

    B. Impact and urgency

    C. Urgency and severity

    D. Severity and cost

8. What of the following are types of incident escalation defined by ITIL?

    1. Hierarchical

    2. Management

    3. Functional

    4. Technical

        A. 1 and 4

        B. 1 and 3

        C. 1, 2, and 4

        D. All of the above

9. What is the best definition of a problem?

    A. An incident that the service desk does not know how to fix

    B. The result of a failed change

    C. The cause of one or more incidents

    D. A fault that will require a change to resolve

10. Problem management can produce which of the following?

    1. Known errors

    2. Workarounds

    3. Resolutions

    4. RFCs

        A. 1 and 4

        B. 1 and 3

        C. 1, 2, and 4

        D. All of the above

Chapter
12

The Other Service Operation Processes

THE FOLLOWING ITIL FOUNDATION EXAM OBJECTIVES ARE DISCUSSED IN THIS CHAPTER:

✓ **Unit 3: Generic concepts and definitions**

- 3-24. Event
- 3-25. Alert
- 3-28. Service request

✓ **5-8. State the purpose, objectives and scope for:**

- 5-81 Event management
- 5-82 Request fulfillment
- 5-83 Access management

In this chapter we take a high-level look at the service operation processes of event management, request fulfilment and access management, and discuss some of the generic concepts and definitions associated with them. These processes happen every day in every IT operations environment. Event management describes how the use of monitoring tools can not only spot faults very quickly, but also automate many tasks. Access management helps protect the organization's data by controlling who is able to gain access to it. Request fulfilment provides a straightforward and efficient way to provide standard services to customers. Each of these processes, if carried out well, will improve the service to customers.

Event Management

Modern infrastructure management depends to a large extent on the use of event monitoring tools. These tools are able to monitor large numbers of configuration items simultaneously, identifying any issues as soon as they arise and notifying technical management staff. The process of event management is responsible for managing events throughout their lifecycle. Event management is one of the main activities of IT operations.

An *event* can be defined as any change of state that has significance for the management of a configuration item (CI) or IT service. Note that this does *not* state that the change of state is a failure. Many events are purely informational. Examples of informational events could include notification of a user logging onto an application (significant because the use of the application may be metered) or a transaction completing successfully (significant because the notification of the successful completion may trigger the start of the next transaction). An event that notifies staff of a failure or that a threshold has been breached is called an *alert*. Examples of alerts could include notification that a server has failed or a warning that the memory or disk usage on a device has exceeded 75 percent. If you consider these concepts in a non-IT environment, a car console may issue an event to say that the system has successfully connected to a Bluetooth device, or it might raise an alert (together with a beep or flashing light) to warn that a threshold has been breached and the car is now low on gas.

There are two types of event monitoring tools:

- *Active monitoring tools* will poll devices to check that they are working correctly. The tool will send a message and expect a positive response within a defined time, such as sending a "ping" to a device. A failure to respond will be notified to support staff. Some tools will have automated responses to such situations, perhaps automatically restarting a device or rerouting data to avoid the faulty CI so that the service is not affected.

- *Passive monitoring tools* do not send out polling messages; they detect events generated by CIs and correlate them (that is, identify related events).

The Purpose of Event Management

The purpose of event management is to detect events, understand what they mean, and take any necessary action. Many devices are designed to communicate their status, and event monitoring will gather these communications and act upon any that need action. Some communications report operational information, such as "backup of file complete," "print complete," and so on. These events show that the service is operating correctly. They can be used to automate routine activities such as submitting the next file to be backed up or the next document to be printed. They may also be used to monitor the load across several devices, issuing automated instructions to balance the load, dependent on the events received. If the event is an alert, such as "backup failed," "printer jam," or "disk full," the necessary corrective steps will be taken. An incident should be logged in the case of a failure.

The Objectives of Event Management

The objectives of event management include the following:

- Detecting all "changes of state that have significance for the management of a CI or IT service" (see the definition of *event* earlier) and deciding upon the correct response, if any. This is then communicated to the appropriate staff to carry out.

- Triggering automated processes or activities in response to certain events. This may include automatically logging an incident in the service management tool in the event of a failure.

- Providing sufficient information to enable an accurate assessment of the performance of a service against the SLA target. This might include analyzing events that show the start and end of a process to enable the elapsed time for its completion to be calculated and compared to the SLA target.

- Using such information and analysis as the basis for service reporting, in particular to measure the success or failure of improvement actions.

You do not need to know the process steps in detail for the exam, but an understanding of the key points will help you understand its objectives. The first step is the notification that an event has occurred. This depends on the monitoring tools being configured correctly to filter out notifications that have no significance. Without this, important events can be missed or lost among hundreds of spurious notifications. The event should then be logged; this may be an entry in the event monitoring log, or an automatic link to the incident management tool may raise an incident record. In the latter case, this interface should not be used until the appropriate filtering is in place to prevent spurious incidents from being raised. An analysis of the event should identify its significance; is it informational, a warning, or an exception? Dependent upon this analysis, any required actions are then taken.

The Scope of Event Management

Event management can be applied to any aspects of service management that need to be controlled and that could benefit from being automated. The service management tool set is an example, including automatically logging incidents in response to emails or events being received, escalating incidents when thresholds have been reached, and notifying staff of certain conditions (for example, a priority one incident being logged).

Configuration items can be monitored by event management tools; this monitoring can be for two different reasons:

- Some CIs will be monitored to make sure that they are constantly available. An example of this is a network device where action needs to be taken as soon as the CI fails to respond to a ping.

- Other CIs may need to be updated frequently. This updating can be automated using event management, and the CMS can be automatically updated to show the new state.

Other areas where event management can be used include the monitoring of environmental conditions. This might be for fire and smoke detection or for other environmental changes.

Using Event Management to Preempt a Major Incident

A large transport organization installed event monitoring across its infrastructure, including monitoring the server room environments. A screen showing current events was installed at the service desk. On the second day after this was implemented, its value was proved. The service desk called the head office 150 miles away to ask the staff there to check the server room, because there were environmental alerts showing on the screen. The head-office staff entered the server room to find that the air conditioning had failed and the room was extremely warm. Had the temperature increased much more, the servers would have failed, causing major disruption to the services. The head office staff members were able to avert the incident by using fans to lower the temperature until the air-conditioning engineer arrived to fix the fault.

Tracking license use is another possible use for event management tools; this ensures that there is no illegal use of an application by ensuring that the number of people using the software does not exceed the licenses held. This may also save money; by showing that there is less demand for concurrent use than was thought, the number of licenses can be reduced. Monitoring for and responding to security events, such as detecting intruders, is another use; the tools can also be used to detect a denial-of-service attack or similar event.

In addition to these uses, event management can be used for day-to-day management of the service. This might be monitoring performance of hardware or network equipment or tracking the use of a particular application.

Monitoring and Event Management

It is important to understand the difference between the two similar but different activities of monitoring and managing events.

- *Event management* is concerned with generating events and detecting notifications that have been produced. These events are produced so that they can be monitored. They provide useful information regarding the status of the infrastructure.

- *Monitoring* detects these notifications but goes further than this. Monitoring includes actively checking CIs to ensure that they are working as they should, whether or not an event has been generated.

As you have seen, event management can be enormously useful in managing large and complex infrastructures. It is often the case, however, that the full value of these tools is not realized. This is usually because there has been insufficient time spent making sure that they are configured correctly to notify staff only for those events where they need notification. Failing to specify the correct thresholds, for example, will mean that far too many breaches are reported. The staff then ignores the events, because they are seldom significant. Of course, this means that significant events are missed. It is all too common that technical management teams have impressive plasma screens on the walls with flashing red warnings that everyone ignores. Sometimes the attitude is that the users will call the service desk if there really is an issue, which of course negates one of the major advantages of using such tools, that of being able to detect and respond to incidents before the user is impacted! Failing to filter the events properly means that the ability to automatically raise incidents cannot be used, because the service management tool would be flooded with multiple spurious events.

Request Fulfillment

The second service operation process we will cover in this chapter is request fulfillment. This is the process for handling requests for standard services, equipment, or information.

The service desk is the single point of contact for users for any aspect of the IT service. We already discussed in Chapter 10 how the service desk handles incidents reported by users. Many of the calls and emails the service desk receives are not reporting anything wrong.

They are all the other reasons that the user needs to contact IT, such as for information, for the supply of equipment, to provide access to a system or data, to reset a password, to add or remove a user, and so on. Often these requests are very standard, low-risk, common changes and as such can be handled by the service desk or second-line support teams, without using the normal change management process. In Chapter 8 we covered standard changes (low-risk, repeat changes that may be preapproved). Many requests are actually requests for changes that fulfill the standard change criteria and so may be implemented without any further authorization being sought. Chapter 8 also looked at "change models"—a set of predefined steps for use in a commonly occurring set of circumstances, allowing particular changes to be handled consistently in an agreed manner. Change models are particularly useful in request fulfillment, because they ensure that repeat requests are handled correctly.

ITIL calls all these *service requests*; they are all opportunities to provide the user with something they have asked for, such as information, advice, a standard change, or access to an IT service (such as resetting a password or providing standard IT services for a new use), and the request fulfillment process is used to handle them.

This process focuses on providing an efficient turnaround of these requests while ensuring that any required authorizations are given. Users appreciate being able to make simple requests and have them fulfilled with a minimum of bureaucracy. By handling these requests at the service desk (and second-line when required), the cost to the IT service provider is also reduced, because more skilled (and therefore expensive) staff members are not used to carry out simple tasks.

Purpose

Request fulfillment is the process responsible for managing the lifecycle of all service requests from the users.

Objectives

The objectives of request fulfillment include providing efficient fulfillment of simple requests to meet the requirements of the business. The process provides a simple means for the business to receive standard services, delivered quickly and consistently, because all the steps required to fulfill the requests (including obtaining any required authorizations) are defined. Users have a single source of information regarding the services available and how to obtain them. If the user wants to comment on or even complain about a service, the same process is used, with a predefined escalation of complaints.

Request fulfillment provides an efficient way to supply standard equipment to users; once an item has been assessed and accepted as compatible with the infrastructure, all future requests can be handled through this process. This encourages the use of standard equipment and software, because it is the easiest and fastest to obtain.

Real World Scenario

Improving Efficiency by Providing a Standard Request Fulfillment Process

A hospital IT department handled requests for hardware and software from the hospital staff. Users would ask for equipment or software that they had seen advertised in magazines or at their local PC store. Often these offered no benefit over the standard equipment in use in the rest of the organization. Each request was handled by the IT staff approaching several suppliers to find the best price and then informing the requester of the cost so that they could raise a purchase order. The money saved by sourcing the cheapest supplier did not cover the cost of the IT staff time it used. The process might be repeated several times a week for very similar requests, because each was handled separately. When the purchase order was raised, the item would be ordered, and when delivered, the support staff would install it; because each item could be different, this meant the staff had to ensure that they were following the installation directions for the particular model or software. The IT department had then to support all these different items and manage the warranty agreements. Occasionally incidents would be caused because these nonstandard items were incompatible with a change. The whole process was expensive and took up considerable IT time. The process was slow, often taking three or four weeks from request to fulfillment, so users would sometimes circumvent it by buying and installing items themselves!

A new standard request fulfillment process was introduced to address these issues. Following discussion with the business, the IT department agreed on a set of standard software and a number of standard devices—a standard laptop and one for "power" users, a standard desktop PC, and a standard office printer. A small stock of each of these was bought and put in storage. Users now ordered from this short list, at a set price, supplying the purchase order at the time of order. The item was taken from stock and installed the same day, while the purchase order was used to replenish the stock. The new arrangement suited everybody; the user was happy to forego the ability to order any item in return for same-day installation, the IT staff had a simpler range of items to support, the IT management was happy to have a less labor-intensive process, and the finance department was pleased that the IT department was able to negotiate a good price from a single supplier in return for a steady stream of orders.

In addition to these benefits, the simpler process meant that the service desk was able to handle the request, assigning the installation to the desktop support team and ordering the replacement. The simple process was very suited to user self-service and became one of the first services offered to users on the new self-service portal.

Take a look at the process flow shown in Figure 12.1; although you do not need to know the process flow in detail for the exam, an understanding of what is involved in fulfilling service requests will help you understand its objectives.

FIGURE 12.1 Request fulfillment process flow

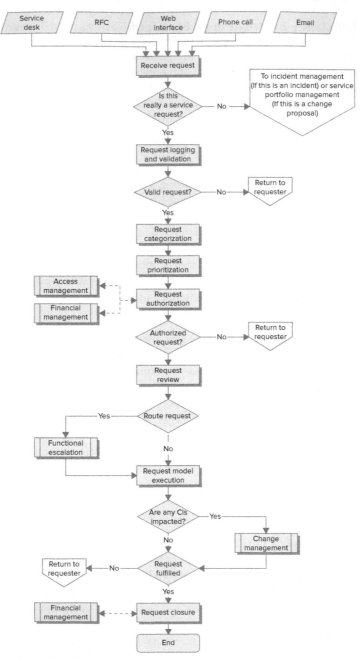

Based on Cabinet Office ITIL® material. Reproduced under license from the Cabinet Office.

Scope

The scope of request fulfillment will vary from one organization to another; it can include any requests that can be standardized and for which organization is happy to use this process. Each request should be broken into agreed activities, with a documented procedure. These procedures are then used to build the request models.

Some organizations will use the incident management process to handle requests, categorizing them as a special type of incident. This has become less common as service management tools have increasingly provided request management workflow capability. There are advantages in treating requests outside of the incident process, because they are very different. Incidents represent a failure in providing the service, and the aim is therefore to reduce the number of incidents. An increasing number of requests, on the other hand, may show that the service offered by the IT department is useful and popular. The targets for incidents and requests may be very different; requests may have specified lead times, which are dependent on other factors (such as the user not being given access until they have attended a training course), whereas the aim is to resolve every incident as quickly as possible.

Where there are a significant number of requests to be fulfilled, a separate process with a different record type should be used. This allows the service provided to be monitored and reported on in a more appropriate way than using incident reporting.

Some organizations widen the scope of requests handled by their service desk or self-service portal to include non-IT requests, such as building management issues regarding cleaning or maintenance issues. Most organizations find that there are also some areas not suited to the process, such as requests for new or changed services, which may be handled by business relationship managers and will involve service strategy and service portfolio management. It would be difficult to have the service desk collect the detail of such a request, and the target lead time would be hard to assess.

Access Management

Access management is the process of granting authorized users the right to use a service while preventing access to nonauthorized users. It also is sometimes referred to as rights management or identity management. Access requirements can change frequently, and service operation is responsible for granting access quickly, in line with the needs of the business, while ensuring that all requests are properly authorized.

Purpose

In Chapter 6, we discussed information security management and its role in defining security policies. The process for implementing many of these policies is access management. This process provides users, who have the required authorization, with the ability to use the services they require. Ensuring that only authorized individuals are given access to data is a concern of every IT service provider; failure to carry this out correctly can be very damaging and possibly breach legal or regulatory requirements. Consider the damage that could be done to an organization discovered to have allowed unauthorized access to medical or banking records because of poor access management processes.

Organizations need to ensure that access is managed not only when a new member of staff is appointed and set up with access to the systems but also when the staff member leaves. A challenge many organizations face is keeping up-to-date with changing access requirements as a staff member moves between departments. Often the new access requirement is requested, but there is no questioning of whether the existing access rights are still required in the new position; therefore, the individual may amass significant rights over a period of years if this step is not carried out. It is dependent, in part, on the business informing the IT service provider of staff movements; the IT provider should routinely query whether existing access is still required when additional access is requested.

There may also be occasions when access is restricted, perhaps during an investigation into suspected wrongdoing, to prevent any evidence from being destroyed. Such requests would normally be made by senior management or human resources.

Objectives

The objectives of the access management process are to do the following:

- Manage access to services, carrying out the policies defined within information security management (see the service design stage).

- Ensure that all requests for access are verified and authorized. This may include requests to restrict or remove access.

- Ensure that requests are dealt with efficiently, balancing the requirement for authorization and control with the need to be responsive to business requirements.

- Ensure (once access rights are granted) that the rights that have been granted are used in accordance with security policies. This might include, for example, the use of Internet access for personal use. Although some personal use may be allowed, there are likely to be categories of websites that may not be accessed.

Scope

The scope of access management, as we have said, is the efficient execution of information security management policies. By carrying these out, the confidentiality, availability, and integrity (CIA) of the organization's data and intellectual property are protected. Confidentiality here means that only authorized users are able to see the data. Integrity means that the data is kept safe from corruption or unauthorized change. Access management ensures that the service is made available to the authorized user; this does not guarantee that it will always be available during service hours, because this is the responsibility of availability management.

A request for access will often be made through the request management process. Some organizations will maintain a specialized team to carry out the requests, but more commonly it is carried out by other functions. Technical and application management functions are involved, and a significant part of the process may be handled within the service desk. There should be a single coordination point to ensure consistency.

You do not need to know the access management process in detail for the exam, but an understanding of the key points in managing access requests will help you understand its objectives.

The first step is to request access. This may be done through the request fulfillment process described earlier or through the completion of a request form. The access request has then to be verified before it can be actioned. The identity of the requestor must be confirmed, and the access requirement must be judged as legitimate. The identity may be confirmed by the requestor providing their username and password or, in the case of a new user, the request having been made by human resources or a line manager. The validity of the request may also be confirmed by requiring authorization from human resources or an appropriate manager.

Once the access has been granted, the status of the user should be monitored to ensure that they still have a valid requirement for the access. In practice, this can be difficult to achieve. Access management should be notified of staff that leave so that their access can be revoked, and many organizations have robust procedures to ensure that this is done. Many organizations encounter difficulty in tracking the changing roles and accompanying access requirements of users, especially those who have been in the organization for many years. In this situation, new access requirements are added to existing rights, with no questioning of whether these existing rights are still required. Consideration should be given to adding questions about existing access requirements to the access request form. The human resources department needs to be made aware of the importance of supplying information regarding changing job roles to access management in order to protect the organization's data.

Access should be revoked when the user leaves the organization; again, the human resources department needs to understand the importance of informing access management quickly in this situation.

Summary

This chapter explored the remaining three processes in the service operation stage, covering the purpose, objectives and scope of each:

- Event management
- Request fulfillment
- Access management

We discussed the key ITIL concepts of events and alerts and how event management can improve availability by preempting failures or reducing the time taken to identify them.

We discussed the key ITIL concepts of service requests and how the request fulfillment process can save time and money in expediting simple user requirements.

We discussed the importance of access management in preventing unauthorized access to data and some of the issues that arise in monitoring access rights:

- Event
- Alert
- Service request

Exam Essentials

Understand the purpose, objectives, and scope of event management.   Be able to describe events (a change of state that has significance for the management of a CI) and alerts (a failure or a breach of a threshold) and the difference between them. Be able to give examples of each.

Understand the role of event management in automation.   Be able to describe passive and active monitoring and the difference between them. Be able to give examples of each. Understand the importance of filtering events. Be able to explain how effective event management can reduce downtime. Although some requests are standard changes, many are not, such as requests for information.

Understand the purpose objectives and scope of request fulfillment.   Know how it benefits the customer and the IT department.

Understand the purpose objectives and scope of access management.   Be able to explain the relationship between access management and information security management. Access management is not just granting access but also restricting or removing it as required.

Review Questions

You can find the answers in Appendix A.

1. The request fulfillment process is suitable for which of the following?

   A. All requests, including RFCs

   B. Only requests that have been approved by the CAB

   C. Emergency requests for change, because the process will ensure a fast implementation

   D. Common, low-risk requests with a documented fulfillment procedure

2. Requests can be fulfilled by the following:

   1. Service desk staff

   2. Second-line staff

   3. Service level manager

   4. Business relationship manager

      A. 1 and 2

      B. All of the above

      C. 1 and 3

      D. 2 and 3

3. Requests must be as follows:

   1. Authorized by the CAB

   2. Authorized by the budget holder when an expense will be incurred

   3. Authorized by technical management

   4. May be preauthorized

      A. 1 and 3

      B. 1 only

      C. 2 and 4

      D. 2 only

4. Which of the following could be defined as a service request?

   1. "Is the service available at weekends?"

   2. "How do I get training on this application?"

   3. "I need this application changed to include a web interface"

   4. "We have a new member of staff starting. Can you set them up on the system?"

      A. All of the above

      B. 3 and 4

      C. 1, 2, and 3

      D. 1, 2, and 4

5. For which of these situations would automation by using event management *not* be appropriate?

1. Hierarchical escalation of incidents

2. Speeding up the processing of month-end sales figures

3. Notification of "intruder detected" to local police station

4. Running backups

    A. 3 and 4

    B. All of the above

    C. 2, and 3

    D. 1, 3, and 4

6. Event management can be used to monitor which of the following?

1. Environmental conditions

2. System messages

3. Staff rosters

4. License use

    A. 1 and 2

    B. 2, and 3

    C. 2, and 4

    D. All of the above

7. Which of the following is the best description of a request?

    A. A standard change

    B. A request from a user for information, advice, or a standard change, or access to an IT service

    C. An RFC

    D. The procurement process

8. Which of the following are types of event monitoring?

1. Passive

2. Virtual

3. Active

4. Standard

    A. 1 and 2

    B. 2, and 3

    C. 1 and 3

    D. All of the above

9. Which of the following is the best description of an alert?

  A. An unplanned interruption to a service

  B. The unknown, underlying cause of one or more incidents

  C. An event that notifies staff of a failure or that a threshold that has been breached

  D. A change of state that has significance for the management of a CI

10. Which of the following is the best description of access management?

  A. Access management enables authorized access to services and data. Information security management removes or prevents access to nonauthorized staff.

  B. Access management grants authorized users the right to use a service, while preventing access to nonauthorized users.

  C. Access management is responsible for setting security policies.

  D. Access management decides what services users should have access to.

Chapter

13

Understanding Continual Service Improvement

THE FOLLOWING ITIL FOUNDATION EXAM OBJECTIVES ARE COVERED IN THIS CHAPTER:

✓ 2-11. Account for the main purpose, objectives and scope of continual service improvement

✓ 2-12. Briefly explain what value continual service improvement provides to the business

✓ Unit 3: Generic concepts and definitions:

  ▪ 3-38. CSI register

  ▪ 3-42. The Deming Cycle (plan, do, check, act)

✓ 4-9. Explain the continual service improvement approach

✓ 4-10. Understand the role of measurement for continual service improvement and explain the following key elements:

  ▪ Relationship between critical success factors (CSF) and key performance indicators (KPI)

  ▪ Baselines

  ▪ Types of metrics (technology metrics, process metrics, service metrics)

✓ 5-9. State the purpose, objectives and scope for:

  ▪ 5-91 The seven-step improvement process

In this chapter, we'll cover the continual service improvement lifecycle stage. This is a separate stage of the lifecycle, but it doesn't work in isolation. Perhaps even more than any of the other stages, this lifecycle stage affects the whole approach for service management. The desire to improve is often the driving force behind using the service lifecycle in an organization, although it may not be recognized as such at the start.

Following an ad hoc approach to improvement will take an organization only so far; the full benefits of a continual service improvement approach can be realized only when the actions taken are done so as part of a regular program.

It is important to understand the purpose, objectives, and scope of this stage so that the full benefits can be achieved. It is also a specified part of the foundation syllabus, and you may be asked questions about it in the examination.

Achieving Continual Service Improvement

Continual service improvement is key to the success of the service management approach, because organizations do not stay static in their requirements. Reviewing performance and identifying improvement opportunities allow the continued development of higher-quality, lower-cost services, in line with the objectives of the business.

Understanding the Purpose of CSI

The purpose of *continual service improvement (CSI)* is to continue to support the business with IT services in the face of changing business needs. Consider for a moment exactly what that may mean in your organization.

In most companies, there are business drivers that cause changes in behavior to meet market forces. Organizations that do not respond to outside forces or recognize the need to change will usually not survive the rigors of the marketplace. The same should be applied to the provider of the IT services that support the business. The idea that an IT service provider will be viewed differently is quite surprising, but this is often the perception in an IT department. Continual service improvement is there to make sure that the changes in business processes that keep the business alive and thriving are recognized and that the IT services that support those processes change with them.

Think about these statements:

- You cannot manage what you cannot control.
- You cannot control what you cannot measure.
- You cannot measure what you cannot define.

Measurement is critical to the success of continual improvement. Without defined measures, it is difficult to manage improvements. CSI is concerned with the improvement of all aspects of the service lifecycle, from strategy through design, transition, and operation. Failure to implement processes that support your services, which are measurable, repeatable, and manageable, will have an impact on the business. It is necessary to engage with your organizational goals and use them to provide clear objectives for your IT services. If defined services and processes do not support business activity, it will become increasingly difficult to keep up with the organization's need for change. Depending on the criticality of the services, the impact on the business may be loss of productivity, higher costs, damage to reputation, or potential risk of business failure. Mitigating against or preventing such an impact is a key driver for continual service improvement. Applying the continual service improvement process across the service lifecycle will enable continued support for business activities.

In addition to this, continual service improvement should be seeking improvements in cost effectiveness and efficiency. This application of continually searching for enhancement should also be applied across the whole lifecycle, including CSI itself.

The Objectives of CSI

To achieve the purpose for this lifecycle stage, the ITIL Continual Service Improvement publication provides the following objectives:

- Review, analyze, prioritize, and recommend improvement opportunities in each lifecycle stage: service strategy, service design, service transition, and service operation, as well as CSI. Regular activity of this type will move the improvement from an ad hoc approach to a genuine improvement initiative.

- Review and analyze service level achievements, according to the service level agreements in place.

- Identify and implement specific activities to improve IT service quality, including improvements to the effectiveness and efficiency of the enabling processes. The overall service quality is partially dependent on the quality of the processes. It can be tempting for IT services to assume that the only metrics that matter are those relating to the technology.

- Improve the cost effectiveness of IT service delivery, without negatively impacting customer satisfaction. Customer satisfaction is an important measure of the value of the service being delivered.

- Ensure suitable and applicable quality management methods are in use to support the continual improvement activities. The quality management methods in use should support the overall quality governance in place in the organization.

- Ensure that the processes in use have clearly defined objectives and measurements, which produce identifiable and actionable improvements. This should be part of the controls around the processes in use throughout the service lifecycle.

- Understand what to measure, why it is being measured, and what the successful outcome should be. Recognizing exactly what is required will enable a better interpretation of the metrics and the behaviors they will drive.

Setting the Scope for CSI

The ITIL Continual Service Improvement publication provides guidance in four main areas:

- The overall health of IT service management as a discipline

- Continual alignment of the IT services with the current and future needs of the business

- The maturity and capability of the organization, management, processes, and people utilized by the services

- Continual improvement of all aspects of the IT service and the service assets that support them

It is only by understanding how the improvements are to be carried out, and what the desired outcomes are, that you can deliver continual service improvement. The activities that support improvement are as follows:

- Reviewing the service performance targets and trends, using the available management information, to understand if the desired service levels are being met

- Reviewing process outputs to understand if the required performance is being achieved to enable the services

- Regularly carrying out maturity assessments on the processes in use to identify areas of concern or demonstrate improvement achievements

- Conducting compliance audits on the processes, ensuring maturity is maintained

- Identifying and making proposals for improvements

- Conducting customer satisfaction surveys as required on a periodic basis

- Reviewing and understanding business trends and projections, maintaining awareness of business priorities

- Measuring and identifying the value created by continual improvement initiatives

These activities will require ownership to ensure that they actually get done. Improvement activities should be planned and be part of a considered approach, managed by individuals who have appropriate authority to carry them out. It is important to make sure that the processes and services are subject to a continual improvement strategy This strategy should ensure that the improvement initiatives are achieving their targets and being kept up-to-date. Specific improvements, which require changes, should follow the change management process. It is easy for improvement programs to fade, so it is necessary for these activities to be monitored as part of the overall continual service improvement approach.

How CSI Provides Value to the Business

The adoption of standard and consistent approaches to improving IT service quality will result in controlled, gradual, and maintainable improvement. Any improvements must, naturally, be cost justified in terms of the return on the investment or, more appropriately, on the value of the investment.

By employing regular reviews of the business needs and ensuring that IT services remain aligned to them, the business can be assured of an acceptable level of support. Because IT services may be said to underpin the success of the majority of organizations, this assurance is critical for business confidence.

One of the key aspects of any improvement is cost, but it is not only the cost justification for the initiative; it is also the benefit that can be achieved in terms of cost. An improvement may be able to create cost savings in real terms or increase capability for additional workload. Because one of the most common themes of budget negotiations is the requirement to achieve more for the same or less than the previous year, this is a genuine long-term goal for organizations. Utilizing the techniques and approaches of continual service improvement will allow for a gradual and sustained increase in capability, because the effectiveness and efficiency of the processes and services are managed.

But it is not only the processes and the services they support that are under the scrutiny of continual service improvement. It looks at all elements that enable the delivery of services to the business. This will include all resources, partners, technology, staff skills, training, and communications. The emphasis on a holistic approach to improvement means that true business benefits can be achieved by delivering cost-effective enhancements across the wider enterprise. For example, renegotiating contracts with third-party suppliers may deliver an ongoing benefit to the business.

To achieve these benefits, it is necessary to ensure that monitoring and reporting on performance across the service portfolio allows for the identification of improvement opportunities.

Utilizing the Continual Service Improvement Approach

We will now cover the approach proposed by ITIL for continual service improvement, illustrated in Figure 13.1.

FIGURE 13.1   Continual service improvement

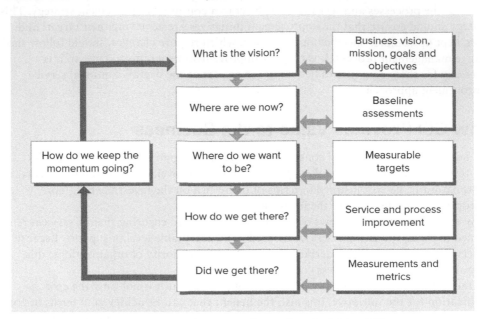

Based on Cabinet Office ITIL material. Reproduced under license from the Cabinet Office.

There are key questions that need to be asked as part of implementing improvements. These are all covered by the continual service improvement approach. The first step is to identify the vision that is driving the improvement initiative. Understanding the high-level focus of the business will allow for the alignment of the IT services and the business strategies.

The question that needs be asked by the IT service provider in this step is "What is the vision?" This enables identification of the ultimate and long-term goals for the improvement.

Once the vision has been established, the next step requires an objective assessment of the current state, namely, a baseline capture of the organization in terms of business, people, process, and technology. Utilizing this information will give a picture of the current service provision and its quality. The question asked at this step is "Where are we now?"

Having established where you are now, the logical next question is "Where do we want to be?" This is not necessarily the achievement of the vision identified at the start of the approach. In fact, it is probably unwise to have that as the answer, because unless it is an easily achievable goal, it is unlikely to be reached. A better approach is to identify an achievable target, one that will enable some quick wins and gain some buy-in for the improvement opportunity. Working in small steps, identifying achievable targets that build steady progression to the overall goal will enable your improvements to be consolidated at each target.

Targets are important, but equally important is the requirement to understand how you achieve them. The next question of "How do we get there?" covers identifying the actions needed to meet the targets. This can take a number of different approaches, depending on the improvement that is required. It could be process improvements, technology improvements, or even training for staff. It is important to ensure that this activity is captured and managed as part of an overall improvement program. The responsibility for monitoring the actions will be critical in achieving the targets, because often improvement initiatives will lose focus and fail at this step. Driving the actions and maintaining momentum will provide the input for the next step of the approach.

That next step is measuring the achievements, and the question that is applied is "Did we get there?" When working on service performance improvements, this is documented as part of the service reviews and performance metrics against the required service levels. Measuring the actual performance delivery and comparing this to the predicted target will provide the answer to "Did we get there?" Specific targets in process improvement may be measured in terms of a maturity matrix, for the efficiency and effectiveness of the process. This is the point in the CSI approach where you understand whether you have achieved the goals when asking "Where do we want to be?" This keeps the momentum of your improvements going, potentially providing quick wins.

You then need to review your overall objective and begin the cycle of assessment, target setting, and measurement again.

 Real World Scenario

Supermarket Improvement Approach

In the United Kingdom, the leading supermarket chain used this approach to reach its current position. Over a period of 20 years, the chain has had as its vision "the commitment to be the most highly valued company for their customers," in other words, to be the first choice for their customers. To achieve this vision, the company made incremental changes to its overall operation, from the introduction of specifically targeted value brands to the improvement in logistics and technology within the stores. By building on each small success, the company consolidated on its position in the marketplace. It has gone from being one of the least successful supermarket chains in the United Kingdom to being the most successful. It proudly proclaims its vision and the approach it takes in its stores and on its corporate website.

This approach can be adopted at all stages of the service lifecycle, from improvements in service strategy to improvements in your approach to continual service improvement itself.

Capturing Your Improvements

Using the CSI approach, you will no doubt end up with more than one improvement initiative running at once. It is therefore necessary to manage your improvement activity, so you need to have a mechanism for capturing these programs and ensuring that you allocate your resources and capabilities efficiently.

The recommendation for best practices is to develop a *CSI register*; Table 13.1 shows an example, where all the individual improvements can be recorded. This means you can apply some categorization and management around the overall CSI approach.

TABLE 13.1   Example of a CSI register

Oppor-tunity no.	Size (small, medium, large)	Timescale (short, medium, long)	Description	Priority (urgent, 1, 2, 3)	KPI metric	Justifi-cation
1	Small	Short	A number of failures have occurred when implementing updated or new applications. This has been caused by the testing procedure in release and deployment using out-of-date test data. The requirement is to update the test data in repository test 4371.	Urgent	n% reduction in failures	Significant reduction in failures after transition and resulting business impact.
2	Medium	Long	Event management: the number of alerts from the ABC 479 module of the payroll suite is still excessive causing unnecessary analysis time. Additional filtering required.	2	n% reduction in spurious events	Will help reduce the amount of analysis time and avoid potential oversight of significant events.
3	Medium	Long	Training issue: Service desk staff would benefit from additional training in the use of the human resources (HR) joiners and leavers application.	3	n% improvement in relevant staff trained in the HR joiners and leavers application	All queries to the service desk on this application currently have to be escalated to the application management team. With some basic training, a number of these could be dealt with by first-line support.

TABLE 13.1   Example of a CSI register   *(continued)*

Opportunity no.	Size (small, medium, large)	Timescale (short, medium, long)	Description	Priority (urgent, 1, 2, 3)	KPI metric	Justification
4	Large	Medium	Change management process: having multiple authorization channels has caused issues with some users because of uncoordinated changes.	3	Alignment to single channel	Redesign of the change management process will reduce confusion and impact to stakeholders.

Based on Cabinet Office ITIL® material. Reproduced under license from the Cabinet Office.

As you can see in the example register, the first level of categorization is to establish the size of the undertaking or task. The suggested approach is to simply use a broad categorization such as small, medium, or large. This will indicate the requirements for resources and capabilities for the initiative.

In addition, you need to establish the timescale for the improvement—can it be achieved in the short, medium, or long term? A brief description of the initiative will provide suitable context for the audience. Also important is to understand the urgency of the improvement, and as always within the framework, urgency and impact based on the business perspective will identify the priority of the action. The register should also provide some indication as to the measures or metrics that will be applied to verify a successful outcome from the improvement. The prediction of achievement is an important factor in determining success, because this will be compared to the actual achievement for the final evaluation.

A brief outline of the justification for the improvement should also be captured as part of the register, but the full details of the initiative will be captured as part of the improvement program documentation. In the example given, there is no contact information or reference to timeframes for completion. Contact information for who raised the improvement and who will be working on it and, of course, the date by which it is required will be necessary. In this example, there are only a limited selection of possible fields; the register should contain whatever information you need, according to the requirements of your own organization, for managing your improvement programs.

The register itself will be classed as a service asset and as such should be managed as an item in the service knowledge management system (SKMS). The CSI manager will be accountable for managing and coordinating the activities.

Capturing the information about the improvements will provide structure and visibility for CSI within the organization. It will be necessary to ensure that the interfaces for all processes likely to generate improvement activities are clearly understood and their outputs effectively managed through the register, such as problem management, capacity management, and change management. This should include service review outputs, because this is a common source for finding requirements for improvements.

Improving Quality with the Deming Cycle

One of the many approaches available in improvement activities is the use of the Deming cycle. W. Edwards Deming is best known for his management philosophy, leading to higher-quality, increased productivity and a more competitive position for the organization. By utilizing the elements of his approach that are applicable for service management, you have the Plan-Do-Check-Act steps that make up the Deming cycle, illustrated in Figure 13.2.

FIGURE 13.2   Plan-Do-Check-Act cycle: Continual quality control and consolidation

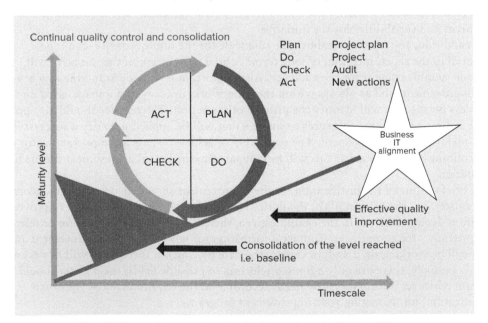

Based on Cabinet Office ITIL® material. Reproduced under license from the Cabinet Office.

The cycle is now commonly referred to as the PDCA cycle, and we will briefly cover each step.

In the Plan stage, you are doing exactly that, planning the activity for the improvement. Ensuring that there is a plan is part of all service management activity, and it is also part of the governance controls within standards such as ISO/IEC 20000 (the Service Management standard). The PDCA cycle is complementary to the CSI approach and the seven-step improvement process. We will cover the seven-step process later in this chapter.

In the remaining stages of the PDCA cycle, you carry out the activity as defined and agreed on in the plan. In the Do step of the process, it is important to capture the activity and make updates to the CSI register. Following this comes the Check step, which consists of checking on the activity that has been carried out. In terms of ongoing improvement, this step and the following step, Act, are used to monitor, measure, review, and implement initiatives. At the conclusion of the cycle, there is a consolidation effort, which, as you can see in Figure 13.2, prevents the circle from rolling back down the slope. The effort of reaching a target may be considerable, but often the effort required to maintain the achievement is just as great. The PDCA cycle allows you to manage this effectively.

The cycle is underpinned by a process-led approach to its management. This means that defined processes are in place, the activities are measured for compliance to agreed-upon values, and the outputs are audited to identify improvements.

The Role of Measurement in CSI

Measurement is a fundamental part of all processes; in fact, it is one of the key characteristics of a process, because all processes must be measurable. CSI cannot take place without the results of measurement, so a key part of this lifecycle stage is to identify the nature of the measures you want to employ and ensure that these are appropriate to identify the improvements that will benefit the organization as a whole.

To be useful, measures must be objective. The role of measurement is to provide the following:

- An assessment of the current status
- The identification of improvement areas
- A measurement of enhancements made

Because your organization's business processes depend on the delivery of services, you must also consider the measures that will be applied to services. Most organizations will measure the following:

- Availability of the service
- Reliability of the service
- Performance of the service

Critical Success Factors and Key Performance Indicators

ITIL describes a *critical success factor (CSF)* as something that must happen if an IT service, process, plan, process, or other activity is to succeed. *Key performance indicators (KPIs)* are used to measure the achievement of each critical success factor.

The CSI manager will be instrumental in assisting the process owners and managers to understand the CSFs for each process and to develop appropriate KPIs to measure their success.

Establishing and measuring the CSF for a process will enable an understanding of the current state of the process, help identify any required improvements, and measure the achievement of any enhancements made.

It is recommended that a service or process have no more than two to five associated CSFs at any one time and that each CSF have no more than two to five KPIs for measuring success. This way, you can be sure of having manageable measurement and meaningful results.

In the early stages of maturity for the process or service, it is probably best to limit the numbers of KPIs still further and measure only two or three. You can add more as the maturity of the service and the service management processes increases, but initially it is important to define the most appropriate measures as a starting point. Over time, the requirements for measurement will change, as the maturity of associated processes increases or new processes are included in the service management scope.

KPIs can be either quantitative or qualitative. It is necessary to identify the specific metrics and measurements required to calculate the desired KPI. The following sidebars show you some examples for both types of KPI.

Qualitative KPIs

CSF: Improving service quality

KPI: 10 percent increase in customer satisfaction rating for handling incidents over the next six months

Metrics Required

- Original customer satisfaction score for handling incidents

- Ending satisfaction score for handling incidents

Measurements

- Incident handling survey score

- Number of survey scores

Quantitative KPIs

CSF: Reducing IT costs

KPI: 10 percent reduction in the costs of handling printer incidents

Metrics required:

- Original cost of handling printer incidents
- Final cost of handling printer incidents
- Cost of the improvement effort

Measurements:

- Time spent on the incident by first-level operative and their average salary
- Time spent on the incident by second-level operative and their average salary
- Time spent on problem management activities by second-level operative and their average salary
- Time spent on the training first-level operative on the workaround
- Cost of a service call to third-party vendor
- Time and material from third-party vendor

Based on Cabinet Office ITIL® material. Reproduced under license from the Cabinet Office.

Another important aspect that you should consider is whether a KPI is fit for use. There are a number of questions you should ask to determine this. Does the performance indicator tell you anything about the goal achievement? If you do not meet the target set for the performance indicator, does that mean you will not achieve your goal? Or if you do achieve the performance target, will you achieve your goal? Performance indicators should be relevant and provide useful information. They should also be easy to interpret and be manageable. By this we mean that it should be easy to change the performance indicator to meet changing requirements, and it should also be proof against external influences. Consideration should be given to the frequency of data capture and the availability required for the output. What conditions will the performance indicator work under, and when will it be impacted sufficiently so that it will no longer work? And lastly, who owns the performance indicator, and who is responsible for collecting and analyzing the data?

KPIs are very important in the overall approach to CSI, and it is important to remember that whatever measures you put in place, they will potentially drive behavior, so you should be careful to ensure that the behavior you create is desirable. A suite of measures is always preferable so that you do not focus on only one particular behavior.

Using Different Types of Metrics

In general, a metric is a scale of measure that allows you to define what is to be measured. It is usually associated with a standard or specific unit of measurement. Metrics are used in a number of different business models including CMMI, COBIT, and Six Sigma and typically are used to track performance in the form of KPIs.

There are three types of metrics that an organization will need to collect to support the activities of CSI and other service management processes:

Technology Metrics   These metrics are usually associated with managing components, using monitoring systems, such as availability monitoring and performance monitoring.

Process Metrics   These metrics are captured in terms of the CSFs and KPIs, as you explored earlier in this chapter. The overall achievement and maturity of the process can be measured in this way. There are four key areas that KPIs can help assess: quality, performance, value, and compliance in following the process. These areas will help identify potential improvement opportunities.

Service Metrics   Service metrics provide a measure of the end-to-end service performance. They consist of the results produced from the technology and process metrics. They are often presented in a customer-facing report.

Using Baselines in CSI

Baselines can be used to provide a clear starting point for any improvement activity, so it is important that when you capture a baseline, you are assured that it's accurate.

Taking a snapshot of the infrastructure, services, and processes at a given point in time is valuable, but in order to use this as a basis for later comparison or as a starting point, the snapshot should be verified against the actual environment before it is declared as an official baseline.

Capturing regular baselines will improve the ability of service management to forecast performance requirements. Ensuring that baselines are documented, recognized, and accepted through the organization is part of the responsibility of CSI. It is important to establish baselines at all levels, including for strategic goals and objectives, tactical process maturity, and operational metrics and KPIs.

When you first start to capture data, it may be inaccurate or lacking in integrity, but it should form the very first baseline, because it is better to have some data rather than none at all. Improvements can be made in the data capture and in the integrity so that future baselines will reflect the improvement that has been made.

The Seven-Step Improvement Process

In this section, you will learn about the *seven-step improvement process*, a crucial part of the success of continual service improvement, as shown in Figure 13.3.

FIGURE 13.3   The seven-step improvement process

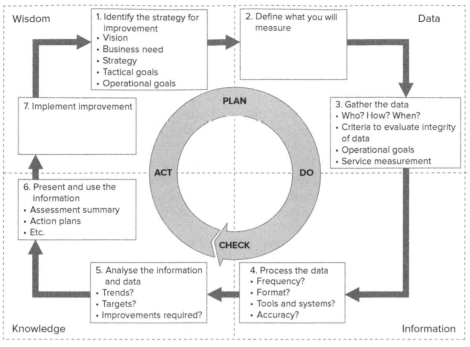

Based on Cabinet Office ITIL® material. Reproduced under license from the Cabinet Office.

The purpose of the seven-step improvement process is to define and manage the steps needed to successfully implement improvements. This includes identifying and defining the measures and metrics; the actions required for gathering, processing, and analyzing data; how the results will be presented; and finally the management of the implementation of the improvement.

The objectives are to do the following:

- Identify improvement opportunities for services, processes, tools, and so on.

- Deliver cost reductions in providing services, while maintaining the levels of service and outcomes the business requires. It will be important to ensure that any cost reduction does not have a negative impact on the quality of service.

- Identify what needs to be measured, analyzed, and reported to establish improvement opportunities.

- Continually align and realign IT service provision with the required business outcomes, and monitor the service to ensure that your service achievements meet the current business requirements.

- Understand what to measure and why it is being measured; define the success outcome.

One of the important considerations for improvement is that it should be cost effective. If the cost of implementing the improvement is not significantly outweighed by the benefit that will be achieved, it must be carefully assessed to ensure that it is actually worth the financial outlay. This means that each improvement opportunity will require justification; in the case of a small-scale improvement, this will be a simple report, but in the instance of a more significant activity, a full business case will be needed.

The seven-step improvement process is not designed to be utilized in isolation and will be fully effective only if it is applied across all aspects of IT service provision, including technology, services, processes, organization, and partners.

The scope should include an analysis of the performance and capabilities of all of these aspects, including an assessment of the maturity of the processes enabling each service. It will also include making the best use of the technology available and exploiting the benefits of any new technology, where it is cost justifiable and provides a measurable business benefit. Also within the scope are the organizational structures and capabilities of personnel, ensuring that the roles and responsibilities are appropriately allocated with the necessary skills.

Each step of the improvement process is designed to assist in the activity of CSI. The process makes it reasonably simple to see what takes place; the challenge is to realize this in the live environment. The seven-step process spans the entire service lifecycle and is the driving force behind continual service improvement.

Step 1: Identify the Strategy for Improvement

Let's consider the steps in turn, beginning with step 1. In this step, you identify the strategy for improvement. The questions you ask here are concerned with establishing the overall vision for the business. What are you attempting to achieve for the business? How can you support the overall business vision, objectives, and plans? What are the future plans for the business—short, medium, and long term? How do your IT services support these goals? This analysis will enable you see where the business can best be aided by your efforts.

It will be necessary to review this step on a regular basis to ensure that you are continuing to align with the overall business objective. Meeting the requirements of the organization should be done according the best possible use of technology, delivering a cost-effective solution that enables the business processes at an appropriate level of cost and complexity.

Any initiative that is considered must be logged in the CSI register. If, after review of the business case or justification (through the change management process), it is rejected, the information can be archived so that you have a complete record of initiatives that have not been successful for later comparison.

Triggers and inputs for the improvement process include the following:

- Business plans and strategy
- Service review meetings
- Vision and mission statements

- Corporate objectives
- Legislative requirements
- Governance controls
- Customer satisfaction surveys
- CSI register

Step 2: Define What You Will Measure

This step is directly related to the goals that have been defined for measuring the services and service management processes to support the measurement and CSI activities.

In this step, it is necessary to define what you should measure, define and agree on what can actually be measured, and then carry out a gap analysis to finalize the actual improvement measurement plan.

To be effective, this step should focus on a few vital, meaningful measures that support qualitative and quantitative assessment of success. These should be usable and provide value to the improvement. IT is usually very capable of producing measures, but often the measures may deliver little value; too many measures will provide a confusing picture and will require rationalization.

Defining exactly what will be measured and the value that it will bring is an important early step. You need to ensure that you have the capability to capture the data and use the measurement. It should also be verified against the needs of the customer; it is not up to the IT department to decide what is of value.

The stages of the service lifecycle that support this step in the CSI process are service strategy and service design; here you should have established the requirements for measurement. It is complementary to the continual service management improvement approach, identifying how you will ascertain both "where you are now" and "where you want to be." By using the gap analysis performed as part of this step, you can identify the requirements of the stage "how you get there" in the improvement approach.

Inputs to this step include the following:

- SLRs and targets
- Service review meeting
- Service portfolio and the service catalog
- Budget cycle
- Measurement results and reports (for example, balanced scorecard)
- Customer satisfaction surveys
- Benchmark data
- Baseline data
- Risk assessments and risk mitigation plans

Step 3: Gather the Data

Gathering the data requires having monitoring in place. It is important to remember that for CSI data capture you are less concerned with real-time monitoring and more interested in the exceptions, resolutions, and trends associated with the data produced. There are a number of ways in which you can carry out monitoring of your services, processes, and technology.

For your technology monitoring, you can employ tools to automate the activity, and these will be part of the component- and application-based metrics that measure performance and availability.

Process measurement is a part of every service management process, and the data captured will assist in identifying improvement opportunities. The tasks associated with this step are as follows:

Task 1: Define monitoring and data collection requirements.

Task 2: Define frequency of monitoring and data collection.

Task 3: Determine tool requirements for monitoring and data collection.

Task 4: Develop monitoring and data collection procedures.

Task 5: Develop and communicate the monitoring and data collection plan.

Task 6: Update availability and capacity plans.

Task 7: Begin monitoring and data collection.

You need to ensure that as part of this step you define the following:

- Who is responsible for monitoring and gathering the data?

- How will the data be gathered?

- When and how often is the data gathered?

- What is the criteria to evaluate the integrity of the data?

It will be necessary to look at the data collected and verify it makes sense in the context of the overall service provision. It is this step that enables you to answer the question "Did we get there?" from the continual service improvement approach.

Inputs to this step of the process include the following:

- New business requirements

- Existing SLAs

- Existing tools and monitoring capability

- Plans from service management processes (for example, availability and capacity)

- Trend analysis reports

- CSI register

- Gap analysis reports (what you should/can measure)

- Customer satisfaction survey

Step 4: Process the Data

This step allows you to convert the data into the required format for the audience. It follows the trail (Figure 13.4) from metric to KPI to CSF, right the way back to the vision, if desired.

FIGURE 13.4   From vision to measurements

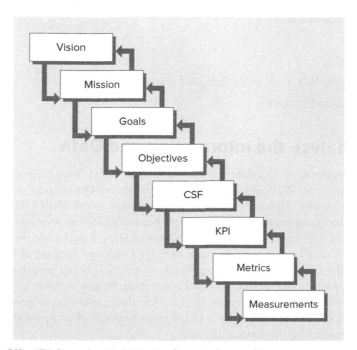

Based on Cabinet Office ITII. Reproduced with license from the Cabinet Office.

During this activity, it is common to use report-generating technology to assist with the transfer of data into information so that it can be analyzed. Processing the data into information allows more successful analytical techniques and will encourage the use of an overall perspective on the measurement, by associating data groups to an overall service.

When processing data, it is important to consider the following:

- The frequency of processing the data. This may be driven by the analysis requirements and the ability to capture trends.
- The format required for the output, which will also be affected by how the analysis is carried out and how the information will be used.
- The tools and systems that are used for data processing.
- The evaluation techniques you will use to verify the accuracy of the data.

Nearly all of the data captured for CSI is likely to be collected by automation, but there will be some elements that require manual capture. When processing the data, it is important to remember that data collected from a manual input may need greater effort in verification. Stressing the importance of accuracy in data entry to support teams and service management staff will help with the ability to process the data.

Inputs to processing data include the following:

- Data collected through monitoring
- Reporting requirements
- SLAs/OLAs
- Service catalog
- List of metrics, KPI, CSF, objectives, and goals
- Report frequency/template

Step 5: Analyze the Information and Data

Analyzing the information and data you have produced so far from the process is crucial to enabling its proper use. Without analysis and understanding the context of the information, you are unable to make informed decisions. It is necessary to establish what the information actually means to the organization. For example, you may have information that demonstrates a downward trend in the volume of service desk calls. But is this a good thing or a bad? It may be that the volume of calls have reduced because of better service quality and availability, or it could be that the service desk is being perceived as ineffective, and users are bypassing the service desk and attempting to seek support elsewhere.

Analyzing the data requires a greater level of skill than capturing or processing the data. It is necessary to understand the context of the information and compare this to the agreed-upon targets identified in the service lifecycle.

It is important to ensure that the analysis answers questions such as the following:

- Are operations running to plan? This could be a project plan or service management plans for availability, capacity, or continuity.
- Are the targets agreed on in SLAs being met?
- Does the analysis show any structural problems?
- Are improvements required?
- Are there any identifiable trends? Positive or negative?
- Is there an identifiable cause for the trends?

Reviewing the trends over a period of time is important for understanding the context and any potential improvement opportunities.

The analysis should be shared with the IT managers and discussed in order to formulate plans for improvement opportunities. This output can then be part of the presentation, which is the next step in the improvement process.

Inputs include the following:

- Results of the monitored data
- Existing KPIs and targets
- Information and perceptions from customer satisfaction surveys

Step 6: Present and Use the Information

In this step, you present the answer to the question "Did we get there?" from the continual service improvement approach. You present the knowledge, represented in the reports, monitors, action plans, reviews, evaluations, and opportunities, to the target audience.

Understanding the audience for the presentation is important so that you deliver the correct format. This needs to be understandable at the right level, provide value, note exceptions to services, identify benefits, and allow the recipient to make an informed decision. This could be at any stage of the service lifecycle—strategic, tactical, or operational.

The created reports should provide emphasis and highlight areas for action to be taken to implement improvements. It is too easy for IT departments to provide too much information to their target audience, without sufficient analysis. CSI should be providing useful and informative reports so that beneficial improvement initiatives can be introduced.

There are four common audience types:

The Customers   Requiring information on IT services and what will be done if the service provision has failed specific targets.

Senior IT Management   Often focusing on CSFs and KPIs and the actual vs. the predicted performance against targets. This may be presented in the form of a balanced scorecard.

Internal IT   Interested in KPIs and activity metrics to help plan and coordinate operational improvement activities.

Suppliers   Interested in KPIs and activity metrics related to their own service offerings and performance.

It is extremely important that you ensure the knowledge is presented in a meaningful way to the audience. For example, using percentage figures for availability may not be useful for the customer, because it is hard to relate a percentage to an actual outage event and understand the business impact.

Inputs to this step of the process include the following:

- Collated information
- Format details—report templates, and so on
- Stakeholder contact information

Step 7: Implement Improvement

In this step, you use the knowledge presented in the previous step and combine it with previous experience to make an informed decision about an improvement initiative.

This stage may include a number of actions, from implementing improvement activities to submitting a business case to justify an improvement. It will involve integration with other service management processes and other lifecycle stages and will include checking whether the improvement achieved its objective.

The decision-making process, applying wisdom to the knowledge provided, should be communicated across the organization, enabling the eventual improvement to be successfully implemented and understood by all stakeholders and practitioners.

After a decision to improve a service and/or service management process is made, then the service lifecycle continues. CSI activities take place throughout the service lifecycle. A new baseline can be established, and the cycle will begin again.

Inputs to this step include the following:

- Knowledge gained from presenting and using the information
- Agreed-upon implementation plans
- CSI register

The seven steps appear to be a circular set of activities, but in fact the seven-step improvement process is actually part of a knowledge spiral. In Figure 13.5 you can see the connection from the presentation of data from operational improvements into the capture of data for tactical improvements, which in turn will feed its presentation of data into strategic improvement activity.

FIGURE 13.5 Knowledge spiral, a gathering activity

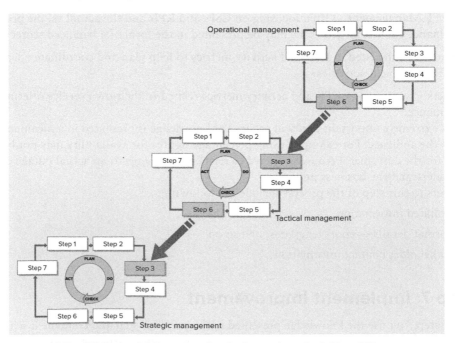

Based on Cabinet Office ITIL® material. Reproduced under license from the Cabinet Office.

DIKW and the Seven-Step Improvement Process

The definition of Data-Information-Knowledge-Wisdom (DIKW) is covered under the process of knowledge management in Chapter 9. You can see the association with DIKW throughout each of the seven steps of the improvement process.

- Data

  2. Define what you will measure.

  3. Gather the data.

- Information

  4. Process the data.

- Knowledge

  5. Analyze the information and data.

  6. Present and use the information.

- Wisdom

  7. Implement improvement.

  1. Identify strategy for improvement.

Data is quantitative, defined as numbers, characters, images, or other outputs. It is a collection of facts, whereas information is the result of processing and organizing raw data. Knowledge can be defined as information, combined with experience, context, and interpretation. Wisdom is defined as the ability to make correct judgments and decisions.

The association between the processes of knowledge management and the seven-step improvement process ensures that the activities are captured as part of the overall management of knowledge in the service knowledge management system.

PDCA and the Seven-Step Improvement Process

In the diagram of the seven-step improvement process, you can see the integration with the Deming cycle. The steps work together:

- Plan

  1. Identify the strategy for improvement.

  2. Define what you will measure.

- Do

  3. Gather the data.

  4. Process the data.

- Check

  5. Analyze the information and data.

  6. Present and use the information.

- Act

  7. Implement improvement.

We covered the Deming cycle (PDCA) cycle earlier in this chapter. This quality improvement approach is complementary to the continual service improvement process.

Summary

In this chapter, you learned about the continual service improvement stage of the service lifecycle. Specifically, you examined the main purpose, objectives, and scope of continual service improvement, as well as the value it provides to the business.

You learned about the seven-step improvement process, namely, its purpose, objectives, and scope, as well as how to manage the gathering, analysis, and presentation of data to enable improvement decisions.

We also covered the continual service improvement approach and its use in the service lifecycle. This approach provides a framework for the improvements identified from the seven-step improvement process. It is used in conjunction with similar approaches such as the Deming cycle. The Deming cycle takes the steps of Plan, Do, Check, and Act to ensure the continuation of quality services.

Improvements are managed through the CSI register, allowing overall management of all improvement initiatives in a centralized register.

Measurement is a vital part of all improvements, and we covered the approach to measurement as part of continual service improvement. We reviewed the types of metrics in use, the relationships between critical success factors and key performance indicators, and the use of baselines for assessing improvement progress.

Exam Essentials

Understand the purpose, objectives, and scope of the CSI lifecycle stage.   It is important to remember that CSI is concerned with maintaining IT services in line with business needs, not simply to meet service targets. This should be done on a regular basis and applied to all areas of service management.

Recall the steps of the CSI approach and of the Deming cycle.   The CSI steps identify the approach taken to manage an improvement initiative and ensure it continues to meet the objectives of the business. The Deming Cycle consists of Plan, Do, Check, and Act, and its aim is to ensure consolidation of achievement and a managed improvement approach to quality services.

Understand the purpose of the CSI register.   The register enables the tracking and management of the improvement initiatives being undertaken by the IT service provider. It is maintained and managed by the CSI manager.

Identify the different types of measures and three types of metrics: technical, process, and service.   Measures include critical success factors, key performance indicators, and how these are used in each service lifecycle process. The three types of metrics interact to provide a complete measurement of the service, which can be presented in a customer-facing format.

Understand the use of baselines.   Baselines are used in continual service improvement as a comparison point for verifying improvement activity.

Understand the use of the seven-step improvement process, and recall the steps of the process.   This process is used to manage the gathering, analysis, and presentation of data.

Know how the seven-step improvement process integrates with the DIKW knowledge model and the Deming cycle.   Understand the interaction of each step of the seven step process with the DIKW and Plan-Do-Check-Act.

Review Questions

You can find the answers in Appendix A.

1. Which of these statements is correct about the purpose of the continual service improvement lifecycle stage?

   1. The purpose of CSI is to continue to support the business with IT services, in the face of changing business needs.

   2. The purpose of CSI is to define the strategic approach for service management across the whole of the lifecycle.

   A. 1 only

   B. 2 only

   C. Both

   D. Neither

2. Which of these statements represents an objective of the continual service improvement lifecycle stage?

   A. To ensure that the changes to the services deliver the anticipated and required business value

   B. To identify and implement specific activities to improve IT service quality

   C. To identify the services and the customers who use them

   D. To set the expectations for the performance and use of the new or modified services

3. The ITIL Continual Service Improvement publication provides guidance in four main areas. Which of these is not one of the four areas?

   A. Continual alignment of the IT services with the current and future needs of the business

   B. The maturity and capability of the organization, management, processes, and people utilized by the services

   C. The development of a strategy that supports business organization improvements

   D. Continual improvement of all aspects of the IT service and the service assets that support them

4. The continual service improvement approach sets out a sequence of steps to follow when instigating and implementing improvements. Which of these represents the correct sequence for the CSI approach?

   A. Where are we now? What is the vision? Where do we want to be? How do we get there? Did we get there? How do we keep the momentum going?

   B. What is the vision? Where are we now? Where do we want to be? How do we keep the momentum going? How do we get there? Did we get there?

   C. Where are we now? Where do we want to be? What is the vision? How do we get there? Did we get there? How do we keep the momentum going?

   D. What is the vision? Where are we now? Where do we want to be? How do we get there? Did we get there? How do we keep the momentum going?

5. Which of these is a key objective in creating and managing a continual service improvement register?

   A. To capture details of the infrastructure and identify risks in their relationships

   B. To capture details of the services that are being delivered across the operational lifecycle

   C. To capture details of improvement initiatives across the service lifecycle

   D. To capture details of the information used to manage services across the service lifecycle

6. Plan, Do, Check, Act are the four stages of which quality improvement approach?

   A. Improvement initiative cycle

   B. Edwards cycle of quality improvement

   C. CSI approach

   D. Deming cycle

7. Measurement is a key part of the CSI lifecycle stage. Processes will be measured by key performance indicators; to what do KPIs relate?

   A. Critical success factors

   B. Critical business factors

   C. Customer success factors

   D. Customer satisfaction focus

8. Using ITIL terminology, there is a difference between a baseline and a snapshot. Which of these statements is/are correct?

   1. A baseline is a point in time that captures a snapshot of the environment and is verified so that it is an accurate reflection of the environment.

   2. A baseline is used for comparison, so it should be captured at regular intervals and recorded.

   A. Neither

   B. Both

   C. 1 only

   D. 2 only

9. The seven-step process is mapped against the Data-Information-Knowledge-Wisdom structure from knowledge management. Which step or steps of the seven-step process align with the Data part of the structure?

   A. 1 and 2

   B. 2 and 3

   C. 3

   D. 3 and 4

10. ITIL identifies four common audience types to whom you present information as part of the CSI process. Which of the four is missing from this list?

> The customers: This group will require information on IT services and what will be done if the service provision has failed specific targets.
>
> Senior IT management: This group will often focus on CSFs and KPIs and the actual vs. the predicted performance against targets. This may be presented in the form of a balanced scorecard.
>
> Internal IT: This group will be interested in KPIs and activity metrics to help plan and coordinate operational improvement activities.

- **A.** Suppliers: This group will be interested in KPIs and activity metrics related to their own service offerings and performance.
- **B.** Business users: This group will be interested in KPIs to help them understand how to improve their use of services.
- **C.** Project managers: This group will be interested in CSFs to help them understand how to improve their project plans.
- **D.** External users: This group will be interested in KPIs and activity metrics to understand their use of services.

Appendix

A

Answers to Review Questions

Chapter 1: Service Management as a Practice

1. D. Auditors are not a recognized source of best practice; they are an external body brought in to check something specific. The other three answers are all sources of best practice.

2. D. ITIL is a service management process framework concerned with planning, designing, transitioning, operating, and improving IT services within budget.

3. B. This is the ITIL definition of a service; all services should deliver value to the customer. A is the definition of incident management, C is an activity of problem management, and D is an activity of supplier management.

4. C. This is the ITIL definition of an outcome, the result of doing something.

5. A. This is the ITIL definition of the makeup of an IT service: the combination of processes (strategic, design, transition, operations, and improvement), the underlying infrastructure and applications the service is dependent on, and the roles required to support the service through the lifecycle.

6. B. There is no "supplier service" type identified. If services are provided by external parties, they would be either core, enabling, or enhancing.

7. C. Both of these statements are correct.

8. D. This is the ITIL definition for an IT service provider, providing IT services to customers.

9. C. There are three types of IT service provider: Type I internally embedded within a business unit, Type II internally shared between business units, and Type III external.

10. A. Functions are self-contained units of an organization with their own resources and capabilities to support an organization. Processes deliver value and define roles for the activities and decisions within that process.

Chapter 2: Understanding Service Strategy

1. C. The strategic phase of the lifecycle is concerned with the high-level planning of a lifecycle approach for all services and the supporting processes of service management to support the services.

2.   B. Strategy is concerned with ensuring business outcomes are met by the services and service management processes. Customer satisfaction and measuring improvements are the concern of continuous service improvement.

3.   C. The value of a service is always based on a customer's perspective. The service is delivered to support a customer's needs.

4.   C. Who designed the service is not a necessary piece of information for defining value; you should focus on the deliverables and cost.

5.   D. The customer is interested in the value the service provides to them and is not interested in the preferences of the service provider.

6.   C. Utility means the service is "fit for purpose" because it has the functionality to support business outcomes.

   "Fit for use" refers to how it is delivered with assurances in relation to capacity, availability, security, and continuity.

7.   A. Financial capital is classed as a resource, and organization and knowledge are capabilities. People can be classed as both: a resource because of the number of people and a capability because of the skill set of the people.

8.   D. Statement 3 is incorrect; the CAB does not assess all changes, and governance does not control this.

9.   B. Calibrate risks is not a stage in the risk management approach. It is important to *identify* risks and to *analyze* these risks to understand how likely they are to happen and the impact if they did occur. Based on that information, an appropriate response is required to control and *manage* the risk.

10.   A. A PBA profile is created to define and understand PBAs to ensure alignment to services. It needs to be classified and to include customer requirements, the capabilities, and the resources required to provide the service in some detail.

Chapter 3: Service Strategy Processes

1.   B. The service portfolio contains details of all services to be under control (pipeline) or live (catalog) or retired. It should provide sufficient detail to ensure the service provider is giving the customers the services required to support business needs.

2.   C. Service portfolio management is responsible for creating and maintaining a service portfolio, which consists of the details of all services to be under control (pipeline) or live (catalog) or retired. It should provide sufficient detail to ensure the service provider is giving the customers the services required to support business needs. Option A is an objective of change management, option B is an objective of service asset and configuration management, and option D is an objective of service-level management.

3.   B. Projects are not captured in the service portfolio; IT services are captured in the service portfolio.

4.   D. Monitoring service performance is performed by service-level management; comparing results of improvement initiatives is carried out by CSI.

5.   A. The service portfolio consists of a service pipeline, service catalog, and retired services.

6.   D. Financial management is concerned with funding IT services throughout their lifecycles.

7.   B. Financial management consists of budgeting, accounting, and charging.

8.   A. All of these are recommended elements of a business case.

9.   C. Business relationship management is concerned with creating and maintaining relationships between the customer and the service provider.

10. D. BRM is concerned with a high-level relationship with customers. The other answers are very specific and may be activities BRM has an interest in but only to suffice the overall objective of building and maintaining business relationship.

Chapter 4: Understanding Service Design

1.   A. All four of these elements are included in the service design.

2.   C. Service design should design services that meet the business requirements but can be improved in the future as business requirements change.

3.   B. Service design does not consider changes to business strategy; this is the remit of service strategy and continual service improvement. Design should be to customer requirements, right the first time, and to the standards and controls agreed on within an organization.

4.   D. This is a description of a service design package, a major output from service design ensuring the service is fully documented and able to pass through transition activities into operations where it can be used, delivered, and managed with appropriate reporting to allow for any necessary improvements.

5.   C. These are the four major areas that need to be considered for a holistic design: people to use the service as well as those to design, transition, and operate it; processes to support design, transition, operation, and improvement of the service; product (technology, such as infrastructure and applications) to enable the service; and partners, which are any external suppliers required to assist with the design.

6. B. All of these are identified as part of service composition. Resources are the actual people, applications, information, infrastructure, and financial capital required to support the service; capabilities manage and control resources appropriately; the functionality requirements (utilities) ensure the service is fit for purpose; and the warranty requirements ensure the service is delivered so it is fit for use.

7. D. The service solution is an output from service design, not a constraint.

8. C. The service design package does not include the organizational business strategy, because that is already in existence within the business. All other items are created during the design phase and reside in the SDP.

9. A. Architecture according to ITIL encompasses the technologies required to create a service—such as infrastructure, application, database, and environments—and how these technologies link together.

10. B. These are the five major aspects of service design. The SDP is an output that would contain a service transition plan. Business strategy has already been considered at the strategy level; it would help shape the requirements that go into designing the service solution, one of the major aspects.

Chapter 5: Service Level Management: Aligning IT with Business Requirements

1. A. This is the purpose of service-level management. Option B is a purpose of business relationship management, option C is a purpose of the service desk, and option D is a purpose of service transition.

2. B. This is an agreed-upon objective of service-level management and reflects the steps of the process. Option A is an objective of change management, option C is an objective of request fulfillment, and option D is an objective of problem management.

3. C. These are the correct statements; the other statements refer to service asset and configuration management and change management.

4. D. Customer-based service provider is not a recognized type of service provider. Embedded is Type I, Shared is Type II, and External is Type III.

5. B. Warranty refers to the achievement of fit for use, assuring levels of availability, capacity, security, and continuity, which usually have agreed-on targets within SLAs and are service-level requirements to assist with shaping the service solution.

6. C. The service-level agreement does not include the definition of business strategy but does contain relevant information about the service(s) supported by the agreement.

7. C. An OLA and a contract support the achievement of an SLA. The OLA is the internal agreement based on the ongoing activities of internal service providers, and the contract is the legally binding document supporting service delivery by an external supplier.

8. D. This is the definition of an underpinning contract as described in the ITIL framework. Contracts are required for external suppliers regarding their commitments to providing service.

9. A. These are the three types of service-level agreement in a multilevel structure.

10. B. These reports are sometimes known as RAG reports, for red, amber, green. Green means everything is within target, amber means there is some concern, and red is an exception.

Chapter 6: The Other Service Design Processes

1. C. Option A refers to an SLA, option B refers to the service portfolio, and option D refers to a business case. Option C is the ITIL definition of the service catalog.

2. C. Retired services are part of the portfolio, not the catalog. ITIL does not define strategic services.

3. B. The service catalog contains customer-facing and supporting services and forms part of the service portfolio.

4. C. Option C is the ITIL definition. Agreed service time is the time a service should be available as agreed on within an SLA or underpinning contract, and downtime is an unplanned interruption to service.

5. B. This is the ITIL definition. It refers to part of a business process that is critical to the success of the business.

6. C. MTBSI stands for mean time between service incidents.

7. D. These are all terms that are part of the availability management process. The others are not ITIL terms.

8. C. Items 1, 2, and 3 are all responsibilities of ISM. Implementing is one of the responsibilities of release and deployment management; no other ITIL process has a responsibility for implementation.

9. A. The SMIS is the security management information system. The KEDB is the known error database that is used by problem management. The other terms are not ITIL terms.

10. D. Supplier management does not deal with internal suppliers; it manages all aspects of contract management with third parties to ensure value for money.

11 C. Trusted is not a supplier type described in ITIL.

12. A. It is service level management that is responsible for negotiating the SLA contents (although the service level manager would consult with capacity management before agreeing on capacity requirements). The other three are core responsibilities of capacity management.

13. A. This is the ITIL definition of the three subprocesses of capacity management.

14. C. This is the ITIL definition.

15. C. It is not the job of ITSCM to ensure that the business has contingency plans; this is the role of business continuity management. ITSCM is concerned with the IT services only.

16. D. This is the ITIL definition.

17. B. Design coordination does not design the solution; it coordinates activities and resources.

18. D. The configuration management system (CMS) and governance requirements are not outputs of this process. They are actually inputs to it.

19. C. The service catalog shows how each operational service supports particular business processes - this is useful to customers. The technical view of the catalog shows the supporting services which make up the service.

20. C. It is the responsibility of the business to plan for business continuity in the event of major disruption, based on business priorities. This will define what level of IT service will be required in that eventuality, and ITSCM is then responsible for planning how this could be provided.

Chapter 7: Service Design Roles

1. B. This is one of the defined responsibilities of the process practitioner, who is responsible for carrying out the process and documenting its activities.

2. D. This is the correct list of role responsibilities in the RACI model as described in ITIL and other methodologies.

3. B. This is one of the process owner responsibilities.

4. A. Managing a process requires resources; therefore, the process manager is responsible for this.

5. B. There can be only one person accountable, and not all activities or decisions need to include Consulted or Informed.

6. D. The RACI model defines who is responsible, accountable, consulted, or informed for each process activity.

7. C. ITIL specifies that the process owner is accountable for the process, and there can be only one person accountable.

8. C. Creating and maintaining the process documentation are the responsibilities of the process owner.

9. D. ITIL does not describe a role of process improvement manager. The process owner and manager roles have responsibility for identifying possible improvements.

10. B. The service owner has responsibility for representing the service, and this includes attending the CAB meeting to discuss any amendments to the service, to ensure that the risk assessment had been carried out correctly, and to minimize the chances of the change failing and affecting the service. The service owner is also responsible for attending service reviews with the business (with the service level manager). The responsibility of maintaining the known error database belongs to the problem manager.

Chapter 8: Understanding Service Transition and the Change Management Process

1. A. This is the purpose of the service transition lifecycle stage, to ensure that the new or changed service is delivered into operation successfully.

2. C. Service transition provides value by delivering services consistently, controlling IT assets and increasing confidence in the success of changes.

3. B. The purpose of change management is to provide controlled change across the whole of the service lifecycle.

4. C. Change management does not cover business, project, or minor operational changes. The change process is used for IT service changes.

5. D. A change model provides predefined steps for handling changes of a similar type. This provides a repeatable and consistent approach to managing changes of similar type.

6. B. A standard change has a low or clearly understood risk, follows a predefined procedure, and has a predefined trigger.

7. A. Change proposals are authorized if the change has a major impact on the business in terms of cost, risk, or resources. A proposal is used to ensure that any major change is justified before raising the request for change.

8. D. The change schedule, projected service outage, and remediation plan are all recognized outputs from the change management process. The change schedule shows the proposed

authorized changes, and the project service outage document shows the outage of the service. A remediation plan is the plan for how to recover in the event of a failure in change implementation.

9. A. Changes are authorized by the change authority. The change authority will depend on the nature, size, and risk of the change being authorized.

10. B. A change record can be closed only once the change acceptance criteria have been met.

Chapter 9: Service Transition Processes

1. A. Transition planning and support provides overall planning for service transitions and coordination of the resources they require. Option B refers to a change management purpose, option C refers to a purpose of design coordination, and option D would be involved in the planning phase of release and deployment.

2. C. These statements are both objectives of transition planning and support, ensuring that transitions are managed effectively.

3. B. The purpose of the SACM process is to identify and control the assets that make up your services and maintain accurate information about these assets. The management of the changes to your service assets is a purpose of change management.

4. D. SACM is a process that supports all stages of the service lifecycle by providing information about the assets that make up your services.

5. C. A configuration record captures the information about a configuration item and records the attributes and relationships. It is stored in the CMDB. Option A is a service asset, option B is a configuration item, and option D is an activity carried out in SACM.

6. A. The layers of the CMS are closely associated to the Data-Information-Knowledge-Wisdom model from knowledge management; the presentation layer allows for decision making based on the analysis and processing of data.

7. B. This is an objective of the SACM process; knowledge management does not cover the detail of the service assets that make up the services.

8. C. SACM is the process that manages the naming convention for the configuration management database. Release management is concerned with the release controls that are specified in the release policy.

9. D. Verification and audit is a step in the process of SACM to ensure the accuracy of the data in the CMS.

10. C. Early life support takes place in the deployment phase, where the handover to service operation takes place.

Chapter 10: Delivering the Service: The Service Operation Lifecycle Stage

1. **D.** This is one of the defined service operation activities. Testing and rolling out are transition activities, and decisions about service retirement are made in the strategy stage.

2. **D.** Design coordination takes place only as part of design. Availability management takes place in service operations, because reasons for downtime are examined and actions are taken to prevent recurrence. ITSCM plans are rehearsed and updated as part of service operations. Performance against service level targets is measured in service operations, and both incident and problem management seek to reduce or prevent downtime that could threaten the achievement of the SLA targets.

3. **C.** These are the four functions described in ITIL. The facilities management responsibility in option A forms part of the operations management function. The infrastructure management and desktop management responsibilities in option B are not ITIL functions; infrastructure management will be carried out by the technical management function, and desktop support is usually part of operations management.

4. **B.** This is the responsibility of technical management. The air conditioning and power management responsibilities are part of facilities management's responsibilities for maintaining the physical operations environment.

5. **B.** The responsibilities of each function defined in ITIL include the activity listed in option B.

6. **C.** This is the responsibility of the problem management process; the service desk deals with incidents and does not resolve the underlying problems that would then prevent the incident from recurring. Service desks should resolve all straightforward incidents in order to provide a faster and more efficient support service than would result from escalating them to the next support level.

7. **B.** The service desk logs incidents and requests and ensures that they are dealt with. It owns the incident and request throughout its lifecycle, ensuring that the customer is happy with the outcome and that service levels are met.

8. **D.** Service desk staff members do not need specialist technical skills, but they need to have sufficient technical ability to resolve straightforward incidents; they need customer service skills to deal with users and business knowledge to assess priority.

9. **D.** These are the two aspects described in ITIL. Facilities management refers to the management of the physical environment of IT operations, usually located in data centers or computer rooms. Operations control refers to the carrying out of routine operational tasks, centralized monitoring, and control activities, usually using an operations bridge or network operations center.

10. **B.** The other three structures are described in ITIL, along with centralized. A local service desk structure will have a service desk co-located with users in each location. Virtual service desk structures provide a number of desks, with calls shared between them. "Follow the sun" will have all calls routed to a service desk dependent on time zones; all calls will be handled by a day shift.

Chapter 11: The Major Service Operation Processes

1. B. This is the ITIL definition. Option A could be describing an incident, but option B is a clearer definition. Option C describes a problem, not an incident.

2. C. Option A describes when a problem, not an incident, should be closed. Option B is incorrect, because the user must agree before the incident is closed. Option D is incorrect because there is no mention of a resolution.

3. B. Incident resolution is about restoring the service; option B is a problem management activity and does not help the user at the time. The other options all attempt to overcome the issue for the user.

4. C. This is the ITIL definition. Normal service is that agreed on and documented within SLAs or contracts.

5. C. This is the ITIL definition of an incident model.

6. D. This is what ITIL recommends. Incidents may also result from events or from technical staff.

7. B. This is the ITIL definition of how to calculate priority.

8. B. ITIL defines hierarchical escalation (going up the chain of command) and functional escalation (passing incidents to more technically knowledgeable teams).

9. C. ITIL defines problems as the cause of one or more incidents. Options A and D are incidents, and option B is a possible root cause.

10. D. Problem management may provide a workaround while waiting for a permanent resolution. This would be documented as a known error. If the resolution required a change, an RFC would be raised.

Chapter 12: The Other Service Operation Processes

1. D. The purpose of the request fulfillment process is to separate the common, low-risk requests and expedite them. Service requests do not need CAB approval. RFCs and emergency requests for change need to go through the appropriate change process.

2. A. Service desk staff deal with many requests, with second-line staff carrying out installations, moves, and so on. Requests do not come under the responsibilities of SLM or BRM.

3. C. Requests that are changes will be standard changes and can be preauthorized; they do not need authorization by the CAB. Changes that needed technical approval would go through the change process, not the request process. If an expense is to be incurred, this will need to be accounted for and authorization granted.

4. D. Option 3 requires a change to functionality that would need to be fully considered and costed; it would need to go through the change process. The others are all requests for information or standard services and are therefore service requests.

5. D. Situation 2 B would not be helped by using events. Situation 1 would detect an alert that a time threshold or a priority condition existed and would carry out the escalation defined. Situation 3 would similarly respond to a particular event such as an alarm and would automatically notify the police station. Situation 4 could use the events signifying the successful backup of each file to automate the start of backing up the next file.

6. C. These are all examples of where event management can be used. Monitoring heat and moisture content can be done through event management, and actions are taken if they breach acceptable parameters. Licenses can be controlled by monitoring who is signing onto applications and raising an alert if the maximum legal number is breached. Staff rosters do not have changing conditions that could be monitored by the use of events.

7. B. This is the definition of a request given in this chapter. A request may involve a standard change, but that may be true only in some cases, so it is not a good description. An RFC is part of the change process, not the request process. A request may involve procurement, but only in some cases, so it is not a good description.

8. C. Types 1 and 3 are the two types of event monitoring described in the chapter. Passive monitoring waits for an error message to be detected, and active monitoring checks periodically on the "health" of the CI. The other two are not recognized event types in ITIL.

9. C. Option C is the definition given in the chapter of an alert. Option A is the definition of an incident. Option B is the definition of a problem. Option D is the definition of an event.

10. B. Option A is incorrect because security management does not remove or prevent access. Option C is incorrect because security management is responsible for setting policies. Option D is incorrect because access management carries out the wishes of whoever is responsible for authorizing access (usually a business manager); it does not make the decision.

Chapter 13: Understanding Continual Service Improvement

1. A. The purpose of CSI is correct in statement 1. This lifecycle stage should ensure you continue to support the business in response to changes in business need. The second statement is the purpose of the service strategy lifecycle stage.

2.   B. Options A and D are service transition objectives; option C is an objective of service strategy. CSI is concerned with the identification of improvement opportunities across the whole of the service lifecycle.

3.   C. CSI provides guidance on IT service management improvements, not on business strategic planning. This includes the continual alignment of IT services with business requirements and the maturity and capability of the service provider. It will include all aspects of the service because everything may be included in an improvement initiative.

4.   D. This is the correct sequence of events for the CSI approach. You can verify this by reviewing Figure 13.1.

5.   C. To maintain and manage improvements, you should be utilizing a CSI register. Capturing details of the improvements that are taking place allows you to manage and coordinate improvement activities. Capturing details of the infrastructure is covered by service asset and configuration management, and the service catalog provides details of the operational services. The service knowledge management system captures details of the information used for service management.

6.   D. Plan, Do, Check, Act make up the four stages in the Deming cycle.

7.   A. KPIs measure critical success factors, which are those elements that enable understanding of the current state of the process, help identify any required improvements, and measure the achievement of any enhancements made.

8.   B. Both of these statements about baselines are correct. Baselines are used by CSI to ensure that you have a regular capture of the state of the operational environment, allowing for comparison to demonstrate or track improvements.

9.   B. Step 2 (define what you will measure) and step 3 (gather the data) are aligned to the Data part of the DIKW structure. In the DIKW model, the starting point of all capture begins with data, and to do this, you should ensure you define the requirements for your data capture activity by understanding what you will measure and then gathering the appropriate data.

10. A. You need to ensure you engage with suppliers who support your services; it's a vital part of your approach to improving the quality of service provision. It is important to ensure you review all of the stakeholders engaged in the delivery of services, as well as those receiving them. External or business users will not be reviewing the key performance indicators to help them understand the use of services, because this information will not be provided by the KPIs. Project managers will not be reviewing CSFs for service management processes, because these will not demonstrate how to improve project plans.

Appendix B

Sample Foundation Examinations

The ITIL® v.3 Foundation Examination

Sample Paper A, version 3.1

Multiple Choice

Instructions

1.   All 40 questions should be attempted.

2.   There are no trick questions.

3.   All answers are to be marked on the original examination paper.

4.   Please use a pen to mark your answers with either a ✓ or x .

5.   You have 1 hour to complete this paper.

6.   You must get 26 or more correct to pass.

Candidate Number: ....

1   What types of changes are NOT usually included within the scope of service Change
    Management?

    a)   Changes to a mainframe computer

    b)   Changes to business strategy

    c)   Changes to a Service Level Agreement (SLA)

    d)   The retirement of a service

2   Which of the following is NOT an objective of Service Operation?

    a)   Thorough testing to ensure that services are designed to meet business needs

    b)   To deliver and manage IT services

    c)   To manage the technology used to deliver services

    d)   To monitor the performance of technology and processes

3   What does the term Operations Control refer to?

    a)   Managing the Technical and Applications Management functions

    b)   Overseeing the execution and monitoring of operational activities and events

    c)   It is the tools used to monitor and display the status of the IT Infrastructure and
         Applications

    d)   It is the Service Desk monitoring the status of the infrastructure when
         operators are not available

4   Which process is responsible for recording relationships between service
    components?

    a)   Service Level Management

    b)   Service Portfolio Management

    c)   Service Asset and Configuration Management

    d)   Incident Management

5   What is the RACI model used for?

    a)   Documenting the roles and relationships of stakeholders in a process or activity

    b)   Defining requirements for a new service or process

    c)   Analyzing the business impact of an incident

    d)   Creating a balanced scorecard showing the overall status of service
         management

6   Which of the following is the BEST description of an Operational Level Agreement (OLA)?

   a)   An agreement between an IT service provider and another part of the same organization that assists in the provision of services

   b)   A written agreement between the IT service provider and their customer(s) defining key targets and responsibilities of both parties

   c)   An agreement between two service providers about the levels of service required by the customer

   d)   An agreement between a 3rd party Service Desk and the IT customer about fix and response times

7   What is the MAIN goal of Availability Management?

   a)   To monitor and report availability of components

   b)   To ensure that all targets in the Service Level Agreements (SLAs) are met

   c)   To guarantee availability levels for services and components

   d)   To ensure that service availability matches or exceeds the agreed needs of the business

8   Which of the following does Service Transition provide guidance on?
   1. Moving new and changed services into production
   2. Testing and Validation
   3. Transfer of services to or from an external service provider

   a)   1 and 2 only

   b)   2 only

   c)   All of the above

   d)   1 and 3 only

9   Learning and Improvement is the PRIMARY concern of which of the following phases of the Service Lifecycle?

   a)   Service Strategy, Service Design, Service Transition, Service Operation, and Continual Service Improvement

   b)   Service Strategy, Service Transition, and Service Operation

   c)   Service Operation and Continual Service Improvement

   d)   Continual Service Improvement

10   Which of the following is an activity of the Service Asset and Configuration Management process?

   a)   Account for all the financial assets of the organization

   b)   Specify the relevant attributes of each Configuration Item (CI)

   c)   Design service models to justify ITIL implementations

   d)   Implement ITIL across the organization

11   Which of the following basic concepts are included in Access Management?
   1. Verifying the identity of users requesting access to services
   2. Setting the rights or privileges of systems to allow access to authorised users
   3. Defining security policies for system access
   4. Monitoring the availability of systems that users should have access to

   a)   2 and 4 only

   b)   1 and 3 only

   c)   2 and 3 only

   d)   1 and 2 only

12   Which of the following would be stored in the Definitive Media Library (DML)?
   1. Copies of purchased software
   2. Copies of internally developed software
   3. Relevant licence documentation
   4. The Change Schedule

   a)   All of the above

   b)   1 and 2 only

   c)   3 and 4 only

   d)   1, 2 and 3 only

13   Which process is responsible for reviewing Operational Level Agreements (OLAs) on a regular basis?

   a)   Supplier Management

   b)   Service Level Management

   c)   Service Portfolio Management

   d)   Demand Management

14 Which of the following is a process owner responsible for?

   a)   Purchasing tools to support the process

   b)   Ensuring that targets specified in a Service Level Agreement (SLA) are met

   c)   Carrying out all activities defined in the process

   d)   Ensuring that the process is performed as documented

15 Which of the following are aims of the Release and Deployment Management process?
   1. To ensure there are clear release and deployment plans
   2. To ensure there is minimal unpredicted impact on production services, operations and support
   3. To authorize changes to support the process

   a)   1 and 2 only

   b)   All of the above

   c)   2 and 3 only

   d)   1 and 3 only

16 Which of the following can be described as "Self-Contained units of organizations"?

   a)   Roles

   b)   Processes

   c)   Functions

   d)   Procedures

17 Agreeing business requirements and service levels for a new service is part of:

   a)   Service Operation

   b)   Service Strategy

   c)   Service Transition

   d)   Service Design

18   The Information Security Policy should be available to which groups of people?

    a)   Senior business managers and all IT staff only

    b)   Senior business managers, IT executives and the Information Security Manager only

    c)   All customers, users and IT staff

    d)   Information Security Management staff only

19   Which of the following are valid elements of a Service Design Package?
    1. Agreed and documented business requirements
    2. A service definition for transition and operation of the service
    3. Requirements for new or changed processes
    4. Metrics to measure the service

    a)   1 only

    b)   2 and 3 only

    c)   1, 2 and 4 only

    d)   All of the above

20   Which of the following are examples of tools that might support the Service Transition phase of the Lifecycle?
    1. A tool to store definitive versions of software
    2. A workflow tool for managing changes
    3. An automated software distribution tool
    4. Testing and validation tools

    a)   1, 3 and 4 only

    b)   1, 2 and 3 only

    c)   All of the above

    d)   2, 3 and 4 only

21   Which of the following statements about Problem Management is/are CORRECT?
    1. It ensures that all resolutions or workarounds that require a change to a Configuration Item (CI) are submitted through Change Management
    2. It provides management information about the cost of resolving and preventing problems

    a)   1 only

    b)   2 only

    c)   Both of the above

    d)   Neither of the above

22   What is the purpose of the Request Fulfilment Process?

    a)   Dealing with service requests from the users

    b)   Making sure all requests within an IT organization are fulfilled

    c)   Ensuring fulfilment of change requests

    d)   Making sure the Service Level Agreement (SLA) is met

23   Which statement about value creation through services is CORRECT?

    a)   The customer's perception of the service is an important factor in value creation

    b)   The value of a service can only ever be measured in financial terms

    c)   Delivering service provider outcomes is important in the value of a service

    d)   Service provider preferences drive the value perception of a service

24   Plan, Do, Check, Act are the four stages of which quality improvement method?

    a)   Business Knowledge Management Framework

    b)   Benchmarking

    c)   Continual Service Improvement

    d)   The Deming Cycle

25   Which of the following should IT services deliver to customers?

    a)   Capabilities

    b)   Cost

    c)   Risk

    d)   Value

26   Which of the following activities is part of the Service Level Management (SLM) process?

    a)   Designing the Configuration Management system from a business perspective

    b)   Creating technology metrics to align with customer needs

    c)   Discussing service achievements with customers

    d)   Training Service Desk staff how to deal with customer complaints about service

27 Which statement BEST describes the purpose of Event Management?

    a) The ability to detect events, make sense of them and determine the appropriate control action

    b) The ability to detect events, restore normal service as soon as possible and minimize the adverse impact on business operations

    c) The ability to monitor and control the activities of technical staff

    d) The ability to report on the successful delivery of services by checking the uptime of infrastructure devices

28 Which of the following should a service catalogue contain?

    a) The version information of all software

    b) The organizational structure of the company

    c) Asset information

    d) Details of all operational services

29 "Warranty of a service" means?

    a) The service is fit for purpose

    b) There will be no failures in applications and infrastructure associated with the service

    c) All service-related problems are fixed free of charge for a certain period of time

    d) Customers are assured of certain levels of availability, capacity, continuity and security

30 A technician uses a pre-defined technique to restore service as the incident has been seen before.
This is an example of which of the following?

    a) A workaround

    b) A standard change

    c) A service capability

    d) An alert

31   Which of the following is a benefit of using an incident model?

   a)   It will make problems easier to identify and diagnose

   b)   It means known incident types never recur

   c)   It provides pre-defined steps for handling particular types of incidents

   d)   It ensures all incidents are easy to solve

32   Which of the following is the CORRECT sequence of activities for handling an incident?

   a)   Identification, Logging, Categorization, Prioritization, Initial Diagnosis, Functional Escalation, Investigation and Diagnosis, Resolution and Recovery, Closure

   b)   Prioritization, Identification, Logging, Categorization, Initial Diagnosis, Functional Escalation, Investigation and Diagnosis, Resolution and Recovery, Closure

   c)   Identification, Logging, Initial Diagnosis, Categorization, Prioritization, Functional Escalation, Resolution and Recovery, Investigation and Diagnosis, Closure

   d)   Identification, Initial Diagnosis, Investigation, Logging, Categorization, Functional Escalation, Prioritization, Resolution and Recovery, Closure

33   Which of the following are objectives of Continual Service Improvement?
   1. To improve process efficiency and effectiveness
   2. To improve services
   3. To improve all phases of the Service Lifecycle EXCEPT Service Strategy
   4. To improve international standards such as ISO/IEC 20000

   a)   1 and 2 only

   b)   2 and 4 only

   c)   1, 2 and 3 only

   d)   All of the above

34   Which of the following is a MAJOR activity of Demand Management?

   a)   Increasing customer value

   b)   Understanding patterns of business activity

   c)   Increasing the value of IT

   d)   Aligning the business with IT cost

35   Which of the following is NOT a type of metric described in Continual Service Improvement (CSI)?

a)   Process Metrics

b)   Service Metrics

c)   Personnel Metrics

d)   Technology Metrics

36   Which statement about the relationship between the Configuration Management System (CMS) and the Service Knowledge Management System (SKMS) is CORRECT?

a)   The SKMS is part of the CMS

b)   The CMS forms part of the SKMS

c)   The CMS and SKMS are the same thing

d)   There is no relationship between the CMS and the SKMS

37   What is the role of the Emergency Change Advisory Board (ECAB)?

a)   To assist the Change Manager in ensuring that no urgent changes are made during particularly volatile business periods

b)   To assist the Change Manager by implementing emergency changes

c)   To assist the Change Manager in evaluating emergency changes and to decide whether they should be approved

d)   To assist the Change Manager in speeding up the emergency change process so that no unacceptable delays occur

38   Which of the following statements about the Service Desk is/are CORRECT?

1. The Service Desk is a function that provides a means of communication between IT and its users for all operational issues

2. The Service Desk should be the owner of the Problem Management process

a)   2 only

b)   1 only

c)   Both of the above

d)   Neither of the above

39 Which of the following are the Four Ps of Service Design?

  a)   Planning, Products, Position, Processes

  b)   Planning, Perspective, Position, People

  c)   Perspective, Partners, Problems, People

  d)   People, Partners, Products, Processes

40 Which of the following represents the BEST course of action to take when a problem workaround is found?

  a)   The problem record is closed

  b)   The problem record remains open and details of the workaround are documented within it

  c)   The problem record remains open and details of the workaround are documented on all related incident records

  d)   The problem record is closed and details of the workaround are documented in a Request for Change(RFC)

ITIL® v.3 Foundation Examination: Sample Paper A

ANSWER SHEET

Answer Key for Exam Paper: ITILv3FoundationSampleA_v3.1

Q	A	Syllabus Ref	Q	A	Syllabus Ref
1	B	05-51	21	C	05-72
2	A	02-08	22	A	05-82
3	B	06-02	23	A	04-02
4	C	05-52	24	D	04-08
5	A	07-02	25	D	01-02
6	A	03-12	26	C	05-31
7	D	05-42	27	A	05-81
8	C	02-06	28	D	05-41
9	D	02-02	29	D	03-01
10	B	05-52	30	A	03-30
11	D	05-83	31	C	05-71
12	D	03-19	32	A	05-71
13	B	05-31	33	A	02-10
14	D	07-01	34	B	05-21
15	A	05-61	35	C	04-10
16	C	01-04	36	B	03-16
17	D	04-04	37	C	05-51
18	C	05-43	38	B	06-01
19	D	03-14	39	D	04-03
20	C	08-02	40	B	05-72

ITIL® v.3 Foundation Examination: Sample Paper A

ANSWER RATIONALES

Rationale for ITIL V3 Foundation Sample Paper A v3.1

Q	ID	A	Syll	Book Ref	Rationale
1	153	B	05-51	ST 46	"A Change Request is a formal communication seeking an alteration to one or more configuration items". The business strategy is not a configuration item
2	28	A	02-08	SO 13	These objectives all appear in Service Operation section 2.4.1 except for "Thorough testing to ensure that services are designed to meet business needs" which is an objective of Service Transition.
3	206	B	06-02	SO 126	"Operations Control, which oversees the execution and monitoring of the operational activities and events in the IT Infrastructure."
4	365	C	05-52	ST 65	"The purpose of SACM is to: ... record ... service assets and configuration items including ... their attributes and relationships"
5	217	A	07-02	SD 189	"Whether RACI or some other tool or model is used, the important thing is to not just leave the assignment of responsibilities to chance or leave it to the last minute to decide. Conflicts can be avoided and decisions can be made quickly if the roles are allocated in advance."
6	493	A	03-12	SD 66	A is the OLA, B is an SLA, C is nonsense, D is a contract
7	135	D	05-42	SD 4.4.1, SD 4.5.1	"The goal of the Availability Management process is to ensure that the level of service availability delivered in all services is matched to or exceeds the current and future agreed needs of the business..."
8	26	C	02-06	ST 16	"The purpose of Service Transition is to:... Plan and manage the capacity and resources required to package, build, test and deploy a release into production...." "Guidance is provided on transferring the control of services between customers and service providers"
9	19	D	02-02	SS 9	Through CSI... "Organizations learn to realize incremental and large-scale improvements in service quality, operational efficiency and business continuity"
10	157	B	05-52	ST 72	B is part of the main activities of the Configuration identification stage of Service Asset and Configuration Management. A would be part of Financial Management C - Service models are not used to justify services D - Although at the heart of ITIL, they are not responsible for its implementation across the organisation.
11	184	D	05-83	SO 68	1 and 2 are both correct: 1 refers to identity, 2 refers to rights. 3 and 4 are both incorrect: 3 is IT Security Management, 4 is Availability Management.
12	482	D	03-19	ST 69	"The DML contains master copies of all controlled software in an organization ... along with licence documents or information". The Change Schedule is none of these
13	125	B	05-31	SD 194	"The Service Level Manager has responsibility for... Negotiating and agreeing OLAs"
14	212	D	07-01	SD 190	"A process owner is responsible for ensuring that their process is being performed according to the agreed and documented process ..."
15	160	A	05-61	ST 84	The two correct answers are included in the bulleted list in ST 4.4.1 Purpose, goal and objective. Option 3 is a responsibility of the Change Management process

ITIL® v.3 Foundation Examination: Sample Paper A

ANSWER RATIONALES

16	7	C	01-04	ST 14	"Functions are units of organizations specialized to perform certain types of work … They are self-contained …"
17	269	D	04-04	SD 31-32	Figure 3.5 and "The areas that need to be considered within the design of the service solution should include: Analyse the agreed business requirements"
18	138	C	05-43	SD 142	"These policies should be widely available to all customers and users…", although the book does not explicitly state that they should also be available to all IT staff, this is clear from the context
19	495	D	03-14	SD 227-229	All the elements describe the holistic nature of Service Design and are included in the SDP
20	498	C	08-02	ST 193	1 is part of the DML, 2 helps Change Management. 3 is Deployment tool. 4 can help within Validation. They are all parts of Service Transition
21	564	C	05-72	SO 65/66	Book answer. They are both valid statements
22	185	A	05-82	SO 56	"Request Fulfilment is the processes of dealing with Service Requests from the users."
23	575	A	04-02	SS 31	D is wrong CUSTOMER preferences drive value perception, Delivering on Customer Outcomes is vital this rules C out. The value of a service can be financial or otherwise therefore B is wrong.
24	694	D	04-08	CSI 29	"The four key stages of the Deming Cycle are Plan, Do, Check and Act…"
25	4	D	01-02	SS 16	The definition of a service starts "A service is a means of delivering value to customers…"
26	122	C	05-31	CSI 91	"…build relationships with your customers by meeting with them on a consistent basis. Share with them your Service Level Achievements, and discuss any future new services or requirements"
27	181	A	05-81	SO 36	"The ability to detect events, make sense of them and determine the appropriate control action" is provided by Event Management
28	131	D	05-41	SD 60	"The goal of the Service Catalogue Management process is to ensure that a Service Catalogue is produced and maintained, containing accurate information on all operational services"
29	35	D	03-01	SS 17	"Warranty is derived from the positive effect being available when needed, in sufficient capacity or magnitude, and dependably in terms of continuity and security."
30	480	A	03-30	SO 64	A workaround is the technique used to restore service based on an Incident that has been seen before
31	497	C	05-71	SO 47	"An Incident Model is a way of pre-defining the steps that should be taken to handle a process…"
32	168	A	05-71	SO 49-53	The correct order is given in the diagram and the headings in SO 4.2.5 Process activities, methods and techniques
33	504	A	02-10	CSI 14	1 and 2 are fine. 3 is wrong, CSI contributes to ALL lifecycle phases. 4 is wrong, CSI does not contribute to updating international standards.
34	113	B	05-21	SS 130	"Patterns of business activity (PBA) influence the demand patterns seen by the service providers …" It is very important to study the customer's business to identify, analyse and codify such patterns
35	500	C	04-10	CSI 61	Personnel metrics would be dealt with outside of the framework of the service

ITIL® v.3 Foundation Examination: Sample Paper A

ANSWER RATIONALES

36	573	B	03-16	ST 147	A is the wrong way round, C is wrong as the SKMS contains more info than the CMS, D is wrong as the CMS is part of the SKMS.
37	150	C	05-51	ST 60	"Where CAB approval is required, this will be provided by the Emergency CAB (ECAB)."
38	198	B	06-01	SO 110	"...should be the single point of contact for IT users on a day-by-day basis" makes option 1 correct. Although the Service Desk may own an Incident Management process it should not own the Problem Management process
39	499	D	04-03	SD 16	The implementation of ITIL Service Management as a practice is about preparing and planning the effective and efficient use of the four Ps: the People, the Processes, the Products and the Partners
40	567	B	05-72	SO 64	A is obviously wrong; the record must remain open as it hasn't been resolved. B is correct with the workaround in the problem record, not the Incident record [C] nor RFC [D]

The ITIL® v.3 Foundation Examination

ITIL® v. 3 Foundation Examination:
Sample Paper B, version 3.1

Multiple Choice

Instructions

1.   All 40 questions should be attempted.

2.   There are no trick questions.

3.   All answers are to be marked on the original examination paper.

4.   Please use a pen to mark your answers with either a ✓ or x .

5.   You have 1 hour to complete this paper.

6.   You must get 26 or more correct to pass.

Candidate Number: ....

1   Input from which processes could be considered by Service Level Management when negotiating Service Level Agreements (SLA)?

   a)   All other ITIL processes

   b)   Capacity and Availability Management only

   c)   Incident and Problem Management only

   d)   Change and Release and Deployment Management only

2   Which of the following statements about a standard change is INCORRECT?

   a)   A standard change is one for which the approach is pre-authorized by Change Management

   b)   Approval for each instance of a standard change will be granted by the nominated authority for that change

   c)   Standard changes are usually low risk and well understood

   d)   Standard changes are only raised by Incident Management

3   Which of these statements about Service Desk staff is CORRECT?

   a)   The Service Desk staff require less training than other members of the IT department

   b)   Service Desk staff should represent customer views during Service Level Agreement (SLA) negotiations

   c)   Awareness of business culture and business priorities is essential for Service Desk staff to do their job well

   d)   Technical skills are more important to the Service Desk than business or interpersonal skills

4   Which of the following statements about demand for IT services is CORRECT?

   a)   It is driven by patterns of business activity

   b)   It is impossible to predict how they behave

   c)   It is impossible to influence demand patterns

   d)   It is driven by the delivery schedule generated by Capacity Management

5   What is the role of Facilities Management?

    a)   The Management of IT services that are viewed as "utilities", such as printers or network access

    b)   Advice and guidance to IT Operations on methodology and tools for managing IT Services

    c)   The Management of the physical IT environment such as a data center

    d)   The procurement and maintenance of tools that are used by IT Operations staff to maintain the infrastructure

6   What are the three sub-processes of Capacity Management?

    a)   Business Capacity Management, Service Capacity Management and Component Capacity Management

    b)   Supplier Capacity Management, Service Capacity Management and Component Capacity Management

    c)   Supplier Capacity Management, Service Capacity Management and Technology Capacity Management

    d)   Business Capacity Management, Technology Capacity Management and Component Capacity Management

7   Which of the following statements about the Known Error Database (KEDB) is MOST correct?

    a)   The KEDB is the same database as the Service Knowledge Management System (SKMS)

    b)   The KEDB should be used during the incident diagnosis phase to try to speed up the resolution process

    c)   Care should be taken to avoid duplication of records in the KEDB. This can be done by giving as many technicians as possible access to create new records

    d)   Access to the KEDB should be limited to the Service Desk

8   Which of these statements about Key Performance Indicators (KPIs) and Metrics are CORRECT?

    1. Service metrics measure the end-to-end service

    2. Each KPI should relate to a critical success factor

    3. Continual Service Improvement (CSI) uses process metrics to identify improvement opportunities

    4. KPIs can be both qualitative and quantitative

    a)   1 only

    b)   2 and 3 only

    c)   1, 2 and 4 only

    d)   All of the above

9   What is described by the following statement? "Maintains relationships between all service components and any related incidents, problems, known errors, change and release documentation"

a)   The Capacity Plan

b)   The Definitive Media Library

c)   The Configuration Management System

d)   A Service Level Agreement

10   Which of the following statements about a Definitive Media Library (DML) are CORRECT?
1. The DML can include a physical store
2. The DML holds definitive hardware spares
3. The DML includes master copies of controlled documentation

a)   All of the above

b)   1 and 2 only

c)   2 and 3 only

d)   1 and 3 only

11   Which of the following statements is/are CORRECT?
1. Problem Management can support the Service Desk by providing known errors to speed up incident resolution
2. Problem Management is the only source of information to Service Level Management about the impact of changes

a)   1 only

b)   2 only

c)   Both of the above

d)   Neither of the above

12   A failure has occurred on a system and is detected by a monitoring tool. This system supports a live IT service. When should an incident be raised?

a)   Only when users notice the failure

b)   No incident should be raised if the technicians have seen this before and have a workaround

c)   Only if the failure results in a service level being breached

d)   Immediately to limit or prevent impact on users

13 Which of the following questions is NOT answered by information in the service portfolio?

    a)   How should our resources and capabilities be allocated?

    b)   What opportunities are there in the market?

    c)   Why should a customer buy these services?

    d)   What are the pricing models?

14 A configuration model documents the relationships between which of the following combinations?

    a)   Services, assets and infrastructure

    b)   Processes, network and Operational Level Agreements (OLAs)

    c)   Procedures, infrastructure and contracts

    d)   Service Desk, assets and technical support providers

15 Which of the following statements about processes is/are CORRECT?
1. All processes must have an owner
2. A process takes one or more inputs and turns them into defined outputs

    a)   1 only

    b)   2 only

    c)   Both of the above

    d)   Neither of the above

16 Which of the following statements is CORRECT for ALL processes?

    a)   They define functions as part of their design

    b)   They should deliver value for stakeholders

    c)   They are carried out by an external service provider in support of a customer

    d)   They are units of organizations responsible for specific outcomes

17   Which process considers the following options?
1. Big bang and phased
2. Push and pull
3. Automated and manual

a)   Incident Management

b)   Release and Deployment Management

c)   Service Asset and Configuration Management

d)   Service Catalogue Management

18   Which of the following is the BEST example of a workaround?

a)   A technician installs a script to temporarily divert prints to an alternative printer until a permanent fix is applied

b)   A technician tries several approaches to solve an incident. One of them works, although they do not know why

c)   After reporting the incident to the Service Desk, the user works on alternative tasks while the problem is identified and resolved

d)   A device works intermittently, allowing the user to continue working at degraded levels of performance while the technician diagnoses the incident

19   Which of the following areas would technology help to support?
1. Self-Help
2. Reporting
3. Release and Deployment
4. Process design

a)   1, 2 and 3 only

b)   1, 3 and 4 only

c)   2, 3 and 4 only

d)   All of the above

20   What are the four stages of the Deming Cycle?

a)   Plan, Measure, Monitor, Report

b)   Plan, Check, Re-Act, Implement

c)   Plan, Do, Act, Audit

d)   Plan, Do, Check, Act

21 Which of the following processes include a need to carry out risk assessment and management against services and supporting assets?

1. IT Service Continuity Management
2. Information Security Management
3. Service Catalogue Management

a) All of the above

b) 1 and 3 only

c) 2 and 3 only

d) 1 and 2 only

22 What is the BEST definition of an incident model?

a) The template used to define the incident logging form for reporting incidents

b) A type of incident involving a standard (or model) type of Configuration Item (CI)

c) A set of pre-defined steps to be followed when dealing with a known type of incident

d) An incident that is easy to solve

23 What roles are defined in the RACI model?

a) Responsible, Accountable, Consulted, Informed

b) Responsible, Achievable, Consulted, Informed

c) Realistic, Accountable, Consulted, Informed

d) Responsible, Accountable, Corrected, Informed

24 In which phase of the service lifecycle would it be decided what services should be offered and to whom they will be offered?

a) Continual Service Improvement

b) Service Operation

c) Service Design

d) Service Strategy

25 Which of the following does Continual Service Improvement (CSI) provide guidance on?
1. How to improve process efficiency and effectiveness
2. How to improve services
3. Improvement of all phases of the Service Lifecycle
4. Measurement of processes and services

a)   1 and 2 only

b)   2 only

c)   1, 3 and 4 only

d)   All of the above

26 Which of the following is a type of Service Level Agreement (SLA) described in the ITIL Service Design publication?

a)   Priority-based SLA

b)   Technology-based SLA

c)   Location-based SLA

d)   Customer-based SLA

27 Which of the following is the BEST definition of an event?

a)   An occurrence where a performance threshold has been exceeded and an agreed service level has been impacted

b)   An occurrence that is significant for the management of the IT Infrastructure or delivery of services

c)   A known system defect that generates multiple incident reports

d)   A planned meeting of customers and IT staff to announce a new service or improvement programme

28 Which service lifecycle phase is responsible for ensuring that measurement methods will provide the required metrics for new or changed services?

a)   Service Design

b)   Service Operation

c)   Service Strategy

d)   Service Delivery

29 Which of the following should be treated as an incident?
    1. A user is unable to access a service during service hours
    2. An authorised IT staff member is unable to access a service during service hours
    3. A network segment fails and the user is not aware of any disruption to service
    4. A user contacts the Service Desk about slow performance of an application

    a)   All of the above

    b)   1 and 4 only

    c)   2 and 3 only

    d)   None of the above

30 Which of the following statements about a change model is CORRECT?

    a)   A change process model should not be used for emergency changes

    b)   A change process model should be constructed when a significant change is
         required

    c)   A change process model predefines steps that should be taken to handle a
         change in an agreed way

    d)   Escalation procedures are outside the scope of a change process model

31 Which is the first activity of the Continual Service Improvement (CSI) model?

    a)   Understand the business vision and objectives

    b)   Carry out a baseline assessment to understand the current situation

    c)   Agree on priorities for improvement

    d)   Create and verify a plan

32 Which Service Operation processes are missing from the following list?
    1. Incident Management
    2. Problem Management
    3. Access Management
    4. ?
    5. ?

    a)   Event Management and Request Fulfilment

    b)   Event Management and Service Desk

    c)   Facilities Management and Event Management

    d)   Change Management and Service Level Management

33   Which phase of the service lifecycle provides a framework for evaluating service capability and risk profile before and during service deployment?

    a)   Service Strategy

    b)   Continual Service Improvement

    c)   Service Transition

    d)   Service Operation

34   Which of the following activities should a service owner undertake?
1. Representing a specific service across the organization
2. Updating the CMDB after a change
3. Helping to identify service improvements
4. Representing a specific service in CAB meetings

    a)   2, 3 and 4 only

    b)   All of the above

    c)   1, 2 and 3 only

    d)   1, 3 and 4 only

35   Which of the following is NOT a goal of Availability Management?

    a)   To monitor and report availability of components

    b)   To ensure that service availability matches or exceeds the agreed needs of the business

    c)   To assess the impact of changes on the availability plan

    d)   To ensure that business continuity plans are aligned to the business objectives

36   Which of the following is the CORRECT description of the Four Ps of Service Design?

    a)   A four step process for the design of effective service management

    b)   A definition of the people and products required for successful design

    c)   A set of questions that should be asked when reviewing design specifications

    d)   The four major areas that need to be considered in the design of effective service management

37 Demand Management and Financial Management are processes described within which phase of the service lifecycle?

   a) Service Operation

   b) Service Strategy

   c) Service Transition

   d) Continual Service Improvement

38 Which of the following statements about Supplier Management is INCORRECT?

   a) Supplier Management negotiates Operational Level Agreements (OLAs) with internal groups to support the delivery of services

   b) Supplier Management ensures that suppliers meet business expectations

   c) Supplier Management maintains information in a Supplier and Contract Database

   d) Supplier Management negotiates external agreements to support the delivery of services

39 Which of the following is NOT a phase of the Service Lifecycle?

   a) Service Optimisation

   b) Service Transition

   c) Service Design

   d) Service Strategy

40 Which of the following is MOST LIKELY to be managed as a service request using the Request Fulfilment process?

   a) A user calls the Service Desk to order a toner cartridge

   b) After a service review, a functionality change is required to an application

   c) A manager asks for a change to an existing global security profile

   d) Users require testing of an element of the business continuity plan

ITIL® v.3 Foundation Examination: Sample Paper B

ANSWER SHEET

Answer Key for Exam Paper: ITILv3FoundationSampleB_v3.1

Q	A	Syllabus Ref		Q	A	Syllabus Ref	
1	A	05-31		21	D	05-46	
2	D	05-51		22	C	05-71	
3	C	06-01		23	A	07-02	
4	A	05-21		24	D	02-03	
5	C	06-02		25	D	02-10	
6	A	05-45		26	D	05-31	
7	B	05-72		27	B	03-24	
8	D	04-10		28	A	04-04	
9	C	03-18		29	A	03-26	
10	D	05-52		30	C	05-51	
11	A	05-72		31	A	04-09	
12	D	05-71		32	A	05-81	
13	B	03-03		33	C	02-06	
14	A	05-52		34	D	07-01	
15	C	01-05		35	D	05-42	
16	B	01-04		36	D	04-03	
17	B	05-61		37	B	05-22	
18	A	03-30		38	A	05-44	
19	D	08-02		39	A	02-02	
20	D	04-08		40	A	03-28	

ITIL® v.3 Foundation Examination: Sample Paper B

ANSWER RATIONALES

Rationale for ITIL V3 Foundation Sample Paper B v3.1

Q	ID	A	Syll	Book Ref	Rationale
1	593	A	05-31	SD 69	"All of the other processes need to be consulted for their opinion on what are realistic targets …"
2	585	D	05-51	ST 48	Standard changes can be raised in many ways, of which by Incident Management is only one
3	397	C	06-01	SO 115	Skills required include "Business Awareness: specific knowledge of the organisations business areas, drivers, structure and priorities" A has no justification, B is SLM's job and D is refuted by the books assertion that only Technical Awareness is needed as a minimum
4	116	A	05-21	SS 130	A is correct since PBA does influence the demand patterns seen by the service provider. B and C are incorrect as the book states specifically that both of these can be achieved and D implies that IT drives the business rather than vice versa
5	207	C	06-02	SO 126	"Facilities Management, which refers to the management of the physical IT environment, typically a Data Centre or computer rooms"
6	144	A	05-45	SD 82-83	Capacity Management is broken down into the sub processes listed in answer as part of the basic concepts. Supplier and Technology Capacity Management do not exist
7	568	B	05-72	SO 66	A - the KEDB is part of the SKMS NOT the same thing. B is correct. C - duplication should be avoided but by RESTRICTING access. D - yes they should use it but NOT the only ones
8	578	D	04-10	CSI 61	1. Better to measure the whole service if possible 2. KPIs are derived from CSFs 3. Process metrics identify gaps in performance. 4. It is better to measure both the quality of the service (customer satisfaction) and quantity (no failed changes)
9	574	C	03-18	ST 68	Part of the book description of the CMS A B and D are all potential Data and information Sources and Tools used within a CMS
10	579	D	05-52	ST 69	The DML is for media only, not hardware spares
11	565	A	05-72	SO 65/66	Only the first option provides a direct interface with the process the second implies that Problem is the main interface with SLM for all changes which is incorrect
12	695	D	05-71	SO 49	The statement "it is usually unacceptable to wait until the user is impacted or contacts the Service Desk" rules out A and C as answers. "Ideally, incidents should be resolved before they have an impact on users" points to D as the correct answer. B is clearly wrong as all incidents must be recorded
13	117	B	03-03	SD 33	Answers A C and D are all in the bulleted list in SD 3.6.2 but answer B is about defining the market, which is not included within a service portfolio. A service will NOT enter the portfolio BEFORE the opportunity has been identified. Therefore the portfolio cannot answer these questions.
14	581	A	05-52	ST 66	"Configuration Management delivers a model of the services, assets and the infrastructure …"
15	485	C	01-05	SD 42-43	Both of the statements are correct and are part of designing a process
16	10	B	01-04	SS 19	B is the definition given of a process. A is incorrect because of the inclusion of functions. C is incorrect as processes are used throughout organisations and not only by service providers. D is a definition related to functions.
17	161	B	05-61	ST 86-87	These are ways software is deployed found in the Release and deployment process

ITIL® v.3 Foundation Examination: Sample Paper B

ANSWER RATIONALES

18	32	A	03-30	SO 64	"In some cases it may be possible to find a workaround to the incidents caused by the problem – a temporary way of overcoming the difficulties…" Option A sees a temporary resolution applied
19	229	D	08-02	SO 157, SO 158, SD 201, ST 193	"Many organisations find it beneficial to offer "Self-Help" capabilities to their users. The technology should therefore support this capability" "The technology should incorporate good reporting capabilities" "These tools and techniques enable…process design" "Specific ITSM technology and tools that cover…..Release and deployment
20	95	D	04-08	CSI 29	"The four key stages of the cycle are Plan, Do, Check and Act…
21	147	D	05-46	SD 126	D part of the purpose goal and objectives of ITSCM relate to conducting Risk analysis with the business Availability and IT Security Management. Though the Service Catalogue is an input it is not directly involved in this activity
22	166	C	05-71	SO 47	C is the book definition of an incident model A. relates to a consistent approach for incident data capture not the steps that have to be undertaken B relates to the component involved. Models are most useful to incidents that are complex and so not limited to the ones easy to solve so D is also incorrect.
23	501	A	07-02	SD 189	Book answer from the list i.e. Responsible, Accountable, Consulted, Informed
24	572	D	02-03	SS 9	Deciding what services you should offer and to whom is an integral part of Service Strategy
25	31	D	02-10	CSI 14	"…looking for ways to improve process effectiveness, efficiency as well as cost effectiveness." "…identifying and implementing improvements to IT services…" "These improvement activities support the lifecycle approach through Service Strategy, Service Design, Service Transition and Service Operation" "That is why it is critically important to understand what to measure, why it is being measured and carefully define the successful outcome"
26	592	D	05-31	SD 67	There are no such SLA types described in SD as Priority-based, Technology-based or Location-based described in the SD book
27	49	B	03-24	SO 35	"An event can be defined as any detectable or discernible occurrence that has significance for the management of the IT Infrastructure or the delivery of IT service "
28	576	A	04-04	SD 15	You must design in measurements and metrics into your service
29	52	A	03-26	SO 56	"In ITIL terminology, an 'incident' is defined as: An unplanned interruption to an IT service or reduction in the quality of an IT service. Failure of a configuration item that has not yet impacted service is also an incident" This means all the scenarios are valid
30	587	C	05-51	ST 46	Change process models can be used for emergency changes (A) Change process models can be used for significant changes but it is by no means necessary (B) Standard escalation paths CAN be used in Change Models (D) Therefore C is correct as the model does pre-define steps for certain types of change
31	97	A	04-09	CSI 15	"The improvement process can be summarized in six steps: • Embrace the vision by understanding the high-level business objectives…"
32	189	A	05-81	SO 46, 36, 56, 58, 68	This list of processes appears in the syllabus and all of them should be covered on the course.
33	466	C	02-06	ST 16	C the question relates to the purpose goals and objectives of Service Transition as it is looking at deployment

ITIL® v.3 Foundation Examination: Sample Paper B

ANSWER RATIONALES

34	430	D	07-01	CSI 134	The three correct answers appear in CSI 6.1.4 Service Owner under the heading "Key Responsibilities". Option 2 is the responsibility of the configuration administrator/librarian
35	699	D	05-42	SD 97	Answer D is a goal of IT Service Continuity Management. The others are goals of Availability Management from the book.
36	67	D	04-03	SD 16	"The implementation of ITIL Service Management as a practice is about preparing and planning the effective and efficient use of the four Ps: the People, the Processes, the Products (services, technology and tools) and the Partners (suppliers, manufacturers and vendors)…"
37	121	B	05-22	SS 97 and 129	Demand Management and Financial Management are detailed in Service Strategy
38	140	A	05-04	SD 149-150	The bulleted list after "The main objectives of the Supplier Management process are to:" includes all of these except for negotiating OLAs, which is a responsibility of Service Level Management
39	20	A	02-02	SS 8	The titles of the core books appear as headings in SS 1.2.3
40	57	A	03-28	SO 55	"The term 'Service Request' is used as a generic description for many varying types of demands that are placed upon the IT Department by the users. Many of these are actually small changes – low risk, frequently occurring, low cost, etc." B, C and D would all most likely need individual approval as risk and resource may be difficult to predict making A the best answer.

Appendix C

About the Additional Study Tools

IN THIS APPENDIX:

✓ Digital Study Tools

✓ System Requirements

✓ Using the Study Tools

✓ Troubleshooting

Digital Study Tools

The following sections are arranged by category and summarize the software and other goodies you'll find from the companion website. If you need help with installing the items, refer to the installation instructions in the "Using the Study Tools" section of this appendix.

 The additional study tools can be found at www.sybex.com/go/itilstudy guide. Here, you will get instructions on how to download the files to your hard drive.

Sybex Test Engine

The files contain the Sybex test engine, which includes two bonus practice exams.

Electronic Flashcards

These handy electronic flashcards are just what they sound like. One side contains a question or fill-in-the-blank question, and the other side shows the answer.

PDF of Glossary of Terms

We have included an electronic version of the glossary in .pdf format. You can view the electronic version of the glossary with Adobe Reader.

Adobe Reader

We've also included a copy of Adobe Reader so you can view PDF files that accompany the book's content. For more information on Adobe Reader or to check for a newer version, visit Adobe's website at www.adobe.com/products/reader/.

System Requirements

Make sure your computer meets the minimum system requirements shown in the following list. If your computer doesn't match up to most of these requirements, you may have problems using the software and files. For the latest and greatest information, please refer to the ReadMe file located in the downloads.

- For PCs: A PC running Microsoft Windows 98, Windows 2000, Windows NT4 (with SP4 or greater), Windows Me, Windows XP, Windows Vista, or Windows 7

- For Macs: A Mac running Mac OS X 10.1-10.3 or higher

- For Linux: Flash Player 9 or above installed

- An Internet connection

Using the Study Tools

To install the items, follow these steps:

1. Download the `.zip` file to your hard drive, and unzip it to the appropriate location. Instructions on where to download this file can be found at `www.sybex.com/go/itilstudyguide`.

2. Click the `Start.EXE` file to open the study tools file.

3. Read the license agreement, and then click the Accept button if you want to use the study tools.

The main interface appears. The interface allows you to access the content with just one or two clicks.

Troubleshooting

Wiley has attempted to provide programs that work on most computers with the minimum system requirements. Alas, your computer may differ, and some programs may not work properly for some reason.

The two likeliest problems are that you don't have enough memory (RAM) for the programs you want to use or you have other programs running that are affecting the installation or running of a program. If you get an error message such as "Not enough memory" or "Setup cannot continue," try one or more of the following suggestions and then try using the software again:

Turn off any antivirus software running on your computer. Installation programs sometimes mimic virus activity and may make your computer incorrectly believe that it's being infected by a virus.

Close all running programs. The more programs you have running, the less memory is available to other programs. Installation programs typically update files and programs, so if you keep other programs running, installation may not work properly.

Have your local computer store add more RAM to your computer. This is, admittedly, a drastic and somewhat expensive step. However, adding more memory can really help the speed of your computer and allow more programs to run at the same time.

Customer Care

If you have trouble with the book's companion study tools, please call the Wiley Product Technical Support phone number at (800) 762-2974, or email them at `http://sybex.custhelp.com/`.

Index

Glossary

A

access management   The process responsible for allowing users to make use of IT services, data, or other assets. Access management implements the policies of information security management and is sometimes referred to as rights management or identity management.

alert   A notification that a threshold has been reached, something has changed, or a failure has occurred.

application management   The function responsible for managing applications throughout their lifecycle.

architecture   The structure of a system or IT service, including the relationships of components to each other.

assets   Any resource or capability.

attribute   Information held about a configuration item, such as serial number, make, model, and so on.

availability management   The process responsible for ensuring that IT services meet the current and future availability needs of the business in a cost-effective and timely manner.

B

baseline   A snapshot that is verified against the live environment, which is used as a reference point.

business case   Justification for a significant item of expenditure, identifying costs and benefits, including options considered.

business continuity management (BCM)   The business process responsible for managing risks that could seriously affect the business and ensuring that critical business functions can be made available following a major disruption, within the timeframe the business requires. Business continuity management defines what will be required from its IT service provider in terms of IT service continuity management.

business impact analysis (BIA)   Business impact analysis is the activity in business continuity management that identifies vital business functions and their dependencies. It is used to identify what the business impact will be if an IT service is unavailable.

business relationship management   The process responsible for maintaining a positive relationship with customers. The business relationship manager's focus is strategic, ensuring that IT will deliver what is required by the business strategy.

C

capabilities   The ability of an organization, person, process, application, IT service, or other configuration item to carry out an activity. Capabilities are intangible assets of an organization.

capacity management   The process responsible for ensuring that the capacity of IT services and the IT infrastructure is able to meet agreed-on capacity- and performance-related requirements in a cost-effective and timely manner. Capacity management includes three subprocesses: business capacity management, service capacity management, and component capacity management.

capacity plan   A plan drawn up to address the current and future capacity and performance requirements of the business. It shows current and historic usage of services and components and the expected increase or decrease for capacity for them over the next 12 to 18 months. It recommends actions to ensure sufficient but not excessive capacity will be available to match these demands; these actions could include purchase of new equipment and storage or reallocation of current devices. The plan considers changes in the business, such as downsizing, changes in the demand for individual services, and technical advances in components, and it puts forward plans to meet a number of possible scenarios.

change   The addition, modification, or removal of anything that could affect IT services.

change advisory board (CAB)   A group of people who support the assessment, prioritization, authorization, and scheduling of changes.

change evaluation   The process responsible for formal assessment of a new or changed IT service to ensure that risks have been managed and to help determine whether to authorize the change.

change management   The process responsible for controlling the lifecycle of all changes.

change proposal   A high-level description and business case of a potential service or significant change. Once the change proposal has been authorized, the service will be chartered.

change record   A record containing the details of a change. Each change record documents the lifecycle of a single change.

change schedule (CS)   A document that lists all authorized changes and their planned implementation dates, as well as the estimated dates of longer-term changes.

configuration items (CIs)   Any component or other service asset that needs to be managed in order to deliver an IT service.

configuration management database (CMDB)   A database used to store configuration records throughout their lifecycle.

configuration management system (CMS)   A set of tools, data, and information that is used to support service asset and configuration management. It may include a federated approach to managing CMDBs.

continual service improvement (CSI)   Continual service improvement is a phase of the service lifecycle. It is concerned with the improvement of services, processes, and service management across the whole lifecycle.

core service   A service that delivers the basic outcomes desired by one or more customers (see enabling and enhancing services).

critical success factor (CSF)   Something that must happen if an IT service, process, plan, project, or other activity is to succeed.

CSI register   A database or structured document used to record and manage improvement opportunities throughout their lifecycle.

customer   Someone who buys goods or services. The customer of an IT service provider is the person or group that defines and agrees on the service-level targets.

D

definitive media library (DML)   One or more secure locations containing the definitive and authorized versions of all software. It may also hold license documentation.

Deming cycle   The Plan-Do-Check-Act approach to quality management.

design coordination   The process responsible for coordinating all service design activities, processes, and resources.

E

early-life support   The extra support given at the end of deployment until the new or changed service is accepted as fully operational. The service is reviewed to ensure that it will be able to meet the service targets.

emergency change   A change that must be introduced as soon as possible, for example, to resolve a major incident or implement a security patch.

emergency change advisory board (ECAB)   A subgroup of the change advisory board that makes assessments and decisions about emergency changes.

enabling service   A service that is needed in order to deliver a core service.

enhancing service   A service that is added to a core service to make it more attractive to the customer.

event   A change of state that has significance for the management of an IT service or other configuration item.

event management   The process responsible for managing events throughout their lifecycle.

F

facilities management   The function responsible for managing the physical environment where the IT infrastructure is located.

financial management   The processes responsible for managing an IT service provider's budgeting, accounting, and charging requirements.

follow the sun   A form of virtual service desk, with calls routed according to the time of day.

function   A team or group of people and the other resources or tools that are used to carry out a process or process activities.

functional escalation   Transferring an incident, problem, or change to a technical team with a higher level of expertise or authority.

G

governance   Ensures that policies and strategy are actually implemented and that required processes are correctly followed.

H

hierarchic escalation   Informing or involving more senior levels of management in an incident, problem, or change.

I

impact   A measure of the effect of an incident, problem, or change on business processes. Impact and urgency are used to assign priority.

incident   An unplanned interruption to an IT service or reduction in the quality of an IT service.

incident management   The process responsible for managing the lifecycle of all incidents. It focuses on restoring normal service as quickly as possible.

incident record   A record containing the details of the lifecycle of a single incident.

information security management (ISM)   The process responsible for ensuring that the confidentiality, integrity, and availability of an organization's assets, information, data, and IT services match the agreed needs of the business.

IT operations management   The function within an IT service provider that performs the daily activities needed to manage IT services and the supporting IT infrastructure. IT operations management includes IT operations control and facilities management.

IT service   A service provided by an IT service provider. An IT service consists of a combination of information technology, people, and processes.

IT service continuity management   The process responsible for managing risks that could seriously affect IT services. IT service continuity management supports business continuity management.

IT service management (ITSM)   The implementation and management of quality IT services that meet the needs of the business.

IT service provider   A service provider that provides IT services to internal or external customers.

K

key performance indicators (KPIs)   A metric that is used to help manage an IT service, process, plan, project, or other activity. Key performance indicators are used to measure the achievement of critical success factors.

knowledge management   The process responsible for sharing perspectives, ideas, experience, and information, as well as for ensuring that these are available in the right place and at the right time.

known error database (KEDB)   A database created by problem management containing all known error records and workarounds where available.

M

mean time between failures (MTBF)   A metric for measuring and reporting availability, or uptime. MTBF is the average of the time between when the configuration item starts working until it next fails.

mean time between service incidents (MTBSI)   A metric used for measuring and reporting reliability. It is the mean time from when a system or IT service fails until it next fails.

mean time to restore service (MTRS)   A metric used for measuring and reporting downtime. MTRS is the average time taken to restore an IT service or other configuration item after a failure. MTRS is measured from when the configuration item fails until it is fully restored and delivering its normal functionality.

N

normal service operation   An operational state that is defined as where services and configuration items are performing within their agreed service and operational levels.

O

operational-level agreements (OLAs)   An agreement between an IT service provider and another part of the same organization that assists in the provision of services.

operations management   This is also known as IT operations management. It is the function within an IT service provider that carries out the daily activities needed to manage IT services and the supporting IT infrastructure. IT operations management includes IT operations control and facilities management.

outcome   The result of carrying out an activity, following a process, delivering an IT service, and so on. The term is used to refer to intended results, as well as to actual results.

P

patterns of business activity (PBA)   A workload profile of one or more business activities. Patterns of business activity are used to help the IT service provider understand and plan for different levels of business activity.

priority   The relative importance of an incident, problem, or change. Priority is based on impact and urgency.

problem   The unknown, underlying cause of one or more incidents.

problem management   The process responsible for managing the lifecycle of all problems. Its purpose is to prevent problems and resultant incidents from occurring.

process   A process is a structured set of activities designed to accomplish a specific objective. A process takes one or more defined inputs and turns them into defined outputs.

projected service outage (PSO)   A document that identifies the effect of planned changes, maintenance activities, and test plans on agreed service levels.

R

RACI   A model used to help define roles and responsibilities. RACI stands for Responsible, Accountable, Consulted, and Informed.

release and deployment management   The process responsible for planning, scheduling, and controlling the build, test, and deployment of releases and for delivering new functionality required by the business while protecting the integrity of existing services.

remediation plan   A plan for actions to be taken to recover after a failed change or release. Remediation may include backout, invocation of service continuity plans, or other actions designed to enable the business process to continue.

request for change (RFC)   A formal proposal for a change to be made. It includes details of the proposed change and may be recorded on paper or electronically.

request fulfillment   The process responsible for managing the lifecycle of all service requests.

resources   A generic term that includes IT infrastructure, people, money, or anything else that might help to deliver an IT service. They are often considered to be assets of an organization.

risk management   The approach adopted to identify, document, analyze, and mitigate against the likelihood of potential impact to a project or service.

risk register   A centralized record of the risks that need to be managed.

S

service   Services are a means of delivering value to customers by facilitating the outcomes customers want to achieve, without the ownership of specific costs and risks.

service acceptance criteria (SAC)   A set of criteria used to ensure that an IT service meets its functionality and quality requirements.

service asset and configuration management (SACM)   The process responsible for ensuring that the assets required to deliver services are properly controlled. It focuses on the management and provision of accurate and reliable information about those assets and ensures that it is available when and where it is needed.

service catalog   A database or structured document with information about all live IT services, which may include services available for deployment.

service catalog management   The process responsible for providing and maintaining the service catalog and for ensuring that it is available to those who are authorized to access it.

service design A phase in the service lifecycle. Service design includes the design of the services, including governing practices, processes, and policies required to realize the service provider's strategy. Its objective is to facilitate the introduction of services into supported environments.

service design package (SDP) Document(s) defining all aspects of an IT service and its requirements through each stage of its lifecycle.

service desk The single point of contact between the service provider and the users.

service improvement plan (SIP) A formal plan to implement improvements to a process or IT service.

service knowledge management system (SKMS) A set of tools and databases that is used to manage knowledge, information, and data.

service-level agreement (SLA) A written agreement between the IT service provider and customer. A service-level agreement describes the IT service, documents service-level targets, and specifies the responsibilities of the IT service provider and the customer.

service-level management The process responsible for negotiating achievable service-level agreements and ensuring that they are met. It manages SLAs and the associated underpinning agreements and contract and ensures that the targets for service provision are agreed and managed.

service-level requirements (SLR) A customer requirement for an aspect of an IT service. Service-level requirements are based on business objectives and used to negotiate agreed service-level targets.

service management A set of specialized organizational capabilities for providing value to customers in the form of services.

service operation A phase in the service lifecycle. Service operation coordinates and carries out the activities and processes required to deliver and manage services at agreed levels to business users and customers.

service portfolio The complete set of services that is managed by a service provider. It includes three categories: service pipeline (proposed or in development), service catalog (live or available for deployment), and retired services.

service portfolio management The process that manages and maintains the service portfolio. It ensures that the service provider has the right mix of services to meet required business outcomes at an appropriate level of investment.

service provider An organization supplying services to one or more internal or external customers.

service strategy A phase in the service lifecycle. Service strategy defines the perspective, position, plans, and patterns that a service provider needs to execute to meet an organization's business outcomes.

service transition   A phase in the service lifecycle. Service transition ensures that new, modified, or retired services meet the expectations of the business as documented in the service strategy and service design stages of the lifecycle.

service validation and testing   The process responsible for validating and testing a new or changed IT service to ensure it meets the requirements of the business.

seven-step improvement process   The process responsible for defining and managing the steps needed to identify, define, gather, process, analyze, present, and implement improvements.

standard change   A preauthorized change that is low-risk, is relatively common, and follows a procedure or work instruction.

supplier management   The process responsible for obtaining value for money from suppliers, ensuring that all contracts and agreements with suppliers support the needs of the business, and ensuring that all suppliers meet their contractual commitments.

T

technical management   The function responsible for providing technical skills in support of IT services and management of the IT infrastructure.

transition planning and support   The process responsible for planning all service transition processes and coordinating the resources they require.

U

underpinning contracts (UC)   A contract between an IT service provider and a third party. The third party provides goods or services that support the delivery of an IT service to a customer.

urgency   A measure of how long it will be until an incident, problem, or change has a significant impact on the business.

utility   The functionality offered by a product or service to meet a particular need or whether it is fit for purpose.

V

vital business function (VBF)   Part of a business process that is critical to the success of the business.

W

warranty   The assurance that a product or service will meet the agreed requirements, fit for use.

workaround   A means of reducing or eliminating the impact of an incident or problem (often by the service desk) for which a full resolution is not yet available.

The Best Study Tools for the ITIL Foundation Exam

Readers can have access to the most comprehensive Study Tool package on the market, including the Sybex Test Engine, electronic flashcards, and database of key terms and definitions.

Get ready for your ITIL Foundation exam with the most comprehensive and challenging sample tests anywhere!

The Sybex Test Engine features:

- All the review questions, as covered in each chapter of the book

- Two multiple-choice Practice Exams with challenging questions representative of those you'll find on the real exam

- An Assessment Test to narrow your focus to certain objective groups

Use the Glossary for instant reference:

- Search through the PDF of the Glossary to find key terms you'll need to be familiar with for the exam

D

definitive media library (DML)   One or more secure locations containing the definitive and authorized versions of all software. It may also hold license documentation.

Deming cycle   The Plan-Do-Check-Act approach to quality management.

design coordination   The process responsible for coordinating all service design activities, processes, and resources.

E

early-life support   The extra support given at the end of deployment until the new or changed service is accepted as fully operational. The service is reviewed to ensure that it will be able to meet the service targets.

emergency change   A change that must be introduced as soon as possible, for example, to resolve a major incident or implement a security patch.

emergency change advisory board (ECAB)   A subgroup of the change advisory board that makes assessments and decisions about emergency changes.

enabling service   A service that is needed in order to deliver a core service.

Use the Electronic Flashcards to jog your memory and prep last-minute for the exam!

- Reinforce your understanding of key concepts with these hardcore flashcard-style questions

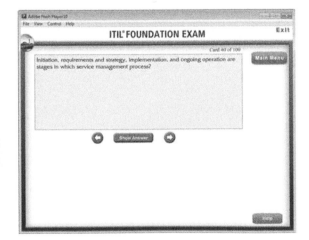

Readers can access the companion Study Tools for the *ITIL Foundation Exam Study Guide* at www.sybex.com/go/itilstudyguide.

CPSIA information can be obtained at www.ICGtesting.com
Printed in the USA
BVOW11s2240220514

354352BV00005B/21/P